D1590279

154477

Wilkinson.
A confutation of certain articles delivered unto the familye of Loue.

Learning Resources Center
Nazareth College of Rochester, N. Y.

NUMBER 279

THE ENGLISH EXPERIENCE

ITS RECORD IN EARLY PRINTED BOOKS
PUBLISHED IN FACSIMILE

WILLIAM WILKINSON

A CONFUTATION OF CERTAINE ARTICLES DELIUERED VNTO THE FAMILYE OF LOUE

LONDON 1579

DA CAPO PRESS
THEATRVM ORBIS TERRARVM LTD.
AMSTERDAM 1970 NEW YORK

WITHDRAWN
LEARNING RESOURCES CENTER
NAZARETH COLLEGE

The publishers acknowledge their gratitude
to the Curators of the Bodleian Library, Oxford
for ther permission to reproduce
the Library's copy (Shelfmark: Tanner 233)
and to the Curators of the University Library, Durham
for their permission to reproduce
the pages: D3 recto, verso, D4 recto, E2 recto, verso, M1 verso,
M2 recto, S3 verso from the Library's copy (Shelfmark: S.R.4.D.11 (2))

S.T.C. No. 25665
Collation: $*^{4}$,☞^{4},A-B^{4},b^{2},C-Y^{4}

154477

Published in 1970 by
Theatrum Orbis Terrarum Ltd.,
O.Z. Voorburgwal 85, Amsterdam
&
Da Capo Press
- a division of Plenum Publishing Corporation -
227 West 17th Street, New York, 10011
Printed in the Netherlands
ISBN 90 221 0279 3

230.3
Wil

A Confutation OF CERTAINE ARTICLES, *deliuered vnto the Familye of Loue, with* the exposition of Theophilus, a suppo *sed Elder in the sayd Familye vpon* the same Articles.

By William Wilkinson Maister of Artes and student of Diuinitye.

Hereunto are prefixed

By the right reuerend Father in God *I. Y.* Byshop of Rochester, certaine notes collected out of their Gospell, and aunswered by the Fam.

By the Author, a description of the tyme, places, Authors, and manner of spreading the same: of their liues, and wrestyng of Scriptures: with Notes in the end how to know an Heretique.

Prou. 30. 12.

There is a generation that are pure in their owne conceit, and yet are not washed from their filthines.

AT LONDON

Printed by Iohn Daye dwelling ouer Aldersgate. An. 1579.

Cum Priuilegio Regiæ Maiestatis.

PErusing ouer this little treatise of M. Wilkinsons, I could not but alowe his diligence and painefull trauell in this heretical, and schismaticall world, and I would hartely wishe of God, that our Church of England might be well weeded from to to grosse errors, for it is high tyme.

Richard Ely.

¶To the right Reuerend Father in Chriſt, and his very good Lord, *Richard* by the prouidence of God Byſhop of Ely: *W.W.* wiſheth all ioye and peace, both in body and ſoule, with happynes in the Lord euerlaſtyng.

Iſe Salomon the ſonne of holy Dauid a pꝛudent kyng, and a peaceable Pꝛince, Reuerēd father in Chꝛiſt: very fittely in his ſweet ſonges reſem= bled the Churche of God vnto a Vine, and the ene= mies thereof vnto raue= nous and greedy Foxes. Foꝛ that the Vine be= yng a ſpꝛeadyng plante diligētly trimmed and paynfully attended vnto, ſtretcheth abꝛoad his ſappy bꝛaūches and bꝛoad leaues, foꝛ a ſuccour and harbour in a ſtoꝛme and is a comfoꝛtable & gladſome fruite to him that eateth it oꝛ taſteth the liquoꝛ of the ſame. Whiche Vine the Foxes ſometymes ſpoyle and endamage by robbyng the fruite, ſometyme by bꝛuyſing the young and tender bꝛaunches therof, befoꝛe they be able by their grouth: to ſuccour themſelues, frō ſo ma= ny ſoꝛtes of aſſaultes moſt daūgerous. And not leſſe aptely our Sauiour Chꝛiſt, the Sonne of God in his holy and diuine Sermons likeneth it vnto a field, wherein good ſeede is ſowne by the paynefull huſbandman, & coꝛrupt ſeede ſcat= tered by the hād of the enemyes. Of both which

Cantic.2.15.
Ezech.13.4.
Eſay.5.1.

Ionas.4.7.

Math.13.24.25.

similitudes albeit many & excellent notes may be gathered, yet the whole scope of them both in my iudgemēt is this: to shew that shootyngs vp and encrease of Gods Church beyng but frō a feeble and weake begynnyng, is continually by Sathan and his mischieuous ministers not a little disquieted, that thereby the gladsome fruite, and looked for encrease therof is much let and hindered.

What the remedy and redresse therof is, I leaue to your Lordshyp to cōsider, whom (with the rest of your godly and learned brethren and Reuerend Fathers,) Gods diuine prouidence Act.20.28. Heb.13.17. hath placed ouer vs (as in a high watchtower) to foresee and discry the subtle assaultes of so slye and cruell enemyes.

And I hartly wish that it might not iustly be affirmed, (or beyng iustly affirmed I would that the losse of the soules of many poore Christians did not auouch the truth of the assertion) that euen frō the tyme, wherein the first scourge (wherewith the Lord afflicted his Churche in the bloudy dayes of Queene Mary) began: neither in, and from that tyme alone, but euen long sithēce also, to the great hurt of Christes church, Math.24.24. Math.13.25. Math. 7.15. & hinderaunce of his chosen, many false Christes arose, and while the watchmen slept, many lying seers, and seducyng Prophets, vnder Lambes skinnes, craftely crept into the sheepfold, priuily whisperyng peruerse thynges, to seduce and beguile the simple. And though the word of

God (his name be prayſed) haue a cleare & free paſſage amongeſt vs, and the bloudy bandoges of the Romiſh Sinagogue be tyed vp, that by thē the ſheepe of Chriſt, are in leſſe daunger to be worryed: yet is not the encreaſe of that heauēly ſeede ſo great, (with grief be that hard, which is ſpoken with ſorrow) as many as do weene & moſt men do wiſh for.

For the roaryng Lion dayly rūneth about, & 1.Pet 5.8.
his miniſters are not idle: zeale in hearyng and charitie in practiſing wareth cold: but ſpecially the continuall labour of Gods huſbandmen beginneth to fainte, thornes & bryers grow vp in the Lordes field, & the deuill transformyng him 2.Cor.11.14.
ſelfe into an Angel of light deceiueth many. The reaſon is (as I take it) that thoſe which ought to be breakers of Gods bread to ſatiſfie & relieue the hungry ſoules of his Saintes cānot breake that, which they haue not: neither are able many of them being vnarmed to withſtād the enemy: or thoſe which are able, either can and will not, bycauſe they are ſleepy: or beyng both able & willing hauing a watchful eye vpō the Lordes inheritaūce, they dare not aduenture beyng diuers wayes diſcouraged with the ſundry & manifold fetches of Heretiques: eſpecially not beyng acquainted with the daunger (of that poyſon which dayly floweth frō our *Louely Familie*) to be ſure of their owne ſafetie keepe them ſelues out of gunſhote.

The cauſe of hereſie is want of preachyng. Math.22.29. Rom.10.14. Eſay.29.9. Ierem.23.2. Zach.11.17. Ierem.50.6. Eſay.56.10. Math.15.14.

Of the Hereſie it ſelfe in one worde to vtter

the truth of that, which almost by the experience and practise of three whole yeares I haue proued to be true, it is the most pestiferous, & deadly Heresie of all others, because there is not almost any one particular erroneous & Schismaticall phantasie, whereof the *Familie of Loue* hath not borrowed one braunche or other thereof, to peece vnto thẽselues this their brokẽ Religion.

HN. his heresie mingled of all heresies.

The encrease of this *Familie* is great, & that dayly, because the withstanders are not many: the defenders are wily as Serpentes & would fayne in lyfe seeme innocent and vnblameable: In profession of the one they boast very much: of the other they walkyng very closely do iustifie them selues, because fewe haue to finde fault with them, yet haue they their lothsome spottes and ougly deformities, as in this booke to the diligent reader playnely may appeare.

Their bookes are many disorderly and confusedly written both for matter, and manner of thynges deliuered in them, their phrases are such as the Scripture speaketh of cloudes without water, and lightenyng without rayne, their blossomes are as dust and their fruite as rottennesse.

2. Pet. 2. 1. 2. Iude, 12.

The proofe hereof I referre to the sequele of the Treatise which ensueth, the which I desire your Lordshyp the rather to accept, because that within this Isle of Ely, and other where, within your Lordshyps Dioces, diuers doe suspect that to be true, whiche common fame re-

por-

porteth, that dayly thoſe ſwarmes increaſe, which in the end (I feare me) will wonderfully diſquiet, (as it hath already begonne in diuers places) and moleſt the Church of God. The Lord vouchſafe when his pleaſure is ſomewhat to cut them ſhorter: and graunt to thoſe vnto whom the care of his Church and ouerſight of his flocke belongeth, vigilant and watchfull eyes, carefull harts, willyng myndes, and ſtrõg and hable bodyes to finde out, and to roote out beyng founde, what ſoeuer doth diſquiet the buildyng vppe of Sion, that we may keepe the ſpirit of vnitie in the bonde of peace, and be but one folde vnder the ſhepheard Jeſus Chriſt our Lord, who bleſſe your Lordſhyp with the fulnes of all ſpirituall bleſſinges, to the honour of his name and profite of his Churche. Amen.

Cambridge September. 30. Anno. 1579.

Your Lordſhyps moſt humbly bounden. William Wilkinſon.

¶ *To the godly and Christian Reader Peace from God the Father, and our Lord Ieſus Chriſt.*

THat which aunciẽt writers and learned men reporte to be the ſingular commendation and eſpeciall prayſe of a good Hiſtoriographer (gẽtle Reader,) to cõceale nothyng of the truth for feare, or to vtter any vntruth for for euill will, neither yet to flatter or claw for fauour: that ſame me thinkes is neceſſarily to be required of all thoſe whiche take in hand to teſtifie of any matter what ſoeuer. For els how ſhould we poſſibly looke for truth of thoſe men: whoſe myndes are wedded to affections, whoſe handes and pennes are let out for lucre, and toungues let looſe to teſtifie an vntruth, who are wholy blinded with diſdayne, and beyng egged on with euill will, haue ſet them ſelues to ſale, committyng what ſoeuer is vnhoneſt with vnſatiable greadines. Cõcernyng my ſelfe, in ſimplicitie of hart I teſtifie, and ſolẽnely proteſt before the whole world, calling God to witneſſe (whom I know to be a ſharpe reuenger and ſeuere iudge agaynſt thoſe which abuſe his bleſſed name to any vntruth) agaynſt myne owne ſoule, if in this treatiſe I haue vttered ought for enuie or malice of thoſe people, againſt whoſe opinions my whole ſtile and writyng is eſpecially directed. I haue truely quoted, rightly alledged, and faythfully as I am hable reported, what ſoeuer I haue either heard by word, or read by writyng concernyng the errour of thoſe men who terme them ſelues to be of the Fami-

lie

lie of Loue. Whiche I haue the rather done beyng thereto required by that dutie that I owe vnto the Churche of Christ, whiche is the felowshyp of the faythfull and societie of the Saintes of God: as also beyng by a Christian Magistrate thereunto cōmaunded I could not chuse (I say) but I needes must testifie the truth of that whiche both I haue heard and sene: which also I am ready at any tyme to auouch before any person beyng called thereunto either priuately or openly. Wherein also I haue not sayd so much as I might truely, and could iustly, hauyng refrayned for their sakes especially, which are my very frendes beyng somewhat ouertaken with the lime of that secte, and are bewitched with the blyndnesse of those vnsauery opinions.

Concernyng my further knowledge in that Heresie, I referre thee (good reader) vnto that which ensueth, most humbly beseeching thee to blesse and further me with thy most feruent prayers, as I hartly desire the promotion and furtheraunce of Gods true Religion, the encrease of a true fayth in the feare of God, the quietnesse of our English Church, and the vtter ruine and abolishyng of all Papistry, Atheisme, and Hereticall sectes, and Schismes whatsoeuer.

Cambridge Septemb. 30.

Readyng certaine bookes of H.N. and conferring with certaine of that Louely Fam. I was by them requested to set downe vnto them in writyng for my further instruction those doubtes whiche (either by meanes of the vnusualnesse of their Methode in writing, the noueltie of their farre fetched phrases, there wrong and wrested Allegories, there Diuinitie not heard of, or their rough trottyng ſtile) I did not vnderſtand, I deliuered vnto them in the moneth of *Auguſt.* 1578. thoſe Articles which follow hereafter in this booke, and deſiryng earneſtly to be fully ſatiſfied in that behalfe, I receiued the aunſwere deliuered to the common carrier in *London*, whiche beyng intercepted by my worſhypfull frend, came not into my handes vntill the third of *Aprill laſt* paſt Anno. 1579. The aunſwere whiche I ſhall ſet downe if firſt I ſhall geue you to vnderſtand what I can teſtifie concernyng them and their Fathers of their monſtruous Hereticall opinions.

¶A brief view of the heresies and errours of *HN*, conteined and confuted in this treatise by pag. as herein they are to be found.

¶With a brief token how to know an Anabaptist, gathered out of Zuinglius, Bullinger, and Caluin, whiche declare the opinions and behauiour of Heretickes from tyme to tyme.

A very brief and true description of the first springing vp of the Heresie termed, The Familie of Loue, which conteineth the places where, and the parties by whom the sayd Heresie was broached.

WHen as long tyme the singular mercy and lenitie of the Lorde (in the happy dayes of good kyng Edward the vj. a Prince of blessed remembraunce) was by the carnall profession of many and loose lyfe of the greatest part abused: in the end by Gods iust scourge ouer England it came to passe (which alwayes ensueth the contempt of so precious pearles) that Amos long before Pro-

Amos,8.11.12.

phesied of the Epicures of Israell: there followed a greuous famine not onely of bread for the comfortyng and susteinyng of the outward man, but also the foode of the soule, whereby our

Math.4.4.
Prou.29.18.

lyfe to Godward is prolonged was taken away. And it was a very daungerous thyng to confesse Christ openly not onely for feare of Excommunication, but for daunger of the losse of lyfe also. And so farre had the Prince of darkenesse confirmed his kyngdome of ignoraunce in this worthy Iseland, that the worshyppers (which worshypped in spirite and truth) durst not openly assemble them selues for feare of the Tyrãnous hatred of the Scribes and Pharisies & the rest of the oiled broode of the Popishe Sinagogue. They were compelled secretly to meete in priuate houses, so fearefull a thyng was it for fleshe & bloud to abyde the extreme fury of the Romish Baalamites which waxed so hoate, and such dayly dãger honge ouer their heades that professed the sinceritie of the Gospel. So scorchyng was the flame of those most bloudy tymes that those men whõ the world was not woorthy of, some of them were tryed by bondes and Imprisonmentes, some of them by most bitter tormentes of Fire and Fagot, such imminent and present perill abode those who professed them selues to be fauorers of Christes truth. which great distresse and calamitie draue diuers of the Children of God to wander from place to place, not hauyng where they durst at any tyme rest long together. In the which tyme of their continuall tossing, sometymes they had ease and comfort by their feruent Prayers, and by the participation of the

the

the blessed word & Sacramentes, they got some space to breath them agaynst that fiery triall, which hourely they looked for. Neither had this affliction (albeit it was mighty) bene so greuous if Sathan there had stayd his rage, but his priuate hatred long concealed, brake forth into open enmitie: who beyng an old Dragon and subtle Serpent dayly raysed vp some, which priuily spake peruerse thynges, entanglyng the simple sorte, and drawyng such weakelynges after them as they dayly met withall to be their Disciples.

The aũcient and famous Towne of Colchester was in the troublesome tyme of Queene Maries persecution a sweete and and comfortable mother of the bodyes, and a tender nourse of the soules of Gods children: which towne was the rather at that tyme frequented, because it afforded many godly and zealous Martyrs, whiche continually with their bloud watered those seedes, whiche by the preachyng of the worde had bene sowne most plentifully in the hartes of Christians in the dayes of good Kyng Edward. This towne for the earnest profession of the Gospell became like vnto a Citie vpon an hill, and as a candle vpon a candlesticke gaue great light to all those who for the comfort of their conscience came to conferre there from diuers places of the Realme, and repairyng to common Innes had by night their Christian exercises, whiche in other places could not be gotten. For proofe whereof I referre the Reader vnto that whiche is truely reported by M. Foxe in his booke of Actes and Monumentes: that at the kynges head in Colchester and at other Innes in the sayd Towne, the afflicted Christians had set places appointed for thẽ selues to meete at, where (least Sathan should bee thought to bee idle or his venemous or deadly hatred agaynst Christes poore afflicted members should seeme to bee lesse then his open professed enmitie) hee styrred vp diuers Schismaticall spirites, whiche euen in that great trouble of the Church sought to be teachers of that wherof they had no vnderstandyng, and thereby turned the knowledge of Gods testimonies (which in many of them though it was small yet somewhat) to vayne and contentious ianglyng, whereby the deare Saintes of God were not a litle disquieted: at such tyme especially as some of them beyng cõdemned to death looked to tast of the same cup, whiche had bene in full measure powred out vnto their brethren. For not onely in the priuate assemblies of the godly did these spidercatchers swarme together to peruert the right wayes of the Lord: but

First Edition, pag. 606. A.

also in diuers prisons in London they kept a continuall haunt, where they scattered their deuilish cocle of abhominable Heresie among such as were committed for the loue of the Gospell. For the testimony of the truth hereof vouchsafe, good reader to read the booke of M. Foxe before alledged, where hee reporteth the letter of a wicked Promoter named Thom. Tye the Popish Priest of Muchebently, and Steuen Norish a false Iudas and betrayer of Gods Saintes in the tyme of their trouble, where he vseth these wordes. There is (sayth this popish priest, one Iohn Kempe, and Henry Harte who is the principall of all those that are called Frewil mē (for so they are termed of the Predestinators) & ẏ sayd Harte hath drawen out xiij. Articles to be obserued among his company, and as farre as I do beleue there comes none in their brotherhode except he be sworne. The other Iohn Kempe is a great trauailer abroad in Kent & what his doctrine is I am not hable to say. Hetherto M. Foxe. And that thou mayest know the better what this Henry Harte was consider I pray thee, what is reported of him. Where that zealous and faythfull seruaunt of God Iohn Careles in his examination by Doctor Martin verifieth that to bee true, whiche in the former place those two were burdened withall by Steuen Norish.

Pag.1605.

* This Kempe is now liuing and is preacher in the Yle of wight, and is by this popish priest slaūdered, the sayd Kemp being a very Godly man, read M. Fox his last booke. pag. 1976. Where he rehearseth Kemps story at large.

M. Fox reporteth his most godly & Christian doctrine. Pag.1976.a. Pag.1530.

H. Harte a peruerse heretique.

Of this Henry Harte sayth Iohn Careles, it had bene good for him if he had neuer bene borne: for many a simple soule hath hee shamefully seduced, beguiled and deceiued with his foule Pelagian opinion both in the dayes of kyng Edward and since his departure.

This Harte write a Confutation of certaine Articles of Christian Religion writtē by Iohn Careles, and sent vnto William Tyms prisoner in the Kynges Benche. The companions also of the same Henry was one M. Gibson who sought to peruert & turne frō the truth xij. godly Christiās which were Martyred. Of this vngracious cōpany also was one Trewe of Kente, who albeit before for the truthes sake he lost his eares (for perswadyng the people from goyng to Masse,) yet afterward happenyng into the cōpany of Pelagians he became deadly enemy to good Iohn Careles, as appeareth by Careles his examination, whiche he with his owne hand penned before he dyed in prison as in this booke of Martyrs is to be sene at large. Now if any man will demaunde, what is this to the Familie

M.Fox. pag. 1531.

agaynst

agaynst whom ye purposely mynde to deale. I aunswere that from this presẽt yeare, in the which this happened the doctrine of HN. began to pepe out, and although it haue a more louely name then the Heresies of the Libertines, Anabaptistes and Pelagians had: yet it is to him that is disposed to see very certaine by that cõparison which in this booke followeth of all ẏ sectes, that the groũd of all these Heresies were brought into England by Christopher Vitels and his complices out of Delph in Dutchland, where it had bene happy for our English Church it with the first Brokers thereof they had bene buryed and forgotten. Theire doctrine was then.

1. *The godly haue in them selues free will to do good.*
2. *They could not away with Predestination.*

Neither cã this Louely Family abide the most blessed and comfortable doctrine of Predestination: as is apparauntly to be sene in their first Epistle to M. Rogers, where they vtter this deuilish & blasphemous speach: *Your brethren in Christ (for their good faythes cause they haue in your licentious doctrine of Predestination and free election) fill all the prisons almost in England.*

But to adde somewhat which is hable by the mouth of a liuyng witnes to be iustified, who in Q. Maries tyme was present at the brochyng of this doctrine by Vitels the Ioygner his testimonie of this Family and their doctrine subscribed with his owne hand is this.

About the third yeare of Q. Maries raigne. *An. 1555.* at Michaelmas or not much after, I Henry Crinell of Willingham in the County of Cãbridge came to the towne of Colchester where I happened into a cõmon Inne. The cause of my repayre thether at that tyme was: that I was desirous to prouide, that my conscience should not be entangled with the Popish pitch: And beyng then there, I met with diuers of myne acquaintaunce as also with straungers, who came thether to conferre concernyng the safetie of their conscience, where William Rauen of S. Iues who came thether at that tyme with me & was my bedfellow hauyng likewise fled beyng in daunger for Religion. Predestination blasphemed by the Fam.

There we founde at our commyng thether one Christopher Vitels a Ioigner, who so farre as I could at that tyme learne held many straunge opinions, and also taught diuers pointes of doctrine scarce sofid and to me before vnheard of. The which Ioigner (as he thẽ priuily dissembled so since he hath bene noted openly for his cunnyng witte and curious phantasies) beyng as it seemed weary of his occupation, left his craft of Ioi-

 gning

gyuyng, and tooke vnto him a new trade of lyfe: so that of a simple scholer he became a great and learned Scholemaister of the doctrine of a man, who liued as he sayd beyond the seas an holy life and an vpright conuersation. This man he praysed very much, and reported many wonderfull thyngs of his Angellike behauiour, whom afterwardes I vnderstode to be one Henry Nicholas a Mercer of Delph in Holland.

The especiall pointes of Hereticall doctrine that the sayd Ioigner did then and there teach, were these.

Vitels doctrine in Queene Maries tyme at Colchester.
1. Infantes not to be Baptised.
2. Kyng Edwardes booke not Gods seruice.
3. Christ not God.
4. The godly sinne not.
5. The Pope no Antichrist.

1. *Children ought not to be Baptised, vntill they come to yeares of discretion.*
2. *He founde fault with the Letany in the booke of Common prayer set forth in King Edwardes tyme, affirming that it was not the right seruice of God.*

1. *Because it was sayd, God the Sonne redeemer of the world: for (sayth he) Christ is not God.*
2. *Because it was sayd, Haue mercy vpō vs miserable sinners, for the godly sinne not (sayth hee) and therefore, neede they not to vse that prayer.*

He affirmed also that the *Pope was not Antichrist, but he which doth not that which Gods law commaundeth, neither fulfilleth the requiring thereof he is Antichrist, & so are there many Antichristes.*

Furthermore at the same tyme one Iohn Barry seruaunt to M. Laurence of Barnehall in Essex came to the same Inne, to reason with the Ioigner about the Diuinitie of Christ, whom Vitels denied to be God. After they had entred cōference Iohn Barry alledged out of the 2. chap. 5. verse of S. Paule to the Phillipiās. Let the same mynde be in you which was in Christ Iesus, who beyng in the forme of God thought it no robbery to be equall with God. &c.

Vitels denyed that Christ is God.

Yea quoth Vitels the same mynde must be in you which was in Christ, the same mynde must be in you which was in Christ, & that there he stopped him: which wordes so oftē he repeated, that thereby he put Barry to silence & blankt him so that he had not a word to say: to the great offence of diuers, but especially of ij. women Gospellers, which came with Barry to heare him and Vitels conferre about that matter. And to say the truth, Vitels babling did so astonish diuers there present and my selfe also, that I was fully mynded to go to Oxford to aske cōsaile of Byshop Ridley & M. Latimer cōcernyng that matter, had I not

met

met with some man, to satisfie my conscience in the meane season.

The truth of the report of this conference I referre vnto the remembraunce of the sayd Iohn Barry him selfe if he be aliue as to others also, who were present at that conflict. The whiche Joigner since that tyme wandryng vppe and downe the Countrey (to visite his Disciples) came to the Towne of Willingham where I dwell, and sent for me to come and speake with hym at an Alehouse, but I sent hym word that I would not come at hym nor haue to doe with him. This is very true and so I testifie with myne owne hand.

By me Henry Orinell of Willingham.

Thus seest thou (gentle Reader) so much as yet hath come to my handes concernyng this matter simply set downe: to the whiche if the Familie shall reply, First that this belongeth nothyng vnto them: I aunswere: This chiefly doth concerne Vitels their Elder and chief Patriarch, who is a great Doctour of their Louely secte, and such Doctour such doctrine, such tree such fruite. &c. Secondly if they shall reply that this doctrine was taught by Vitels lõg since, and since by him recanted openly, and vpon harty repentaunce, which then he shewed he hath bene receiued into the Churche, and needeth not now to be feared for teachyng of any such doctrine: I aunswere (albeit the Famely deny that euer he recanted, yet seyng many witnesses aliue can auouch it to be true) if he since haue bene sory from his hart, and vppon his repentaunce be restored into the Church, God make him to be a member, not a molester of the Church, least in the end his repentaunce proue not to be as the sorrow of Simon Magus: but as Simon Peters who earnestly and with teares bewayled the deniall of his Maister: to whom sith he standeth or falleth, I will not iudge him: the Lord make hym both to bee and to continue of the number of his children. Amen.

Obiectiõ of the Familie.

Aunswere.

Vitels some tymes an Arriã God graunt he now be founde in that point.

Actes.8.24.
Math.26.75.

¶Notes vpon the booke entituled *Euangelium regni*, gathered by the Reuerend father in Chriſt *I. Y.* Byſhop of Rocheſter, with the aunſwere of the *Familie* vnto the ſayd Notes.

Generaly HN. his Euangelye is to be miſlyked for.

AS the Latin (a) *is meane, ſo is the ſtile or* (b) *maner of writyng darke and obſcure in many places: and although the Author had not ſet to his name, yet it ſhould ſeeme to be of ſome Friers doyng or ſome other that fauored the Church of Rome.*

Aunſwere of the Familie of Loue.

Odious compariſon of the Fam.

FOr (*a*) the firſt part where ye take exception at the meannes of the Latin (which yet perhaps ye would hardly match, much leſſe better it all thynges conſidered) me thinkes ye might out of reaſonablenes conſider, that ẏ meannes of the Latin in any worke, is not any hinderaunce to a right and good matter: for the more common the Latin is, the eaſier it is to be vnderſtanded of the ſimple Clerkes, and therefore that is not worthy of note to take exception at, for the ſingle and lowly mynded reſpect more the intent of a matter, then the floriſhed ſtile or ſpeach. &c.

Fam. maketh Gods word hard to be vnderſtode, ſo doe the Papiſtes contrary to the ſcripture. Prou. 8.8.9. Pſalme. 19.7.8. All without the Fam. fleſhly and worldly minded.

(*b*) Secondly whereas ye finde fault at the obſcuritie and darknes of the Authors writyng, I might aunſwere that it might ſeeme ſo much the more to be the ſame, that it geueth forth it ſelfe for (*videl.* a worke proceedyng from the ſpirite of the Lord) and therfore hard to be vnderſtode of all myndes of the fleſh, and out of the induſtrious prudencie of the manly reaſon or knowledge. (For then ſhould they right wel vnderſtand it, for the world can vnderſtand her owne) whoſe wiſedome maketh all men (in their manly wiſedome) meere fooles, compaſſing the wiſe in their wiſedome, and prouyng their thoughtes to

be

be but vayne will, therfore as S.Paule and likewise the Prophet affirmeth destroy the wisedome of the wise and reiect the vnderstandyng of the prudent. For it hath ben euermore an order with the holy ons of God, in the bringyng forth of the holy thynges, to expresse it more out of the authoritie of the spirite, and with power (I meane out of the efficacie of the Lord had by their essentiall operation in their inwardnes) thē with the entising wordes of manly wisedome, that our fayth might not stand or rest grounded in the wisedome of man, but in the power of God: by which meanes the naturall man perceiueth not any thyng of the spirite of God. Yea the thynges of God and his wisedome, are mere foolishnesse vnto him. And therefore he shalbe founde happyer that becommeth deceiued with such a godly deceit, then shall those which are borne in hand to be in a right way and a good case beyng yet in the meane tyme directed with the dreames of mans fantasie in steade of cleare truth. &c.

Vntruth for the Prophet Esay, and the rest are very eloquent

All, without the Fam. directed with dreames of mans fantasie.

Rochester.

THe greatest part of this boke is nothyng but a brief discourse either a rehearsall of the story of the Bible, as appeareth frō the. 5. chapter, to the. 27. &. 28. chapters. And his collectiō is none other, but such as any meanly learned may gather by diligēt readyng of the Scriptures.

The Familie of Loue.

HOw well soeuer the greatest part of the booke bee iudged by you to be nothyng, but a bare brief discours or rehearsall of the histories of the Bible: whiche any meanly learned (as you say) might do the like yet seemeth it to me to be of greater force neither haue I euer in my tyme heard or by readyng perceiued that the greatest learned among the prudent wisenesse (which rest grounded more on ẏ litterall knowledge of the Christiā veritie then on the beyng of the same) haue atchiued the like or

No booke of any wrighter like HN. his Euangely.

brought the match therof to light (all thyngs considered.) For it is not onely an euident declaration of the singular good will and operations of God towardes his creatures in respectyng and tenderyng their saluation, darckly figured foorth in the Bible: but also and expresse manifestation of the approchyng of tyme, wherein the purpose of the Lord drawen a long and begon as the tyme state and age of the worlde would permit the same touchyng the disposing of the wicked world with her ministers and adherentes, & the erectyng of the righteous world to florish there ouer in vigour for euermore becōmeth as he there testifieth. Full accomplished through the same seruice of God, or ministrations of his loue expressed or mencioned in the same booke accordyng to the promises. To the which ministration God hath chosen the Authour as he there alledgeth to be a right minister, and prepared him thereto, in the fourme and sorte mencioned in the head of his booke, vnto which like function and holy annoyntyng no conceited Scripturelearned or Doctour of the letter, that I can any way marke or perceiue hath in these dayes attained or reached. And whether that be a pretendyng of the Ghost or no, that will well appeare and be seene in his tyme by the sequele thereof (to weete) in the perseueraunce and foorth goyng of the same among and with all such as shall endure to see the triall therof. &c.

HN. his Euangelie in Exposition of darke figures in the Bible.

No learned mā in these dayes like HN.

Rochester.

THe Authour doth much pretend the holy Ghost, and entituleth his booke, An Epistle written from the holy Ghost, which is to be suspect of hygh Reuelations, daungerous to deceiue the simple.

Familie of Loue.

This is aunswered in the Section before.

Rochester.

Intrea-

INtreatyng of Antichrist in the 28. chapter, he teacheth no certaine doctrine, who he is, or where to be founde, that we may know him & beware of his doctrine, but it seemeth altogether doubtfull, in so much that the Note in the margēt sayth, O that this Antechrist were knowen. Whereas if the Authour would haue dealt plainly and according to the scriptures, he might easly haue shewed that Rome is the seate of Antechrist. And that the succession of Popes, and that body and kingdome is the very Antichrist mencioned and described in the. 2. Thessal. 2. Apocal. 13. 17. &c.

¶In the Chapter 31. 32. the Authour *HN.* bewrayeth him selfe to be a Papist.

1. FIrst, he calleth the Church of Rome, the communion of all Christiās, whereas it is but a particular Church fallen away from the vniuersall Church of Christ. HN. a Papist.

2. Although he seemeth to cōfesse that the Church of Rome hath not that perfection of Religion, whiche it had in tymes past (which the Papistes do and must graunt) yet he seemeth to allow and speake reuerently of all Popishe orders as they be now.

The Pope hee calleth the chief annoynted, the chief Byshop, or high Priest, who hath his beyng in the most holy sanctuarie of true and perfect holynes, most holy Father. Chap. 31.

Next vnto him he placeth the Cardinals whom he calleth most holy and famous, and hee sayth that they are next the most auncientest and holy Father the Pope in most holy Religion and vnderstandyng.

Next vnto Cardinals he reconeth Byshops whom he calleth chief Priestes.

After Byshops, he nameth Curates, Deacons. &c.

After those he maketh mencion of Monkes, whom he commendeth as men addicted to holynesse, and separated from the world, and all carnall desires.

But most playnly the Authour sheweth him selfe a frend to the Church of Rome, saying: that many through conten- Chap. 31. sent. 4

tion and discorde did cast of the Church of Rome, and dyd blaspheme her with her ministeries, and of their own braynes pretendyng the Scriptures, haue brought in other ministeries and Religion: they spoke much of the word of God. Who doubteth that this is the voyce and iudgement of Papistes agaynst Protestauntes and true Christians.

Familie of Loue.

Where as you furthermore complayne of the insufficiencie of the expressing of *Antechrist* (as to say who he is and where to be founde) because the Authour applyeth him not to the Pope and his succession in the Church of Rome, it seemeth if the matter were well looked vnto, that mē should finde that *Antechrist* euen in the very selfe same place from whence you gather your exception flatly detected: (although he is not so employed to mēs contētations) for if men could see what Christ accordyng to the spirite is, as he is a liuyng power of God, were whereas his whole scope & drift of writyng stretcheth) they should then right well perceiue thereout that the man of sinne and child or broode of the Deuill and cōdemnati[illegible]n (beyng a right aduersarie or an expresse contrary beyng vnto Christ, the righteousnes of God the father) and raignyng in all states of men generally. Beyng fleshly Popes or other, from the tyme of the declinyng of the man from the true fayth in Christ the light of lyfe to the addictyng of him selfe to the lye or darcknes or euer such tyme as they become conuerted to their God and are regenerated in the spirite of their mynde, is the greatest *Antichrist* which also frō the very begynnyng as likewise in the very corporall appearaunce, of Christ in the flesh (like as S. Iohn also expresseth) impugne it and persecute it in the truth of God (and that in the inwardnesse of the man to the establishyng of all vnrighteousnesse in him, and not onely a certaine disordred or abused *Papistrie* (yea or euer the *Papistrie* was thought of) which no

Christ what he is according to the Familie.

Antichrist nothing but sinne according to the Fam.

Pope

Pope also (or such outward fleshly creature) could or can euer worke or bryng to passe. And therefore deceiue not your selfe in the point, to iudge the Author to be a maintainer of any fleshly or creaturelike Pope with his adherentes in their abusion of Ceremoniall seruices & Ceremonies: but he driueth his matter onely (as in his worke beyng well noted you may sée) to this point (to wit) that after the entraunce of the darknesse once chaunced (the manly ge...erations beyng falne away from the fayth towardes God, which was established by Christ in his Apostles and Disciples) the old Fathers grew out of a zealousnes of the mynde towardes God and his righteousnesse, to institute certaine Ceremonies and seruices (so neare as they could out of their insight and comprehendyng, that they by their diligent study and searchyng of the Scriptures had attained vnto concerning Gods truth hit the same) that resembled or were conformablest to the holy and diuine Scriptures to a commemoration of the thyngs wrought and brought to passe before with Christ and his holynes in the very true beyng to the susteinyng and staying vp of the ignoraunt people in the tyme of darknes from fallyng into any greater absurdities, enormities and errours, that might haue happened vnto thẽ and which also did happen vnto many such as maliciously and obstinately, not rightly seyng but rather in meanyng to set vp some better, degressed and winded of them selues there from and maliciously blasphemed and continewed the same, tell that the light of Gods truth might spryng foorth agayne or be erected in the seruice of the loue, accordyng to the promises and goeth not about to establish the same in, and of their ceremoniall (much lesse abused) seruice and Ceremonies (where about men presently so greatly striue and varie) now in this present tyme of the light of loue) whiche he affirmeth to be ẏ day of the cleare & righteous iudgemẽt of God: wherein god will restore all thynges to their right (to wit) bryng or set the lye in his lying beyng to be condemned in the hellish caue, and the truth likewise in his right fourme or degrée, to wit to preuayle florish and beare sway ouer the vnrighteousnes for euermore.) Whereby that the will of God might euē so be accomplished in earth as in heauen. Wherefore me thinkes that should be very small discernyng in such as can not distinct the shadowes figures or image of a thyng from the body it selfe, or the very true beyng either substaunce of the same. And that he speaketh of mens ignoraunce in that place, and touchyng their slender knowledge & vnderstandyng in Gods worde that layeth he forth flatly to the effectuall word and not the imagelike or written word wherein the right Christians are not iniuried but the conceited Christians detected.

Two kyndes of Gods worde after HN. his Familie.

Rochester.

THe rest of the booke from the 34. Chapter vnto the end is of the callyng of the Gentiles, and of the grace of God offred to the world in the last age of the world, which seemeth to be the best part of that booke.

Familie of Loue.

IT is well that ye like some part of the booke, and if ye could therewithall note that there were a defectiō frō the truth, and that there were also by that meanes no difference to bee had, betwixt a ceremoniall either letter doctour Christian, and an vncircumcised Heathen so had ye then somewhat for your part.

Rochester.

THus haue you a tast of this booke gathered as the tyme would serue, whereby it appeareth to be no such precious price of worke as of some it is supposed to be. Such fayre shewes and glorious titles may soone deceiue the simple to haue such bookes in more admiration then the holy Scriptures. But we haue Moses and the Prophetes let vs heare them and iudge all others by them.

Luke. 16. 28.

Family of Loue.

I do not so collect by the authors wrighting that he would prefer his writing aboue the scriptures geuen by inspiration of God, and brought forth, and written by the holy Fathers in times past. But if you had well marked or considered the same, he witnesseth as by a concordable, and uniforme testimonye, either by record of the same their writynges what the Lord will now accomplish in these last dayes, wishing euery one in the same booke to search the Scriptures, whether that they also mētion and record not the very same: affirmyng also therewith that God is not ne cannot be a God of contentatiō but of peace & unitie. And that God moreouer, hath stirred him vp to bee a seruiceable instrument, or as his elect minister to bryng downe (accordyng to his promises written in the Scriptures) all controuersies growne among men about their misunderstanding of the scriptures to bryng ẏ same to an end. And doth also in ẏ same booke, vncouer sundry secret thinges which they that haue seing eyes may by ententiue reading of the same together with the Lordes assistaunce well perceiue and understand: that no selfewise, or enuious scripture learned could or can euer attaine unto it agayne. What iniurie were it (seing that it proceedeth by the same spirite) to valew it equall with those same sacred scriptures, that were tofore written by the holy one of God.

A notable vntruth for HN. no where in his bookes doth wish mē to read the Scriptures.

Horrible blasphemie HN. his booke of Euangelie made equall with the word of God.

Also ye may remember that the fleshly Iewes had also for their aunswere to Christ enuying agaynst him being the truth it selfe, the same testimonye that ye alledge, to weete, that they had Moses and the Prophets: &c, But who were in the meane time greater persecutours of him then they.

Rochester.

WE are sure that the holy Scriptures were wrighten by the (spirite of Loue, and truth) the holy ghost: And conteine all true and necessary and sufficient doctrine for our Ephe.5.21. *saluation, let vs not hould vpon men: proue all thinges, hould* 1.Iohn.4.1. *that which is good, beleue not euery spirite but proue the spirites.*

Family of Loue.

I Graunt that right discerning is good, and commeth from the Lord, and through him from them, whome he and not themselues placeth, and by them that are set in the right place of iudgement by the Lord himselfe, and not by those that sitt on their owne stoole: for it is to be doubted that so many as take vpon them that office of iudgemẽt, or medling with gods matters or euer Christ be come vnto them, or haue a liuing shape in them, that they all will comme to short in their reconing. &c.

I may not deny but that there is conteined in the scriptures geuen by inspiration of God (being rightly vnderstanded, followed, and obeyed,) necessary and sufficient doctrine of saluation: but for want of these three principall pointes, many haue small profite truely. I could also with all my hart wishe that man with man committed not filthines, nor depended one vpon an other: but to stay them onely on the Lordes truth, and not on flesh and bloud, so were then all controuersies at an end.

No man may iudge of doctrine but the F..milye.

It were well also to proue all thinges: but not as semeth me by the crooked rule of mans owne iudgement, or fleshly minde and concerning, nor by his imagination (without the light of Gods truth, or spirite of righteousnes and loue:) taken on in constructing, and wresting of the right sence and minde of the scriptures which being seperated from the light of lyfe, as he in the same worke alleadgeth is a closed booke, or a darke word without light, and the seruice administred thereout as a dead bodye without a soule, or as a dead wife deceased from her husband, which could bring fourth no children of lyfe. For what can the naturall man iudge, that is altogether ignoraunt of the thinges of God, or yet open the holy

thinges

thinges without the key of Dauid, or behould the Paradice of God, when as men can not frely enter the Seraphin with his fiery sword not being taken away: or yet iudge of an other which hath ouercome, and attained to haue a new name, written in the white stone: that lyeth himselfe, yet in the meane time altogether bewrapped and buried vnder the bondage and subiectiō of the earthly being, and vngodlynes. &c.

Consider therefore euery thing in his right degrée (if you be endewed with ghoastly vnderstanding, and possessed with the right spirite of iudgemēt,) and then out of your spiritualnes iudge all thinges according to the ballance of equitye, and trying squaire or measure line of righteousnes in the lyfe and truth. Trie also the spirits by the same rule, and be not vnbeleuing towardes the right spirit, but follow and embrace that which is good. For if you can shew vs any passinger God of Israel, or any better lawe, rites, and ordinaunce: then is his lawes, rites, and ordinaunces, or anye perfecter life then the loue: whereon Christe with his holy ones haue heretofore testified, (Whereto also the Author presently as a concordable witnes with the same doth only point and direct vs) or that there be any better thing then the eternall lyfe and the loue it selfe. So let not thē that same most best, be withheld from vs (whilest that we onely enforce vs thereunto) that we might serue euē to the onely liuing God in vniformenes of hart, and vnpartialitye of minde together with an vpright righteousnes, and holynes.

Take this briefe freindly & well meaning aunswere to your exceptions in good part, and way it not as a matter done to defend the worke by the way of contending: but rather as one out of goodwill doe but geue you occasion thereby to weigh more distinctly, and reasonably of that which commeth so lyuely, & freindly to your hands, out of grace, to your profit and welfare. Therefore saue labour for making any further reply hereunto, least you doe but lose your trauaile herein, for Christ with his holy ones will not now in this same day of the Loue (lyke as doe the princes of the earth whose kingdome is of this world) set vp and maintayne his kingdome with contention, and discorde, but with peaceablenes, louing kindnes and long suffering. But if one listed to see wrestlers bestirre them in their play: then for to graunt them leuill ground, he might not well denay. And yf one should trauers the right of his case: then must the Judge sit vnparciall in iudgement place, so shall then all matters in equalitye out fall: but otherwise be peruerted and oppresse right we shall.

Louely Poetrie of the Familie.

Vale ꝗ. F. L.

Errours and absurde asseuerations out of HN. his Euangelie, gathered by William Wilkinson.

Preface sent.2. Resurrection is appeared vnto HN.

HN. Sayth the day of Loue (by him preached) is the appearyng of our Lord Jesus Christ in the Resurrection. Esay. 26. c. 1. Cor. 15. f. of the dead, wherein the law and the Prophetes, and all that is written of Christ becommeth fulfilled. Luke. 24. e.

Law and Prophets & all fulfilled in HN. his Loue day.

Preface. sent. 3. HN. taketh on him Iohn Baptistes office.

HN. sayth he is the Aungell of the Lord, or messenger before him for to prepare his way. Math. 3. a. Math. 11. b. and to publish an euerlastyng Euangelie. Math. 24. Apoc. 14. a. vnto all generations, languages and peoples accordyng to the promises.

Sent. 4. HN. his writinges the Gospell.

All the testimonies of HN. set foorth in the Glasse of righteousnesse, are the Gospell.

Sent. 6.

HN. sayth the *Familie* is the rest of God prepared frõ the begynnyng, for the people of God, and for all repentaunt persons: and is appeared in the last tyme accordyng to the promises.

Cap. 1. sent. 4. Libertie of Religion.

HN. permitteth to euery nation, what Religion they will, so they hold with his heresie of the Loue.

HN.

HN. receiued this message of his Euangelie, from the mouth of God him selfe. Chap.2. sent.1.

HN. maketh the day of the publishyng his Euangelie, to be the last commyng of Christ in iudgement with thousãds of Saints. For proofe he citeth Esay.3.b. Math. 24.d. and.25.d. Jude.1.b. Fol.4.

HN. buildeth vpon miracles without Scriptures. Cap.2.sent.1.

HN. sayth he will declare the secret misteries of God, and make relation of thynges hidden before the world. Cap.2.sent.11.

HN. sayth the former kyngdome, wherein man was set (that is Adam before his fall) is brought agayne in the lowlynes of the vpright beyng. Cap.4.sent.1.

HN. sayth of the Preachers, that they vaunt and geue foorth them selues for Christians, and as illuminated men, that are Maisters of the Scripture, beyng craftie, subtill, peruerse of hart, darcke in their vnderstandyng, of a peruerse nature. Cap.4.sent.4. HN. rayleth on the Ministers & Preachers of Gods word.

HN. sayth that no man how wise and vnderstandyng soeuer he be in the knowledge of the Scripture, can by any meanes vnderstand or comprehend the wisedome of God, but they onely that be of his *Familie.* Sent.5. Onely HN. his Familie wise.

Therefore hope we (sayth HN.) with much ioy ouer the dead whiche dye in the Lord, or are dead in him, (to wéete) that they in their Resurrection from death shall liuyngly come vnto, or méete with vs. For all the dead of the Lord, or the members of Christ shall now liue and arise with their bodyes, and we shall assemble with them, and they with vs. Sent.15. Resurrectiõ cõmeth to passe in HN. his new day.

This day of the Loue is the last commyng of Christ. Heresie sent.18.

Abell was slayne through the wicked nature of sinne, through the handes of his brother *Cain.* Cap.5.sent.1.

HN. depraueth the whole Historie of Abraham, from Gene.16. vnto the 27. Chapter by turnyng it into an Allegorie. Cap.8.sent.4.5.6.8.&c.

The greatest must serue the lesse, that is sayth HN. the great righteousnesse of the law, with the great knowledge or prudence of the fleshe, or of the earthly beyng, Cap.9.sent.7.

which is borne out of the letter, shall serue the litle mynded simplicitie of Christ.

Cap.13.sent.3. HN. peruerteth the fourth Commaundement.

Cap.13.sent.4. HN. sayth the Ceremoniall law is needefull to be obserued.

Cap.19.sent.5. HN. termeth our Baptisme an handfull of water.

Sent.11. Who soeuer is not Baptised accordyng to the forme or maner of Iohn: that is with the water of repentaunce confessing their sinne, he is no Christian.

Cap.23.sent.2. No man sayth *HN*. can Minister the vpright seruice or Ceremonies of Christ truly, but the regenerate.

Cap.23.sent.2. HN. denyeth the outward admission of Ministers.

Cap 25.sent.6. The *Familie* shalbe in all perfection euerlastyngly vpõ earth, to the end, that Gods will might be done in earth as it is in heauen.

Cap.25.sent.6. HN. boasteth perfection in this lyfe *and in many places.*

Cap.25.sent.6. HN. sayth that this testimony and publishyng of the ioyfull message (*videl. his Gospell*) is the kyngdome of perfection, and that all the seruices, and prophecies, which are gone out from God doe lead hereunto, and rest and cease herein.

Ibid. No dissembling is lawfull by HN. HN. his sayth *Familie* must not conceale or dissemble their Religiõ, but they must hold it out before euery one, whõ the Lord stirreth vp in their wayes.

Sent.10. In HN. his *Familie* is the true, most holy of the euerlastyng beyng of God, from whence the vpright seruice of the *Familie* is ministred: whereunto all seruices and prophecies, which are gone out from God, and his truth, do lead, as to the right and very true perfection: that God might euer be declared vpon earth.

All prophecies doe lead and end in HN. his Fam.

HN. sayth of all preachers without his *Fam*. that they are vnilluminated, vnregenerated, vnrenewed, vngodded vnsent, good thinkyng, which out of their literall knowledge come into the sheepefold of the beleuers, besides the Church of Christ. Which Christ calleth theeues, wolues, murtherers, false hartes, and Scripture learned.

Cap.28.sent.4. HN. raileth vpon preachers.

Cap.30.sen.5.6. HN. alloweth confession of sinnes in his *Familie* and forge-

forgeuenesse of the same, and clensing whiche he calleth *Purgatorie*. HN.liketh of purgatorye.

HN. sayth that the *Romishe* Church hath obediently grounded it selfe on the seruices and ceremonies, which are the prefiguration of true Christianitie, and her seruices, and with diligence and feruēcie obserued the same to a good discipline, or ordinaunce of the congregations. Cap.31.sent.1. HN.Fauoreth poperie. Popish discipline good by HN.

HN. sayth that the annoyntyng with oyle, which the Papistes vse, is a Sacrament of the holy Churche of Christ: and signifieth vnto vs the annoyntyng of Priests, and Elders, with the holy Ghost. Cap.31.sen.4.7. Orders a Sacrament by HN.

HN. alloweth of the Pope, (because sayth he) through his seruice of the holy word, the true clearenes of Christ was spread abroad in all landes. Sent.5.7. The truth spred in all landes by the Pope sayth HN.

HN. of the Popish *Hierarchie* namely Cardinals, Bishops, Parish priestes, signifiyng the Leuiticall Priestes Deacons or helpers of the Parish Priestes, Sextons, or keepers of holy thynges. Sent. 8. 10.14.17. 18.19.

Monkes whiche signifie such as dwell alone, and are through the loue of righteousnes sanctified, and therfore seperated from the world, and all that is fleshly: for to liue euen so as sanctified ones of God. Sent. 23.

All the aforesayd (sayth HN.) hath bene vsed in tymes past in his true beyng, whē the light of lyfe had his clearenes, but now is become darkned.

HN. condemneth as many out of their knowledge, whiche they take out of the Scriptures: brought in certaine seruices, and ceremonies in any other wise and order, then the Churche of Rome appoynted: as vnorderly reiectyng and blasphemyng the Catholique Church of Rome, and rentyng the consent, and nurturable sustentation of the same. Cap.32.sent.4.

It is mere lyes and vntruth which the Scripture learned, through the knowledge whiche they get out of the Scripture institute, preach and teach. Cap.33.sent.11.

HN. sayth God raysed him vp (which lay altogether dead without breath and lyfe) from the death annoynted Cap.34.sent.1. Blasphemye.

 him

him with his godly beyng, named him selfe with him, and Godded him with him selfe.

Cap.35.sent.1. All the Scripture speakyng of Christ, of his sæde, of his commyng in his glory, is in this day of the Loue fulfilled.

Cap.35.sent.3.4 5.6.7. HN. sayth that the prophecies. 1. Edras.4.d. Esay.3. e.and.11.b.Ezech.39.c. Soph.3.b.Zach.2.b.are in this day of Loue fulfilled.

Sent.8. Resurrectiō passed already saith HN. Moreouer the raysing vp, and Resurrection from the dead, commeth to passe also, in this same-day through the appearyng of the commyng of Christ, in his maiestie, ac-accordyng to his saying, John.6.c. I will rayse him vp agayne in the last day.

Cap.36.sent.13 Cap.37.sent.1. and.14.and.cap. 38.sent.1.3. Cap.4. sent.7. In this day are all prophecies fulfilled.

The seruice of Loue is the perfection it selfe.

All (sayth HN.) shall perishe without the *Familie of Loue.*

¶ Hereticall affirmations, and vngodly expositions of Scriptures by HN. out of the documentall sentences.

Even thus haue the seruices of the testimonyes of the holy spirite of Loue their ministrations among the perfect ones: and do remoue the midle wall: which is betwixt ÿ perfect and vnperfect ones. To make euen so of twayne that it be one namely God, and the man in one true being of Jesus Christ. cap.1.sent.4. Scripture vildly abused by Allegories.

Nothing can come from the true perfection, but all humble and méeke vertues and righteousnes which flow out of perfection. cap.1.sent.7. Nothyng commeth from HN. his perfect ones but perfection.

He alledgeth that there is a perfection in his lyfe, to proue it, he quoteth 1.Cor.13.b.cap.1.sent.9.10.2.Pet.1.d. Perfection.

The perfect can bring forth nothing but all good, and loue, quoted as a profe. John.13,14.16. he leadeth thē into all truth. Cap.2.sent.1.

¶ Christ is taken on

Videl.	1.	With an imagination of knowledge.	Cap.2.sent.1.
	2.	Good thincking of the hart.	
	3.	Or out of the text of the letter.	

No man can teach the word of doctrine of Christ but such as haue bene disciples obedient of the Loue. cap. 2.senten.1.

Unilluminated Scripture learned and vnsent preachers. cap.2.sent.2.

The word that is ministred speakeable or in letters out of the Loue, and out of the true lyfe, is also Christ after the fleash. cap.2.sent.4. Christ after the flesh what?

For euen so among the beleuers of the word, the word became flesh, and dwelt among them, and Jesus was in

Christ tooke no flesh the virgin, but doctrine. &c

such sort borne of the virgin Mary out of the seede of Dauid after the flesh that is of pure doctrine, out of the seede of the Loue, and whosoeuer feadeth of the ouerflowne word, and his lyfe beleuingly in his soule, he eateth truely the flesh of Christ, and drinketh his bloud: and is raysed vp by Christ in the last day to eternall lyfe, and becommeth euen so in his new birth, Consubstanciated with Christ after the spirit. cap. 2. sent. 5.

As also for that the seruauntship of the Law should be noe Gal. 3. c. c. heire with the beleuer. cap. 3. sent. 10.

That same was the complaint of Abraham, which he or euer he had a sonne, or an heire complayned before the Lord, that he had obteined no. Gen. 15. a. seede out of the beliefe. And supposed euen so that his seruaunt (that is his seruauntship out of the law) should be his heire, but the sonne wich shall be borne out of the spirite, that is out of the fayth of Abraham. cap. 3. sent. 11.

HN. his perfect ones not subiect to Gods worde alwayes.

As long as the young ones are childish, and not yet growne vp vnto the Elderdome of the perfect being, they are yet vnder the ordinance of the Lord or his word: not that they should alwayes remaine as subiect thereunder, but vntill the appoynted tyme, vntill the manly old age in the godly vnderstanding of the holy word: (that is) tell sinne in them be subdued, sayth HN. cap. 3. sent. 12.

Shrift.

Let euery one confesse his sinnes wherein he falleth before his Elder in the holy vnderstanding, and make manifest before him all his dealyng, and conuersation. cap. 4. sent. 3.

Scripture vntruly Expounded. 1. Cor. 15. cap. verses. 50. 53. 54 Resurrectiō denied.

Verely the mortall wherof S. Paule witnesseth is not any creature of earthly flesh & bloud, but it is the liuing word or being of God: which in the beginning was mortall in the manhode, and is in vs for our sinnes cause become mortall. cap. 6. sent. 3.

The letter slayeth. 2. Cor. 3. 6. namely the administration of the law after the letter, or ministration of Christ after the flesh: that is nothing els but that the letter acording to the requiring of Christ, pointeth, and leadeth vs to the death of sinne, and withdraweth euen so our mindes, and thoughtes, from all that which is vngodly. cap.11.sent.6.

A man which loueth the vpright righteousnes cannot apply hinselfe vprightly thereunto, before he haue wholy geuen ouer himselfe to the gratious worde, and seruice of Loue, for to be obedient vnto the word: and euen so to be admitted thereto by his elder in the holy vnderstanding, and minister of the gracious word, for to become taught therein. cap.13. sent. 1.

The Family wil haue all the whole man or nothyng at all. Admission into the Familie.

He that is admitted into the Famil. promiseth before God and his holy ones, that he will cleaue onely to the word, and his requiring, and shew faythfull obedience out of his whole hart and minde, and not seperate himselfe therefrom for euer. cap. 13. sent. 4.

Admissiō to the Familie with an othe. Herodes oth in the Familie. Why few Fambles returne frō HN. his doctrine.

But if they (*our ould sinnes which he calleth our Paramours which in tymes past we loued. sen.7.*) take or lay hold on vs with force, and violence, and that then although we cry there commeth not any power or helpe vnto vs, for to withstand their force and violence: and that they euen so rauish vs agaynst our will: so are we guiltles of the transgression, for we haue cryed for to be released from the tyranny of the euill, and there is no helpe come vnto vs, *Ergo*, if we sinne, we are guiltles. Of the which guiltles transgressing, the law likewise witnesseth, where it sayth: Deut. 11.27.

Giltles of particular sinnes. Antecedent. HN. his argument that we may sinne.

A woman which is violently taken in the field, whereas there is not any help, and so rauished (and although she haue cryed aloud and gotten no helpe) she shall be guiltles of the transgressing. cap.13.sent.8.

Scriptures wrested.

If it chaunce that any man through weakenesse doe sinne, yet let him not couer his sinnes: but let him confesse them before his Elder, in the holy vnderstandyng, and repent him, so shall then the Lord be gracious vnto him and forgiue his sinnes. *Cap.13. senten.8. and Cap.11. senten.6.*

Shrift.

This is the day which God Actes. 17. e. hath appointed

HN. taketh to him that is pro-

 ted

per to Christ. Agge.2.7. Heb.12.27. HN.1.Epist. cap.1.sent.2.& pub.of the peac. sent 14.

ted for to iudge in the same the cōpasse of the earth with righteousnesse, through his word, in whom he hath concluded his iudgement. *Cap.15.sent.4.*

Shrift worse then Popish.

They of the *Familie* must manifest them selues and their whole hart, dealyng, and inclination, to the Elders in the Familie of Loue. *Cap.16.sent.4.*

Conference denyed.

Haue not much prate or disputation with straungers, nor with thē that fall away from the seruice of the Loue, nor with the vnwillyng ones & resisters. *Cap.16.sent.18.*

O ye adioyned ones, and incorporated ones to the word ye shall not hold you, Math.18.and.c.1.Cor.5.b. 2.Thessal.3.b.

HN.his holy bread dayly eaten at Tables. Scripture wrested.

Common with straungers and decliners from the seruice of Loue, for to eate dayly with them at your Table the holy bread John.6.d.Actes.2.f. But breake and eate the same among ech other. *Cap.18.sent.10.*

Beare in no wise any enmitie to any one, but shew alwayes your brotherly loue, which ye haue amongest ech other. *Cap.16.sent.11.*

Sinnes forgiuen in the Familie onely.

Come now all and turne you to this mercy seat of the Loue of the holy spirite of Jesus Christ, and obtaine the forgiuenes of your sinnes. *Cap.19.sent.2.3.*

ARTICLES

Which I exhibited vnto a frend of *mine, to be conuaied vnto the Familie of loue,* that I might be certified of the doubtes *in them contayned. Which for my further instruction* one *Theophilus* sent me with a letter, and an *Exhortation annexed vnto the sayd Articles,* with his exposition, in manner following.

THEOPHILVS

TO the collector of these after expressed Articles (that out of his malitious minde peruerted the sence, and true minde of the Author, and framed sundry of them into errors,) and to the rest of his Assistants in these and such vncharitable dealinges, wheresoeuer they be, greeting.

W. WILKINSONS TITLE.

ERrors out of the bookes of HN. *faythfully, and truely* (if sayth THEOPHILVS such preachers as be vncircumsided both in tongue and eares be to be beleued in these dayes) *gathered, and quoted as in his booke by Chapter, and Section they are to be found.*

THEOPHILVS.

YE might rather in truth haue affirmed, vnfaythfully, lyingly, slaunderously, and malitiously, or vncharitably. Gay Rhetoricke of the Familie.

W. WILKINSONS CONFVTATION.

MArke (I pray thee gentle Reader) what a chollorick, and taunting spirite these Familers be of, and yet they needes will be called the Familye of loue: as though all that com-

 meth

meth from them, were nothing but loue, and the very pefection of it selfe, (For so they affirme of themselues. Now if these be their swéete and amiable wordes, and louely phrases, what cutting tearmes shall wée then looke for, when they shall sée vs that wée withstand their enterprise, and controule their doctrine: especially seing that I did neither by worde, nor writing, euer geue thē any occasion. But if this be their loue, and perfection, then truely I confesse that I meane not to walke with them. I enuy not their happines, neyther care I amōgest them to be reckoned vnperfect. In déede these speaches be such as the Anabaptistes vsed agaynst the preachers of the Gospell, which withstode their heresie, they rayled on them calling them Lutherans. Fol. 254. False and carnall Gospellers 255. erroneous and vnskilfull preachers 256. succeders of the Pharisies. ibid. Hypocrites, blinde guides, fooles, serpentes, generations of vipers, hirelinges, 2576. fellowes of théeues whome Dauid maketh mention of Psal. 50. These were the flowers of Anabaptistes Rhetorique: but S Paule teacheth vs another kinde of Eloquēce, which becometh the children of God. Let all thinges (sayth he) be done in loue, and the fruite of the spirite is loue, ioy, peace, long suffering, gentlenes, goodnes, fayth: Loue suffereth long, it is bountifull, it enuieth not, it doth not boast, it is in déede and truth, not in tongue and worde onely. Now whether this family haue bene taught in the schole of the holy ghost, or in the schole of the Anabaptistes, I leaue it to the indifferent reader to be considered. But if any man shall muse to sée such enuious speaches to flowe from so louely a familye, I aunswere: No merueile at all, for such a fountayne, such water: men gather not grapes of thornes, nor figges of thistles. And true it is that our Sauiour sayth, out of the aboundance of the hart the mouth speaketh.

Docum. sentences 1. Chap. sect. 3.7.

Bullenger agaynst the Anabaptistes.

1. Cor. 16.14. Gal. 5.22. 1. Cor. 13.4. 1. Iohn. 3.18.

Math. 7.16. Luk. 6.44. Math. 12. 34.

ARTICLE

ARTICLE. 1. No Church.

THe house of Loue sayth HN *is the Church of God. 1.Exhor.cap.7.s.37.*

Theophilus his exposition.

FIrst note that it is all one to say the house of Loue and the house of God: the familye of Loue, and the family of God: and then proceede.

William Wilkinson.

DArke wordes & double speaches, haue bin allwayes the starting holes of heretiques, playne meaning men walke openly at noone, lewd and euill disposed persons vage, and wander abroad at midnight. For he that euill doth, hateth the light, neyther commeth to the light least his déedes should be reproued. Yée speake in a riddle, neither doth your reason follow. Because it is framed *A petitione principij*. You take that to be graunted which is in controuersie (or rather cleane false.) For what proprietye of speach is this, or how doth this reason follow: The house of God is the Church of God: therefore *the good willingones in England*, which are named *the Familye of Loue*, are the Church of God. But if you will in playne wordes affirme, that you onely which are of that familye, and no man els which is not of that societye, is of the Church: First I aunswere, that the *Anabaptistes* did lykewise of their conuenticles affirme that they were the true Church: Next I say: that when I shall vnderstād your meaning better, I will tell you more. In the meane time I would you knew, that you are not of the Church, but yée haue made a Schisme from the Church. Christes coate without seame ye haue rent in péeces. Truely sayth a learned father: whosoeuer doth cut a sunder the vnitye, and disturbe the peace of the Church, whereby the fellowship of the faythfull is torne into diuers partes, he is a Schismatique. *Such*

Iohn.3.20.

Fam. of Loue in the briefe rehearsall the title.

Bulling. 1.boke chap.8.leaf.18.a

Cyp. de simpl. August. ad Crescon.2.boke 7.chapter.

Schismatiques, who.

Num. 16.1.

2.Cor. 1.12.

Actes.20.28.29
30.verses.

Rom.16.17.18.

Fam . bred and
brought vp a-
mong the Pa-
piftes.
Deut.27. 18.

Math.18.7.

1.Cor.11.19.
Reuel.3.11.

1.Tim.3. 15.

Math.24.5.24.

1.Iohn.4.1.

Ezech.33.4.

were Chorah, *Dathan*, and *Abiram* agaynſt Moyſes : ſuch were they which diſquieted the church of Cozinth by hol= ding ſome of Paule : ſome of Peter: ſome of Appollos, ſome of Chziſt. Such are they whome *S. Paule* bad the Elders of Epheſus take hæde of, foz they ſhould be gre= uous wolues not ſparing the flock , who ſpeaking per= verſe thinges, ſhould dzawe diſciples after them. Of ſuch *S.Paule* ſayth: I beſeech you brethren marke thoſe, which cauſe diſſention amongeſt you, contrary to the doctrine which you haue receiued, and auoid them.&c.

As foz you of that Familie , neither were ye of vs , noz went from vs. So ye haue choked the wozd in many weake bzethzen, laying ſtumbling blocks in the wayes of the ſimple. Ye haue led the blinde out of their way, therefoze are ye by Gods mouth accurſed. And albeit that offences muſt nædes come, yet woe be to him by whome they come, it were better a milleſſone were han= ged about his neck, then to offend one of the litle ones. There muſt be hereſies in the Church to try the fayth= full, and happy is he that holdeth faſt leaſt another take his crowne . When ye can ſhew me by the ſcripture, that your Familie is the houſe of God , the piller of the truth, I ſhall confeſſe my ſelfe to be in an erroz. Chziſt hath geuen vs warning to take hæde that no man de= ceiue vs, for many ſhall come in his name , ſaying, I am Chriſt , and ſhall deceiue many: and there ſhall ariſe falſe Chriſtes, and falſe Prophets &c. but he hath told vs befoze that we ſhould not beleue them, noz goe after thē. Beleue not euery ſpirite (ſayth S. Iohn ,) many falſe Prophets are gone out into the world . Thus are wee warned in the mouth of the ſonne of God, & if the ſwozd come and take vs away , our bloud ſhall be vpon our owne head.

HN. His aſſertion.

1.Epiſt. cap. 2.
ſent.2. 6.
1.Exhor. cap. 7.
ſent.38. leaf.16.

IT is the hill of the Lorde whereon his houſe is builded, to the which he that ſubiecteth not himſelfe, is a falſe hart.

hart, and standeth minded agaynst God, and his Church.

Theophilus exposition.

THat is spoken of the loue it selfe, and not of the Family: (For how is an house to be builded on an house?) which thing also may not be denyed, for so much as God is loue, and the other must consequently or necessarily follow.

William Wilkinson.

FIrst to the text of HN. and to *Theophilus* his exposition. The familye sayth HN. is the hill of the Lorde whereon his house is builded, for prouse hee quoteth. *Esa. 2. 2. a. Mich. 4. 1. a.* It shall come to passe in the last day, the mountaine of the Lordes house shall be prepared in the toppe of the moũtaines, &c. The sence of the which places of the prophets is, that in the last day vz. in ẏ first comming of the sonne of God, the Church shall by him be restored to her glorious beauty, the which places in HN. his new gospell 3. chap. 3. sent. are applyed to HN. himselfe, and to the time of his appearaunce in these wordes. Now shall the law be taught out of Sion: and in the 4. sent. for this is the day of promise: Psal. and ver. 24. c. which the Lord hath made: which first place is directly vnderstode of Christ, and the building agayne of the Church by him. The other place of the psal. declared that *Dauid* being appointed by God to be king ouer Israell, should deliuer the Arke out of the handes of the *Philistines*: wherein he foreshewed that by a figure which was true in Christ. Ephe. 4. verses. 4. 8. 11. 12. 13. the which HN. presumptuously taking vnto himselfe, grossly erreth in applying the scripture, & gracelesly blasphemeth ẏ sonne of God. First making Christ lesse carefull of his Church, than he is in dede: Secondly he is openly impious in this, that whereas Christ sayth, All is finished: (meaning all types and figures,) HN. maketh all vnperfect, affirming that in him and his appearaunce all

Scripture abused.

Last day.

Euang. cap. 3. sent. 3.

Psal. 118. 24.

Ephes. 4. 4.

Marc. 15. 28.

Iohn. 20. 30.

Euang. præface. sent. 2.

becommeth fulfilled. His wordes be these: *The day of Loue* Psal. 118. ver. 24. c. *is the appearing and comming.* Mat. 24. c. Luk. 17. c. Actes. 24. *of our Lorde Iesus Christ in the resurrection of the dead.* Esa. 26. c. 1. Cor. 15. f. *Wherein the law of the Prophets and all that is written of Christ becommeth fulfilled.*

Luke. 24. c.

Scriptures quoted in vaine.

All which places by him quoted are very playnely ment of the resurrection, that is, the second resurrection from death, & the secōd comming of Christ to iudgemēt: whereby HN seemeth to emply the resurrection of the body, and the second comming of Christ to iudgement to be past already, which is heresie: or els quoting those places for his first comming he alledgeth them amisse, which is ignoraunce.

HN.

TO the which he that subiecteth not himselfe is a false hart.

William Wilkinson.

Cyp. de simpl. prælat.

August. ad petrum. dia. cap. 34 6. Epist. 1. boke.

Cyp. ibid. throughout.

Iud. 6. vers.

IT is very true, he that submitteth not himselfe to the Church of God is a false hart. &c. For he shall neuer haue God for his Father, which hath not the Church for his mother. The Church is Noahs Arke out of the which he that is must nedes be drowned. *Christianus non est, qui in Christi ecclesia non est* sayth Cyprian. He is not a Christiā which is not of ẏ Church of Christ. They be Antichristes which goe out of the Church, and deale agaynst the Church. The which Church of Christ if your Family be, Shew me out of the scriptures these markes wherby the Church ought to be knowen: this if you can truely doe, I confesse that you haue the Church: if ye cannot, beware least the further ye wander from the shepfold, the further ye goe astray from Christ, and encrease your owne damnation. Therefore loke well to your standing. The doctrine is very true, yet the place quoted by HN *Fol, 16. sent. 38.* out of *S. Iude* to proue it is be-is very impertinent hauing no such proofe in it as he alledgeth it for. For how hangeth this reason together. *God hath reserued vnto the Angels (which kept not their first estate, but left their owne habitation) euerlasting chaines vnder darknes vnto the iudgement of the great day, which S. Peter calleth their damnation. Therefore he that turneth away from the cominalty of Loue (which as you tearme is the Church of God) bringeth euen so ouer himselfe the iudgement of his condemnation.* But it were hartely to be wished that his fault in abusing Scripture were the least (which in the eyes of God is damnable) so should not his cancred and poysoned Heresies, besides his owne guilt, draw with them likewise the soules of those that stumble vpon him. And thus much for HN his text. Now to *Theophilus* exposition. 2. Pet. 2. 4.

Theophilus.

YOu say that this clause: It is the hill of the Lord: is spoken of the loue it selfe, and not of the familie.

W. Wilkinson.

THen belike you would haue me take your meanyng to be this. *The loue* (ẏ is God ye say, for so in the next clause ye expound it) *is the hill of the Lord, whereon his Church is builded.* What a perplexitie of speach is this, ẏ ye can not vtter your mynde so, ẏ I may vnderstand ye? If you meane ẏ God is onely ẏ foũdation of his Church. I graunt: yet hath not your Paraphrasis vpon HN. his wordes as yet forced thus much. *Ergo*, God is the foundation of your Loue Familie. Ye take in hãd to explicate HN. his meanyng, but the old Prouerbe will still belike be true: An euill expositor marreth the text. For herein you do but rayse dust with your shufflyng: & tell vs there is a marke if we could see it, when ye haue dimmed it with a darke exposition so, that it can not be sene. For in my simple iudgement you leaue the wordes very doubtfull. For whereas you make a circumloqution and say, *it may not bee denied, for as much as God is loue and the other must consequently or necessarily follow*. I vnderstand HN. very well, when he sayth God is loue, it is very true, and therefore I take it that in diuers places he vseth this diffuse terme *the loue*; for *the Lord our God* as a worde that is equiualente of signification. But whereas you say the other must consequently or necessarily follow, I vnderstand not yet what you meane, for it is as though ye bad me looke stedfastly and yet shut myne eyes: For what is *the other* which you adde. Is the sence this? the Familie of Loue (by you pretended) is Gods Church: & that God is the grounde of that your Familie? Geue me leaue to vse your own wordes, neither is *the consequent good:* nor doth it *follow of necessitie* for which you induce it. For to let passe your learned and weightie Parenthesis (*for how is an house to be builded on an house?*) with a sad interrogatorie ministred in the same, what a necessarie consequēt is this? God is the hill of the Lord: or this, God is the foundation of his Church *Ergo*, your pretended Familie is the Church of God. How this consequent doth halte in his followyng, he that knoweth what a consequent meaneth can easely consider. But it seemeth that you are no great gatherer of necessary consequentes: albeit ye iumbling stumbled on these wordes: To follow consequently or necessarily vnwares. But if hereafter vppon a further deliberation by you had you shall enforce your *consequent* more *necessarily*: I shall hit on your meanyng the better & so shape you a fitter aunswere. And thus much of the first Article.

An addition to the first Article, out of HN.

1.Exhor.cap.12. sent.42.fol.27.

THe Familie and cōmunaltie of the same house (vid. of the loue) is Gods chosen people of Israell, and he him selfe with them is. Ierem.24.a.& 31.d. Ezech.27.c. Apoc.21.a. their God, and will likewise bide their God, from generation to generation-

neration,euerlaſtingly. And if they chaunce to tranſgreſſe in any thing, God will then, 1.Chron.3.chaſtẽ teach and informe them: but he will no more withdraw his grace and mercy frõ them. Pſal.89.c.d. For God hath choſen none other houſe, nor Ierem.7.b. Temple, but 1.Cor.3.b.c.& 2.Cor.6.b.c. the godly childrẽ, or Communialtie of loue. For the F.of L. is the mercy ſeate of the loue (that is of the Lord,) the ſchole of grace: Exhor.Cap.12.44.Heb.5.a. The reſt prepared from the beginnyng, for the people of God and all repentaunt perſons. It is the Sion and Ieruſalem from whence the law was propheſied Eſay.2.Mich.4.to come. The Familie of Loue is the true tabernacle of God, which ſhall in all perfection be euerlaſtingly vpon earth. For ſo it hath pleaſe d God to the end that his will and iudgemẽt of his righteouſnes may be done vpõ earth, as it is in heauen Math.6.Luke.11. All propheſies & miniſtratiõs, which are gone from God doe tend or lead (to the Familie of Loue) as to an euerlaſting, very true, perfect, good & moſt holy ſeruice of the loue (that is the Lord) which ſhall remaine in the ſame clearenes in his miniſtery euerlaſtingly to the end that the ſame moſt holy Prophet good frõ henceforth might perpetually be declared vpon earth.

1.Exhort.cap. 20,ſent.7.fol.49

Dictata.cap.19. ſent.3.

Euang.præfac. ſent.6.&.cap.23 ſent.7.

Euang.cap.3. ſent.3.fol.4.

HN. wreſteth. 3. Article of the Lordes Prayer.

Euang.cap.24. ſent.9.

W. Wilkinſon.

Theſe haue I (good Reader) put downe as a taſt, that thou mighteſt bee ſomewhat acquainted with their horrible blaſphemies: and thereby thou knowyng them, mighteſt more carefully eſchew and auoide them.

ARTICLE. 2. HN. *No truth.*

HN. *ſayth that he can not perceiue nor find the true belief in Ieſus Chriſt amongeſt any people vpon earth, that walke without the Communialtie of loue, and liue vnto them ſelues: and that ſame is appeared and manifeſted vnto the holy ones of God in the Communialtie. 1. Iohn.1.3.a. of the loue, through the appearyng. Mat.25.3.d. Act.1.11.d. of the comming of*

Iesus Christ, out of the most high heauen. So can not likewise the same most holy belief become rightly witnessed or confessed by any other people, nation, or communialities, but onely by the 1. Cor. 12, a. b. Ephes. 4. b. communialitie of the holy ones in the loue, or by such as walke and liue.. 1. Pet. 1. b. 1. Iohn. 3. b. &c. 4. b. obediently vnder the gracious word and his seruice of loue.

W. Wilkinson.

HN. *sayth, he can not perceiue or finde the true belief. &c.* to this I aunswere, that it is Gods iust, though secret, iudgement, that when men aske amisse they do not obtaine, when they knocke at the wrong dore, they are not let in, and beyng on sleepe when the bridgrome commeth and wāt light in their lampes, they enter not in, with him into the Mariage. That HN. *hath not founde nor perceiued the truth,* the reason is he wil not learne. Pro. 8, 8, 9. he stoppeth his eares charme the charmer neuer so wisely. Psal. 58. 4. 5. The Lord will guide thē that be meeke in his way. Psal. 25. 9. but knowledge entereth not into a froward soule, and a foole that seeketh wisedome findeth her not: for the Lord withstandeth the proud & geueth grace vnto the humble. 1. Pet. 5. 5. The Israelites sought God as a people desirous to know his wayes, but because the feare of him was learned by mēs preceptes Esay, 29. 13. & they were selfe conceited wise Esay. 5. 21. Therfore did they heare and not vnderstād, see and not perceiue, their hart was fat, their eares were heauy and their eyes were shut. Esay. 6. 9. 10. Where note (curteous Reader) that this holy *Praphet* (for so wil the Ioigner neede haue vs for to take him) HN. and our *Papistes* vse the selfe same weapō, and by the same knife seeke to cut the throate of gods Church, which they hādle after this sort. *Your Church ye Protestātes was not alwayes visible neither did it alwayes appeare vnto the world. Therefore it is not the true Church.* What a faint Consequent and weake reason this is (especially with our *Papistes,* which can not abide, an Argument drawen from the Negatiue)

Iam. 4. 3.
Math. 25. 11. 12.
Prou. 8. 8. 9.
Psal. 58. 4. 5.
Popish chaleng 9. Artic, 8. demaun.
D. Fulkes boke.
Stapletō. Controuer. 1 lib. 4. cap. 9. pag. 121.

gatiue) by this which followeth beyng the like may easely be proued. I see no sunne (sayth the blind man) neither heare I any swetnes of song or pleasaũt Musicke, sayth the deafe man. *Therfore* there is no sunne sayth the one, nor song quoth the other. HN. the sonne of perdition, and the *Romish* brode of old Hipocrites can not see the truth, or will not: therefore there is no truth at all. *The communialitie of the holy ones in the loue* (for so vnlesse ye terme them they will bee angry out of measure) creepe in corners as owles doe at none, euen as did the *Anabaptistes* in the first spryng tyme of their heresie: therefore there is now no Familie of Loue, neither were there any *Anabaptistes* any where in tymes past: this Argument as it is euidẽt in the one, so will it not be denied by ẏ other. Albeit in dede it be a feble kinde of disputyng & farre swaruyng from all rule of reason. For the seyng or not seyng of mortall man doth not approue or disprone the truth of the immortall God. Pharao kyng of Egypt saw Moses and Aaron, and confessed the miracles by thẽ wrought to be true miracles: yet saw he not a reason to perswade him to let Israell goe. John Baptist did as it were point out Christ with his finger, saying: Behold the lambe of God. The Jewes cõfessed that Christ had done all thinges well. The Pharisies saw their thoughtes disclosed yet reasoned they thus: The Scribes and Pharisies and rulers beleue not on him: but onely the rude and accursed multitude. Therfore is he not the Messias. And if I should vse the like forme of Argumẽt as this is: trow ye the Familie would thinke the consequent necessary? Before the dayes of Queene Mary, or An. 1555. at the furthest, this Louely Familie was neuer sene nor heard of, onely the hatchers of this Familie, the Libertines, the *Arriãs*, the *Anabaptistes*, the *Free will men*, and *Catharistes* were than extant: but as yet this brode of *Locustes* had not broken out of the bottomlesse pitte neither had it the name of Loue, which it now hath. Therfore the *Familie of Loue* neither is the Church of God, neither is the holy

Simlers epist. fol. 1.

Exodus.

Iohn. 1. 36.
Marc. 7. 37.

Math. 9. 4.

Iohn. 7. 48.

Fathers of the Fam. of Loue.
Apoc. 9. 3.

truth of God in that their conuenticle: but vnto them and their *Patriarch* HN. I leaue such kind of reasonyng, most hũbly besechyng God to giue them eyes to see, & tongues to confesse the truth to Gods glory and the safegarde of their soules in the appearaunce of his Christ.

After HN. had told his Disciples, where he could not finde the truth, now he telleth them where he foũd it. *vz.*

HN.

THe same is appeared and manifested vnto thẽ holy ones of God in the Communialtie of Loue.

W. Wilkinson.

SO that then belike, vnlesse it be graunted him that he founde it there, all his labour is lost. Secondly it was not founde out there before he founde it, and to that purpose it is whiche in his new Euangely he sayth. *He will declare the secrete misteries of God, and make relation of thynges hidden from the world vntill his new day. &c. And he is annointed with the holy Ghost: Godded with God in the spirite of his loue: made heyre with Christ in the heauenly goodes of the riches of God: elected to be a minister of the gracious worde, which is now in the last tyme raysed vp by God accordyng to the promise. Ierem. 33.* Which is ment of Christ, wherein HN. blasphemeth. What if for all these, his great boastyng crakes, his swellyng wordes of vanitie turne to smoke out of the fornace, and dust before the winde? what then? if for all his outfacyng of the simplicitie of the Gospell, and shouldring out the sonne of God, the Lord lay opẽ his folly to the world and his shame vnto the sonnes of men? And if he founde no truth, or if it be truth, yet not of his findyng. Was there no truth before he told it? Was there no Gospell before his heape of confusion and huge lompe of shapeles and vnshamefast heresies? If there was (as most vndoubtedly there was) a light before darkenes, and an Arke of God before *Dagon*

Cap. 2. sent. 11 leaf. 7.

Cap. 1. sent. 1. fol. 3.

the Philistian Idoll, why boasted he then thus presumptuously, that the truth was of his findyng onely? Neither is it yet agreed among his new peruertes, concerning the age of this new founde heresie. For some of his Sectaries beyng demaunded where his Church was from the Apostles tyme, vntill the appearaunce of HN. this new found *Prophet* of theirs, he aunswered not onely obscurely to the question, but also fondely to the purpose, and vnfittely to satisfie a waueryng conscience. *It was in the land of the liuyng among the holy ones.* But thus doth the Lord suffer their eyes to dazell, who are quicke sighted to seeke out Phantasies to feede the it itchyng eares of them whõ no doctrine can content.

Truth from Christ and the Apostles tyme vntill HN. where the Fam. affirme it was.

HN. alledgeth. 1. John. 1. a. for proofe: The wordes be these, That whiche we haue sene and heard declare we vnto you that ye may also haue fellowshyp with vs, and that our fellowship may be with the Father, and with his sonne Iesus Christ. Where S. Iohn teacheth he is a true witnes, because he saw and heard: secondely he was a profitable minister, because he kept it not to him selfe but declared it vnto others. Thirdly the profite that doth ensue to the Children of God by S. Johns declaration: that ye may haue fellowship with vs. Lastly to make his message more amiable in the sight of men, and mẽ to embrace the same more greedely, he addeth: that our fellowship may be with God the Father, & with his Sonne Iesus Christ, and to entise them more effectually to take hold of Christ, he sheweth that Christ commeth not bare or naked, but clothed and accompanied with all his mercies, to the encreasing of his children and comfort of the godly. This worde fellowship geueth vs to vnderstand, that among the godly there ought to be a mutuall feelyng of infirmities, with a supplying of all comfort both in thynges spirituall and temporall. This doctrine conteineth the true Exposition of the Article of our belief. I beleue the communion of Saintes. So that HN. might euen aswell haue founde his Communialty, (nay with much

1. Iohn. 1. a.

Communion of Saintes expounded.

more ease and lesse labour) in the belief as in S. Iohn the Apostle.

But let vs see the application of this place of S. Iohn. *The faithfull haue fellowship with the Apostles and God the Father, in or with Christ Iesus: Therfore this fellowship is in the familie of your loue onely, and there is no societie in truth but yours.* Not so. For many a day before HN. was heard of was there a Communialitie of Saintes, neither was it a Communialitie of goodes, of which the *Anabaptistes* did dreame, neither that filthy and graceles Communialitie of the Femal kinde of wiues, virgins &c. whiche the *Nicholaitanes* did dote of: But this it was that made HN. so farre to ouershoote him selfe, that wheresoeuer he founde this word Communialitie or fellowship, straight way he imagined that it might proue vnto vs the Familie of his new inuention. For neither did the woordes Actes. 2. 44. Act. 4. 32. And all that beleued were in one place, and had all thinges common (meanyng that *quoad vsum* to helpe and releiue the necessity of such as could not labour, there ought to bee a mutuall contribution among the faithfull of their temporall blessynges, as there is in all Churches rightly gouerned) proue *quoad possessionem* accordyng to priuate right no man ought to enioy any landes or other possession to the mainteinance of his callyng and nourishyng of his familie, though in holy Scripture it bee set downe for an vnfaillible truth that Phillip the Deacon had a house: so had Mathew and Peter, and Ioseph of Aramathia, Lidia a purple seller and Cornelius the Capitaine had priuate abidyngs and great wealth: so had Philemon a faythfull Preacher and companion of Paule the Apostle both house and seruauntes, yet no Communitie.

Apoc. 2. 6.

HN.

How HN. foūd the truth.

THyrdly hee telleth them how hee founde the truth: *Through the appearyng of Iesus Christ out of the highe heauen.*

To

W Wilkinson.

TO proue that Christ appeared vnto him hee citeth. Math. 25. d. wherein is conteined how Christ shall come in his second commyng, to seperate the shéepe from the goates &c. Act. 1. 11. b. the men in white garmentes sayd he shall come agayne, so as ye haue sene him go into heauen. Thus then yf Christ did appeare in his body (to HN.) and in his second commyng, or if he appeared not otherwise, than did he not appeare to HN. at all: and doth the mighty Rabby of ẏ Familie ly: which is very like to be true: or els with the Sadducies hee denieth the resurrectiõ, or with Himeneus and Philetus he affirmeth that the resurrection is past already. Math. 22. 23. 2. Tim. 2. v. 17. 18.

HN.

THe same most holy beliefe cannot become vprightly witnessed, nor confessed by any other people. &c.

William Wilkinson.

THis is the last part of HN his assertion, wherein he sheweth where onely the truth and true beliefe is to be looked for: that is in the Familye of Loue, of his coigning and not els where. The morter whereby he laboureth to build, is vntẽpered, the stones are very precious but neyther fitte nor coucheable in that place wherein he sayth they shall be layd. The place by him alledged 1. Cor. 12. a. b. proue that although there be diuersitye of giftes in Gods Church, yet is it thereby builded vp. For there is but one spirite whereby, and one Lord to whome the Church is builded. And this he amplifyeth by diuers examples and similitudes of the body of man. &c. And Ephe. 4. b. he sheweth that there is but one Church, one Fayth, one Baptisme, and yet are there diuers functions instituted of God for the building vp of the Church as Apostles, Euangelistes, Pastors and teachers, yet doe all these diuers giftes tend this one, and the same Where HN. foũd the trueth.

end. 1. to the gathering together of the Saintes. 2. to the edification of the Church. 3. to the vnitye of faythe. And to touch *S. Paule* his meaning and scope: Therefore Christians ought to liue charitably together in loue. Doth this then proue, that if men should agrée, they had the truth, and none but they that doe agrée? doth vnitye of mindes proue a truth in doctrine? S. Peter and the rest of the Apostles in their feruent prayer affirme that 1. Pontius Pilate. 2. the gentiles. 3. the Iewes agreed to put Christ to death. Act. 1. 27. 28. Was here truth because they had vnitye? Euen so though I graunt all to be true that S. Paule affirmeth (as no doubt it is very true) yet hath not HN fitly alledged these places. 1. Cor. 12. b. Ephe. 4. b. to proue that the truth is no where taught but in his Familye.

Vnitie not alwayes proueth the truth.

HN.

11. Epist. cap. 5. sent. 4. and. 1. Epist. cap. 1. sent. 5.

VVIthout the Familie, is nothing but good thinking, tedious trauaile, labour, and misery.

Theophilus.

SO then this is very true (sauing that you haue put truth, for true beliefe) the rest of the wordes are spoken or referred to the rest which God hath reserued to his chosē in that house, and to the seruice of that house. Loke better on the text.

William Wilkinson.

VVHensoeuer any man shall be without or depart from the Church, he shall neyther finde rest in bodye, nor peace in conscience: as they doe very well knowe, who haue departed and falne away from the knowne truth, or which at any tyme suffer their consciences to wauer & halte betwixt God, and Baal, truth, and errour, light, and darknes. God for Christ his sake keepe vs from falling away from the truth, or standing in mammering therof, knowing that Neuters, and Hipocrites

pocrites, with Lukewarme brethren shall be spewed out of Gods mouth, which HN and his Familye must take heede and harken to, whiche geueth any man liberty (so he be of their Familye) to embrace, and lyke of what religiō he list, in his new *Euangely*. cap. 1. sent. 4. HN. geueth libertie of Religion.

Now if there be nothing but trauaile, misery, &c. Why wishe ye peace and health unto them, which are dogges, and not of the houshold of Fayth, permitting them what religion they will. But hereby ye thought to stretch your Familye, from sea to sea, and from one end of the world to another. So that here you shewe what kindred & acquaintaūce your Heresie hath with ÿ *Anabaptistes*, who affirme that for their quietnesse sake they may confirme them selues to any Religion of the people amongest whō they dwell. How neare you and these mē iumpe, I leaue to the discrete Reader to discerne. M. Bullinger his censure on them is this. Of this iudgement was that beast Dauid George (sayth he) and this sect is the most pestilent of all others. Thus much sayth M. Bullinger who was acquainted with thē as hee him selfe testifieth. I did put *truth* for *true belief*, thinkyng them to be all one, neither as yet haue ye shewed any difference betwixt them. I haue *looked on* HN. his *text* sufficientlye, God geue you grace to looke better on the Testament: and to come backe to the truth whence ye haue slydden, and kéepe me in that which I doe and haue professed.

Bullinger agaynst the Anabap. 2. booke. 4. Chap.

Bullinger 1. booke. 4. chap. leaf. 9. b. line. 17.

HN.

THe true light hath not bene declared by any of them all, that haue taken on, set forth and taught before the same, and without the same Familie of Loue. Heb. 9. b. & 10.

HN. 11. Epist. cap. 5. sent. 4. 1. Exhort. cap. 16. sent. 9. leafe. 42.

Theophilus.

YOu shuld do wel to alledge the text as it is, and not your owne imagination, which is that there is, hath bene or can be any more thā one true light (vz. Christ) or the loue whiche presently is appeared to his chosen in the house of loue or of God. For before and without the Church and his seruice there cā be no truth taught.

W. Wilkinson.

That our blynde southsayer told vs, there is not any truth to be foūd, without his fond Familie, although it hath by me bene handled, in that part of this Article, which immediately goeth before, yet this learned Elder of this Louely Familie barketh and brauleth stil against vs, and will not suffer playne and manifest truth to stop his mouth. And although the place by me alledged out of HN. be verbatim and word for word as I alledged it, yet will he not be satisfied, but as it were facyng me out with a carde of x. he seeketh to ouerrunne me with his eloquēce, & sayth to blanke me withall, that I haue mistaken and falsified the author. But because he taketh me vp for an Imaginer of the text, vouchsafe gentle and curteous Reader to way myne Imagination, as he pleaseth to terme it. The place by me cited out of the 1. Exhort. of HN. *Cap.16. sent.9. fol.42.* is in the very first line thus. *Therefore the holy nor the most holy, the true nor the most true light (which the most highest hath presently in his most holy seruice vnder the obedience of the loue geuen vnto vs, for to be declared forth) hath not Heb.9.b.10.a. bene declared by any of thē all, that haue taken on, set forth, and taught any thyng before this same or without this same our seruice of the loue.* Are not these my very wordes sauyng that for breuities sake I pretermitted your long and vnnecessary Parenthesis? Haue I not delt truly with your housholdfather in that I truly and faythfully as from his owne mouth did report his wordes? Am I not vniustly charged and falsely blamed for my Imagination in the text of so worthy an Author? But seyng it is not expedient that I be myne owne iudge of myne innocencie, I refer me to the sentence of the indifferēt Reader, whom also I desire to be aduertised, that he hath heard me take an Elder halting in his word, whē as the faith of their Familie (HN. I meane) in the booke by him intituled. *Dictata per* HN. *or documentable sentences* sayth, *nothing can come from the true perfection, but all humilitie and meeke vertues and righteousnes floweth from all perfection*. Now if to slaunder and misreport be a worke of righteousnesse and worthy of their perfection, let them glory therein, I had rather in that sort be vnperfect. As for me and those that desire not hand ouer head to receiue all that comes from euery mā, it is sufficient and shalbe that if they lauish out any vntruth, that I be pardoned for not sealyng vnto it, before I way it in Gods ballance, least it proue light, and try it at the touchstone least it be counterfeite.

Theophilus vttereth an vntruth wittingly. 1. chap.7.senten.

The places of Scripture by HN. quoted are very impertinent and absurdely alledged, hauyng not any thrée wordes that sounde toward such a sense as he would father on them.

Theophilus.

THere hath not bene, is, ne can be any more thā one light which is presently appeared vnto his chosen in the house of loue, or as HN. sayth, our house of loue.

W. Wilkinson.

WHy then haue ye left the Churche, into the which ye were Baptised? why did ye promise ye would manfully fight vnder Christes banner, and continue his faythfull souldiour and seruaunt to your liues end, and now lyke a runnagate Apostata & a cowardly souldiour or rather a traiterous Iudas ye betray his Saints to Sathā, & breake truce with the son of God, into whose obedience ye were sworne? Why do ye like children past grace insolently taunt and checke your mother, and impudently tread vnder your féete the Lordes pearles as most filthy swine? why come you not to ẏ light that your workes may be sene how they are wrought in God? what meane

HN. and his schollers traytors of Christes Church.

you to frame and imagine to your selfe a new Churche? For whereas so oftē you affirme, that you haue no church but ours, no assemblies but ours, why doth HN. terme it *our Familie or seruice?* doth not this word, *our Familie*, note a particular secte or faction in the possession of a few. Ye say very truely there can not bee any truth without the Churche. If this be true then your doctrine is false, for there is but one Lord, one fayth, one redeemer, one spirite of sanctification, one Abrahā the father of the faithful, one Isaac, one Iacob, one body wherof we all are mēbers. The Churche hath but one head and one body. As for deridyng and scoffing *Ismaell*, he shall be cast out with the bondmayd his mother: prophane *Esau* shall haue no part in the Lordes inheritaunce, neither your Schismaticall Familie vnles ye repent hartely for that which is past. The *Iewes* cryed the *Temple* of the Lord, & yet were they a stiffenecked people: you cry the *schoole of grace* the *mercy seate, the Familie* of the Lord, and yet all is but hypocrisie. For the *Iewes* had an externall tabernacle instituted of God. Therfore they might boast better thā you. You haue coined and inuented a Schisme, & yet very cōfidently you affirme, your conuēticle is the Church without the which is no truth to be loked for.

Ephes. 4. 4.

An Addition of HN. vnto the 2. Article.

Euang. cap. 4. sent. 5.

Sent. 7.

1. Exhort. chap. 16. sent. 16.

NO mā (sayth HN.) how wise soeuer he be in the knowledge of the Scriptures, can by any meane vnderstand or comprehend the wisedome of God, but onely they that be of the Familie: who soeuer is without the Familie is inueigled with wiles, subtletie, and falsehode. For no man rightly accordyng to truth of the Scriptures, nor accordyng to the spirituall vnderstandyng of the godly wisedome, can deale in, or vse the true Gods seruice, nor the seruices of the holy worde, but onely the Illuminate Elders in the godly wisedome whiche walke in the house of loue.

Euang. chap. 23. sent. 6.

The wise men of the world and the Scripture learned haue not knowen the veritie of the heauenly truth, nor yet obteined or gotten the clearenes with Christ.

It is mere lyes and vntruth, what the Scripture learned through the knowledge they got out of the Scriptures, institute or teach.&c. Euang.cap.33. sent.11.12.13.

They preach in deede the letter and Imagination of their knowledge, but not the word of the liuyng God. Therfore sayth he they are mē whose knowledge doth imagine much in them. 1.Exhort.cap. 16.17.18. Cap.16.sent.5.

ARTICLE.3.of HN. *No Baptisme.*

Without the Familye of Loue (sayth HN*) there is no true Christian Baptisme.* 1.Exhort.cap.7 sent.10.11.32. fol.12.

This same is the schole of grace, to an euerlasting remission of sinnes ouer all such as cleaue there vnder. and.cap.12.sent. 44.fol.27.

There is no true Christianitye but the Comminalty of the holy ones in the loue of Christ Iesus. Ioh. 17.c. Ephe.4.a.b. &.cap.16.sent. 20.fol.43.

All other that haue not the Christian doctrine of the seruice of the loue forgoing their Baptisme, It is not meete and conuenient, that men should count such vnbeleuers, and vnbaptised ones for Christians: neither yet also for men, at whose handes one should any way suppose or trust to finde any word of Ioh.1.a. 3.a. gods truth or yet any workes Mar.1.a. righteousnesse or Gods seruice, that God regardeth or accepteth. They are without Christes body. Euang.cap.23. sent.7. &.cap.4.sent.57.

Theophilus.

COnsider better of the text. Rather vnder the obedience of the father and his loue, vnder the obedience of Christ, and his beliefe, and the obedience of the holy ghost, and his renewing of the lyfe, and minde &c. to be baptised in the name of the father, the sonne, and the holy ghost. &c.

William Wilkinson.

WHat account HN. maketh of our Church, and the truth therein taught, is already declared. Now followeth it to be vnderstode, what his opinion is of our Sacramentes. And first to speake of baptisme (For of the holy Sacrament of the supper of our Lord he hath written very litle) what he attributeth to our Church therein is playne, that vnlesse we haue our foregoing in the doctrine of the loue, we are not to be counted of him, and his Fam. to be baptised ones. To the which I will aunswere briefly, if first he shall satisfy me in this demaund: Whether when there was no Family of Loue, there were no vpright baptisme in England? If he say there was a lawfull baptisme, than is there an vpright baptisme without the foregoing of his louely doctrine, and without his Family a true Christian baptisme. If he say there was none, than doe I aunswere, that these Famelers in England are not rightly baptised, & speake the truth, & worke righteousnes, or an acceptable worke in the sight of God. To the which, if the Familye shall further aunswere, though then they were not, yet since they haue bin rightly baptised. This it may be, *Vitels* the Ioyner will aunswere to approue his hereticall behauiour at *Colchester*: and to this I am to reply, that if the Fam. acknowledge a *rebaptization*, then are they hypocrites all the sort of them. For they in their last confession (being *a rehearsall of their doctrine, beliefe, and religion*) affirme, that *they doe deale simply, and playnely. &c, We haue (say they,) nor vse any other Ceremonyes, lawes, statutes, nor Sacramentes: of Baptisme, and supper of the Lord, then such as are ministred in the Church of England.*

Confes. leafe. 7.a.
Ibid. 6. leafe. v.

But I say that the Church of England vseth no rebaptization. Therefore if they be rebaptised, they be double faced dissemblers, Furthermore if they shall affirme that they vse no other Sacramentes &c. than is vsed in the Church of England, that is: in their Fam. in the Church of England, because it was sayd in the first Article, that we haue no Church without their Family: I aunswere: They pretend in their confession, they deale faythfully with all men: If this be their fayth, what I pray you

is

is their falshode. Furthermore I let passe to repeate, much lesse to confute, that fond opinion of those vaine heads, which thought the partyes baptised of heretiques, ought to be rebaptised agayne. Of this opinion the Fam. of Loue semeth to lyke very well, for because they affirme before, that without this Fam. there is no Christian baptisme.

And thus much for this Article is sufficient. As for you frend *Theophilus*, ye huddle vp so, that no man can vnderstand you: when you shall learne to speake out of the mouth, and leaue to fumble with your. &c. I will tell you my minde more art large.

An addition of the 3. Article of HN.

HN. *Reproueth our doctrine with this terme, an handfull of water, an Elementish water. Whosoeuer is not baptized according to the forme and manner of Iohn, who baptized the people confessing their sinnes, flowing with the water of repentaunce into their hartes, he is not rightly baptized, neyther may he boast els that he is a Christian.* HN. Euang. cap. 19. sent. 5. 6. Sent. 11.

ARTICLE. 4. HN. *No forgeuenes of sinnes.*

W*Ithout he Familye sayth* HN. *there is no forgeuenes of sinnes: for this is the true Christianitye the Familye of Loue, wherein God himselfe 2. Cor. 6. b. Apoc. 21. a. dwelleth, liueth, aud walketh.* 1. Exhor. cap. 7. sent. 40. & cap. 12. sent. 44. Euang. chap. 41. 7.

Theophilus.

FOr so it is agreable with the Scripture.

William Wilkinson.

The truth of this exposition, I must gladly graunt, and willingly confesse. viz. No pardon of sinnes without the Church of Christ. For truely it is sayd. No man must seuer or put in sunder, that which God hath lincked together, and so in our Creede the Communion of Saintes, and forgeuenesse of sinnes are ioyned together. And S. Paule sayth, that Christ gaue him selfe for the Churche, to satisfy it, and clense it, by the washyng of the water through the woorde, that hee might make it a glorious Church spotlesse and without wrinckle. &c. And I know very well that we are naked in our selues and poore, but in Christ, and his Churche so many as are members of that head are clothed richly, with the manifold graces of God, and continually enriched. And to this purpose fitly sayth the spirite of god by Esay the Prophet, God is in the Churche: and the 21. of the Apocal. 3. a. is fitly alledged, and the truest hetherto that HN. hath cied. As for his place out of the Corinth, there is no such thyng, nor any steppe of such a sence as he seemeth to alledge it for. All the Article if it should be geuen, yet shall you not thereby proue that without your particuler conuenticles, and Schismaticall assembles, is no remission of sinnes. For the promise of the keyes, and the remission is geuen to the Church which is Christes spouse, not to an harlot, and shameles strumpet. Ierusalem aboue is free, and is the mother of vs all: but your Agar is in bōdage, and is cast forth with her children. The Lord geue you grace to consider in what case you are. There is no fauour of God to them that forsake his truth, and cleaue vnto errour. Most of your *illuminates* haue ben professors, though now most deriders of the ghospell, and skoffers of Religion, making a profession of religion, but inwardly hauing denied the power thereof. The further you walke in darcknes, the greater is your daunger.

Ephes.5.25.26.27.
Esay.45.14.
2.Cor.6.b.
Math.16.19. &.18.18. Iohn.20.23.

An addition to the 4. Article.

THe same doctrine is in diuers other places affirmed that there is no pardon. &c. 1. Exhort. cap. 13. sent. 10. & cap. 15. sent. 29. & cap. 18. sent. 7. Euang. cap. 41. sent. 7.

ARTICLE

ARTICLE. 5. HN. *No Miniſtery.*

WE muſt haue reſpect vnto the ſeruice miniſtred in the Familie by the Elders thereof. For God hath choſen vnto him ſelfe the Familie of loue, and this ſeruice of the holy and gracious word: for their miniſtration is the ſafemaking miniſtration. 1.Exhort.cap.12 ſent.40.41.42. 43.44. &.cap.16, ſent. 16.

Neither is there any miniſter of the worde rightly called but by their Familie. Lam. cōp, ſent. 31.

Theophilus.

BEcauſe their exerciſe is obedience and loue accordyng to the requiryng of his word.

William Wilkinſon.

TRue it is that Gods miniſtery is an holy and ſacred thing, in thought not to be violated, in word and deede greatly to be had in reuerence. For they which are Gods meſſengers doe bryng the glad tidynges of deliueraunce from ſinne and Sathā vnto the people of God. They are Gods watchmen and do warne vs of the commyng of the enemy, which like a roaryng Lion goeth about ſeekyng how hee may deuoure vs. And becauſe their mouthes ſhould keepe knowledge, of them muſt wee aſke for the vnderſtandyng of the word, and enquire after the will of our God: yet doth not all this proue, that that miniſtration which is by you, of that faythleſſe Familie forged, is the true and holy miniſtration. For ſometyme (as now in your Familie) it cōmeth to paſſe, that falſe Prophetes will ſay, thus ſayth the Lord, and yet the Lord hath not ſpoken. They will preſume to preach without a viſion, and propheſie without a burthen: runne when God biddeth them not go, & take the teſtimonies of the holy ones in their mouthes, when yet the Lord ſendeth them not. Heretiques will with a face of the Churche ſeeke to out-

Euang.cap.52.7 Math.4.14. Ezech.33.7. 1.Pet.5.8. Luk.22.31. Malach.2.7.

face both the children of God and the truth also.

Thus then not every one that pretendeth is called in déede, for some come not in at the doore, but clyme in at the windowes, and as many as come before Christ, and set downe a contrary requiryng (as ye do) he is a Wolfe & séeketh but to rauin. Not every one that crieth Christ, *Regeneration, the spirite, a perfect, and true incorporatyng into the vpright, beyng a consubstantiation and counityng with God*, is a true teacher and faythfull Christian. Nor every that taketh vpon him to expounde knoweth the meanyng of the word. For many of you, when as ye would be Doctours of the word, had néede to be instructed in the very principles of fayth, and first grounde of Religion. So the true Ministers haue both a publicke and externall callyng by man: as also a priuate and internall callyng by God, which who so hath not he is an hereticall intruder and no propheticall Minister of God, nor Preacher of the most holy one. The whiche internall and externall callyng to the Lordes haruest to be a true labourer, if any man shall pollute with his lewde life, and light conuersation, he is at the Lordes hand to be beaten with stripes without number. Yet if any man shall say well and doe euill (whiche God forefend) with man it may discredit him that doth speake well and yet do amisse: with God euill déedes doe not disanull the truth of doctrine, as good déedes proue not euill doctrine to be true. A ring of gold in a swines snowt ceaseth not to be a ryng of gold though a swine weare it: pearles are pearles before dogges or swine. The broad seale of England, is highly to be honored, for the Maiestie of the Prince therein appeareth: though some tyme the partie that may cary it may bee a lewde person and a Godles Atheiste. The word and Sacramentes ministred by wicked men cease not by their administration to haue their force. For the wickednes of man can not ouerthrow the institution of God. Where, I in good conscience testifie, that I speake not to defend corrupt life in any man, but to vphold the truth, of good

Bulleng. 1. boke. 8. chap. leafe. 17. verse.

liquor

liquor in an unsauery vessell, and gods good worde, and sacramentes in a minister of an euill lyfe, and conuersation. For that Iudas, and Iames in their ministery gaue the same word, and wrought to the same wonders, yet the one a reprobate, the other an holy one, and a perfect Saint of God.

So then this reason that in corners your froward Familye useth to whisper agaynst euill men (though Gods Ministers) is Anabaptisticall. *Your Ministers liue not as they teach. Therefore their doctrine is not true.* In Scripture I know this reason is often used: Your lyfe is not according to the law & your profession: Therefore you are hypocrites and dissemble with me sayth God. The former fond argument I neuer hard of any man that is sound for iudgement, and sincere for godlynes. Bullen. 2. boke. 7. chap. leafe. 97. Esay. 58.

The same reason is by your Familye, and by your good minded brethren the *Papistes* alledged agaynst the truth, now preached after this sort. *We worke better then you, therefore our religion is truer then yours.* The first exposition (if you know what proposition meaneth) I deny, and also the argument. More than we they marke I graunt (so had they neede that will haue heauen by desert, or els will naue none of it) but better they doe not. *Quod non est ex fide peccatum est.* What is not of faith &c. The Pharisie gaue more almes, tithes &c. than the Publican, yet was the Publican more iust by much then the Pharisie. Not to worke, but to worke well in Gods sight is commendable. *Non tam quid, quam quomodo operamur, inquiret dominus.* Not so much what as with what fayth we worke, that will God demaund. Luke. 18. 11.

Thus haue I *obiter* and by the way touched your Families Papisticall, & Anabaptisticall argument, whereof the one will be saued by the fulfilling of the lawe, the other will haue markes concurre with fayth in the matter of Iustification, cleane contrary to *S. Augustine* who sayth, *Opera sequuntur iustificatum, non praecedunt iustificandum.* The workes we doe follow as fruites and goe Bullen. 2. boke. 8. chap. leafe 18. Euang. cap. 13. sent. 4.

not before as the efficient cause of our iustification. And thus much of the worthines of the Ministery, and ministers thereof, Whome I counsell you to reuerence in better sort, both in worde, and writing, than ye haue done. For you know what Christ sayth: he that despiseth you, despiseth me &c. and reade further Exod. 16. 8. 1. Sam. 8. 7. Num. 16. chap. throughout.

The dignitie of the Ministrie. Math. 10. 40.

I haue in this place (gentle and indifferent reader,) to desire thée diligently, to marke the sly and crafty dealing of this peuish Familye. For in my Articles which I exhibited vnto them for my further satisfaction, I added this clause of the outward calling of the minister, which then I did suspect they denyed, and since by their faythles demeanour of concealing that clause, I am certainely perswaded to be true, where also it shall not be amisse if besides their fond behauiour (in ouerhipping that which they néedes must confesse to be truely reported of them by me) to consider also how guilefully they protest that. No man is able iustly to blame, accuse, detect, or burthen them as transgressors of the lawe beit agaynst any the Quéenes Maiesties proceadinges in causes Ecclesiasticall &c. And yet in this place by me quoted out of the *lamentable complaynt*, *sent*. 34. They deny without their Familye there is no lawfull calling of Ministers. Their wordes be these. *For to be a teacher or minister of the holy worde is not euery mans office but his only, which is thereunto, euen lyke as was Aaron, called and elected of God, whose rodde or staffe greeneth, blossometh, and beareth fruit, as lykewise his which is a true disciple of the worde, and louer of the truth, hath receiued the learning and administration of his holy word, with integritye or singlenes of hart of the Elders in the house of Loue, obediently, and euē so is growē vp vnder thobediēce of the loue in the holy vnderstādings, till vnto the Elderdome of the man Christ, and taught to the kingdome of God.* And the same is by thē in playne wordes affirmed, but more skoffingly, and contemptuously in the same booke. sent. 34. But of that

Fam. conceale that maketh agaynst them.

Confes. pag. 4. confuted by Theoph.

Lam. Compl. sent. 34. of HN.

place

place more hereafter in the addition to the Article.

They with their cauill,as it is common vnto them with their brethren the *Papistes*,and *Anabaptistes*, (who alwayes, not being able to criminate,and blame the doctrine taught, flye straight wayes to the persō of the preacher) demaunde, A Syr what auctoritye haue you to minister,and who layd handes on you , who called you? &c. as also their forefathers the old *Pharisies*, which demaūded of *S. Iohn* the *Baptist* the same question , with that learned man *M. Musculus*. I aunswere, *Qui legitimé vocati non sunt,quæstionem de vocatione mouent*, They which are not called lawfully , first moue a controuersie about a lawfull calling : which obiection M. Bullenger in his booke agaynst the Anabaptistes doth aunswere learnedly and at large . Bullenger agaynst the Anabaptistes 3. booke . 4. chap. 90. leafe.

Zuinglius agaynst the Catabap. fol. 188. Iohn. 1. 22. 25.

Musculus Common places title of Ministers. pag. 182.

An addition to the 5. Article of an outward calling.

SUch an one as is euen so with his vnderstanding , and thoughtes, become incorporate in all obediēce of the word to the truth of God , and lyfe of Christ , and euen so acknowledge the truth , the same verily bideth rightly in the doctrine of Christ , and is apt to minister the holy word of truth, and to be a teacher of the people. &c. No man can teach the word of Christ,and his doctrine ,but such as first haue bin obedient disciples of Loue.

Lam. Compl. sent. 33. 34.

Docum . sent. 13. cap. sent. 1.

No man ought to busy himselfe about the word , but the Elders in the Familye . &c.

1. Exhort. cap. 16 sent. 16.

No man knoweth Christ nor the father nor yet also the seruices or Ceremonies of Christ, but euen onely those which are euen so through Christ, as we haue rehearsed, renewed or regenerated in their spirite and mynde : neither doth it also behoue or belong vnto any other to set forth any seruices or Ceremonies of Christ nor to preach or declare the Euangely: but such are those whiche are sent of Christ him selfe, for otherwise it is all false . The Disciples of Christ could not vnder-

Euang. cap. 23. sent. 2.

stand the clearenes of Christ before the fifty day, that the holy Ghost was poured vpon them: much lesse then verely can now the Scripture learned, which haue not kept the passeouer from death into lyfe, and from flesh into spirite with Christ, nor yet atteined through the power of the holy Ghost to the clearenes of Christ, vnderstand out of the knowledge of the Scripture, the clearenes of the word of Christ, nor yet set forth or teach accordyng to the truth his ceremonies or seruices, nor also preach or declare the Euangely of Christ.

ARTICLE. 6. of HN. *Of vniting into God.*

1. Exhor. 13. chap. 18. Cap. 16. sent. 16.

AND the Elders of the Familie (sayth HN.*) are illuminated from God they are Godded with God they are incorporate into God, with whō God also in one beyng, is Hominified, or become man.*

Theophilus.

1. Cor. 6. 17. 2. Pet 1. 4.

WHat errour is this if it were rightly sene vnto? whilest the vine braunch is to be vined in the vine Iohn. 15. & he that is ioyned vnto the Lord is one spirite with him, and are made partakers of the godly nature. 2. Pet. 1. 4.

William Wilkinson.

Caluin. vpon Math. 26.

TRue it is that a certaine godly and learned man affirmeth, writyng vpon the fall of S. Peter, When God leaueth vs to our selues there is no hope to stay from rūnyng headlong into sinne, right so it fareth in Gods iudgement with this coale Prophet HN. and his dreamyng Disciple *Theophilus.* For the maister on still fallyng from phantasie to phantasie, and from one errour into an other and the scholer bringeth in stones and morter to build vp the confused heape of all impietie.

In the former clause was shewed that they vtterly cōdemne and mislike all Ordination, and Election of Ministers with their Familie: now it followeth to be handled what priuiledge and prerogatiue his Elders purchase

vnto

vnto them selues, by the admission they haue into that blynd societie.

HN. affirmeth very soberly as it seemeth that *the Elders of his broode are illuminated and Godded with God or incorporated into God.&c.* his scholer *Theophilus* laboureth to strengthen his Assertion with the testimony of Scripture to that ende by him wrested and wrongly alledged: wherein seyng he cã not slippe the coller with me as erst he did in leauyng the former sentence, now to outcountenaunce the truth with the impudencie of his forehead, hee asketh. *What an errour is this if it were rightly seene vnto?* what errour do you aske: truly an horrible & palpable errour it is, flat against the truth of ẏ sacred scripture, straungely sauoryng of those dregges, whiche you haue deepely dronke both at the hand of the *Anabaptisticall Sinagogue,* and also of *the Romish harlot* & sea of Antichrist. But whereas you adde a Caueat which is: *If it be rightly sene vnto?* I aunswere: he that putteth on the Christall spectacles of Gods word, and taketh in his hãd the Lanthorne of holy write to looke diligently to your steppes, shall straight trace out a theefe and a rebell agaynst the Lord.

But first to procede orderly let me aunswere your authorities, and then in a word or two, wil I set downe the horriblenes of that opinion.

You say: *The vine braunche is vined into the vine.* I finde no such wordes in the place by you quoted out of *S. Iohn,* neither doth the Greeke or Latin translation afford any such termes of *vinyng into a vine* as ye seme to import. There is to abyde or remaine in the vine vers.2. and 6. and in the 7. vers. he expoundeth what his abidyng meaneth *vz.* If you abide in me and my wordes in you. &c. but be it graunted that ye quoted it (for perhaps you you followed the translation of HN. his Dutch Bible) it it I say be graunted that you haue not wroõg in the errour, by writyng out of a false meanyng of S. Iohn his wordes, Know yee not, nor haue ye euer heard, that Pa-

Scriptures falsified.

rables in the Scripture are rather to be considered in the end, whereto the doctrine they containe is applied then in euery part of the *Allegory?* is ech circumstaunce to be sifted and stode in? The cunnyng Archer respecteth more to hitte the marke, than the curious watchyng of the clouē ayre, which parteth in sunder at the end of his arrow, or the fallyng of his fethers: euen so the spirite of God doth rather respect the end of the similitude and the doctrine conteined there vnder with the especiall applicatiō therof, thē the waying of euery word or ech singular cir-
Luke. 16. cumstaunce therein comprehēded. The estate of the godly and the wicked after this life is most liuely painted out by the Parable of the riche man and poore Lazarus by S. Luke chap. 16. of the which Parable if I should stand in euery particular circūstaunce therof, I should very much entangle my selfe with vayne and idle questions, and disturbe the vnitie of the Churche, whereof the one were hurtfull to my selfe, the other intollerable to others. By
Luke. 15. 8. the similitude of the lost groat ẏ Lord shewethe the great and vnspeakeable ioy, which he conceiueth at the conuersion of a sinner: now he that besides this nedes will descant out for Allegoricall or Anagogical sence, as what the besome signified wherewith the woman swept, what the the candle, what the neighbours called in; &c. He that is curious thus vaynely to hunt after euery sillable, shall, as others haue done before, styrre many coales & yet finde small light, rayse much dust and yet see the meanyng and marke of the Scripture not any whitte the sooner. The word of God is *Lex vitæ ad bene agendum* not *ansa rixandi ad contendendum*. A rule to lead our lyfe, thereby to attaine euerlastyng happynes, not an occasion to contend or quarell to endles and nedles ianglyng. Which I note the rather because that in your loue house it is accōpted an high matter, to be hable to fetch a farre and an vnhard sence out of the wordes of Scripture: yea and higher thā to be humbly obedient to that, whiche is reuealed in the Scriptures, And to speake with profe to auoyde cauill,

the

the straunge stretchyng of the place of Christes driuyng the deuils out of the mã possessed into the heard of swine, *videlic.* the sinnes and sinnefull beyng of the earthly, and as yet vngodded man, is driuen vnto the soules of the sinfull worldlyng, who fall thereout into euerlastyng damnation. This their vayne and Godles exposition is very much rewed of the godly, and loathed of them who tremble in hart to heare the name and word of God thus impiously prophaned and horribly abused. Math. 8. 32. Fam. of Loues Exposition.

Now to come to the sence of S. Iohn his meanyng, which is this: By nature we are dry and naked, so is the vine braunch not abidyng in the stocke. Christ is the author and fountaine of all goodnes and graces, wherewith plentifully floweth and vnmeasurably aboundeth for his deare spouses sake the Church, and those that be his children, which none do any longer enioy, then while they stand in deede, and liue to that whiche in tongue they doe professe. So is it betwixt the braunches and the tree. He that is not of this misticall body in this lyfe, shall neuer triumph with him in the lyfe eternall: so doth no braũch florish in sommer, which abydeth not in the vine in sharp stormer of winter. If wee suffer with Christ, wee shall raigne with him. &c. Of the cõparison betwene the vine and the Church Read. Psal. 80. 9. 6. Esa. 3. 13. cap. 5. 7. b. and Ierem. 2. 21. d. and 12. 10. Ose. 10. 1. a. Iohn. 1. 6. 1. Pet. 13.

Where also it is worthy the notyng to consider, that Christ is not sayd to bee a naturall vine, but is by some qualitie of the vine resembled vnto vs: So are not we *naturally Godded* with God in his substaunce, but in qualitie with the image, whereunto mã was first created Gen. 1. 26. 27. Ephes. 4. 24. and Luke. 1. a. Here then we may easely vnderstand, that this your reason doth not follow necessarily: because your Parables and similitudes accordyng to the old Prouerbe, proue not a thyng to be, but manifestly and clearely argue a thing taught and proued by an euident and vndeniable example.

S. Paule to the Ephesians handlyng our coniunction Ephes. 5. 32.

with Christ sayth. I tell you of a great secret or mistery: which mistery if it were fleshly, than to the carnall & outward man, it were very easie to be understanded, but beyng spirituall it is of more difficultie: For the carnall and earthly man can not so easely perceaue the thynges which are of God.

Now followeth your second place out of the 1. Cor. which proueth that the Children of God are with him, Joyned and vnited together in one spirit.

Somewhat cōcerning our vniting, which hath bin touched before. To absolue all the doubt which ariseth in this place, this question is here to be demaunded. What is it to be made one spirite with Christ? If you shall aunswere that to be our spirit &c. is to haue our spirit confoūded with Christes spirite in the same substance, than doe I reply: that this your aunswere is a darke and vnreasonable *Paradox*. For onely bodily and corporall substāces are confounded, and mingled, so that incorporall and immateriall essences cannot be coupled in the same third matter, as farre as yet my reason can comprehend. A

Luk. 24. 49. spirit sayth our Sauiour Christ hath not flesh and bones: that is: there is a spirite no earthly or corruptible matter, or corporall substaunce. Therefore our ioyning and knitting vnto Christ, is not in matter, or substance, or being: but in spirit, and fayth. Thus see you than that your imagination is but the shadow of a slomber, whereof you doted all this while, that you demed our earthly and terren nature, to be embodied, and incorporated with him in perfect being, that is in his heauenly and diuine nature: and so we being men to become Gods to him, and he being God doth become man to vs. This

Cap. 6. sent. 3. your fantasye is more apparant in HN. his dictata or documentable sentences: but all your fantasies are but as mistes before the sonne, and the sleepes of a sick man, whose dreames hang together.

To be vnited in spirit, what it is. To be vnited and conioyned in spirite with God is nothing els, but to draw nearer vnto the image of our

first

first creation: wherein first we were created vnto holynes of lyfe &c. to be heauenly affected, to sauour spirituall and goastly thinges that belong vnto the soule. Briefely (I say M. Peter Mart. whose great iudgement I know how much the learned esteame) we are one spirite with god, when we are ioyned vnto him by the operation of his spirite, and the inward working of the holy Ghost: Yet doth not this vniting of vs with God auaile vs so far that we thereby should be equall with him, onely Iesus Christ the sonne of God according to the deuine nature is so vnited with God, that he is one in spirite with his father, and wholely equall with him, wherein we of right and worthely are far vnequal, & inferior vnto him. Ephes.4.24. Mart.1.Corin.6 17.

And thus much out of him concerning the meaning of this place of S. Paule, whome ye wrest to approue your errour, and yet in the iudgement of the best interpretours, your blinde exposition and forced minde of that place is cleane ouerthrowne and confuted: for we are sayth he *farre inferiour vnto God* and our vniting vnto him is, that in the preaching of the word, and ministration of sacramentes, he stoupeth and lispeth with vs that we may vnderstand him.

Now concerning the last place by you alledged out of S. Peter. which is this, we are made partakers of the heauenly nature, therefore say you, your Elders are illuminated from *God & Godded with God. &c.* Truely, yf ye had read any learned wrighter vpon this place, or if ye had but waighed with your selfe the purpose of S. Peter in that place, comparing the place, you cited with that which goeth before, and that which euen in the next wordes follow after, I trust ye would haue bin better aduised before ye had wrested the place so violently, to the purpose that ye haue applied it. For in the very wordes following doth he expound his owne meaning in this sort. *To be made partaker of the deuine nature*, is nothing els but *to flee the corruption which is in the world through lust*, which S. Paule calleth oftentimes in his Rom.6.6.7.8.

Rom.6.6.7.8.
Rom.7.6.&. 8.5
&c.
Leuit.11.44.45.

r.Pet.1.15.16.

See Byſhoppe
Iewels replye
where hee ex-
poundeth this
place of S. Pe-
ter pag. 434.
lin.24.

Epiſtles to be dead to ſinne, and not to be in the fleſh, and agayne let not ſinne raigne in your mortall bodyes that ye ſhould obey the luſt of it: but euen as the Lord is holye ſo muſt we be holy, for we are the temples of the holy Ghoſt, and the Lord God through Chriſt doth dwell within vs.

But let me demaūnd this one queſtion of you, to the which if ye will directly aunſwere, ye ſhall ſæ all this controuerſie betwixt vs about this place of S. Peter ſone diſcuſſed, tell me but this? *What is the nature of God which we are partakers of?* is it not his euerlaſting trueth, his righteouſnes, his wiſedome? &c. Is it not peace of ſoule, ioy of conſcience, and all goodnes which cannot be imagined? is not he thē which is made partaker of theſe good graces of God, both in body and ſoule, rightly ſayd to be made partaker of the heauenly nature? yes verely. Then may ye very playnely ſæ, and eaſely diſcerne, that by theſe wordes, *the nature of God*, Wee are not ſayd to be partakers of his ſubſtance or eſſence, but of the deuine and heauenly qualityes which are in God. Of this place

Chap.11.ſect.10
Chap.25. ſect.
10.
Actes.17.27.28

read *Caluins inſtitutions* 3. boke. I know in dæde the heathen Poet Aratus, out of whome S. Paule doth al-ledge a verſe in the *Actes of the Apoſtles*, ſayneth that we ſpring out of the generation of G D D. But what haue we to ſtand to his fond fantaſie and idle dreame. True it is, the *Manicheis* held the ſame errour, that we were ſprong of the ſame offſpring and ſæde of God, and after we haue run the race of our lyfe, we ſhall returne to our fiſt original. And I know that in the former times of our fore fathers, there were ſome frantick men which imagined that Gods nature is ſo powred into vs, that it wholy cauſeth our nature, & being to loſe the force there-of. Right ſo dreameth your Fam. and as they quoted

r. Cor.15.28.

for profe, God muſt be all in all. Therfore are we who-ly reſolued and turned into the nature of God. To the ſelfe ſame purpoſe haue ye as fondly as they alledged in this place, this text out of Saint Peter: but right ſo may
　　　　　　　　　　　　　　　　　　　　　　　　it be

it be affirmed of you which is sayd of them, such a dotage as this neuer once entred into the minds of the Apostles. Foolish therefore and vngodly are they (whosoeuer they be) which out of this place imagine that the essentiall nature or being of God is poured into vs, our owne being there vtterly vanishing away. And thus much for the meaning of these wordes of S. Peter We are made partakers of the heauenly nature. And for a further exposition hereof, reade the Byshop of Salisburyes reply agaynst harding. pag. 331. 5. Article. 7. diuision.

Now to satisfy your questions which ye aske of me: *What errour is this yf it were rightly sene vnto?* I aunswere *Looke you rightly vnto it and ye shall see it is the errour of* Manes, of Seruetus a Spanish Arrian burnt at Geneua, the errour of Osiander concerning the essentiall and substantiall iustice, more largely expounded by HN. in his Euangelie. 1. chapter and first sentence. From the which heresie good Lord deliuer vs. The which opiniōs because I feare they will more hurt the simple people by repeating, then doe you good in confuting: of purpose I let them passe reseruing you for a more fuller and perfect instruction to M. Caluins institutions by whom the heresies aforesayd so are clearely cōfuted, that no godly Christian can or will desire a more absolute resolution. Goddyng into God what error and whose. Cal. Institut. 3. booke. 11. chap. sect. 5. 6. 7. 8. &c.

Not meaning any further to busie my selfe with the confuting of the opinions of our Romish Catholiques, who in this point agree with you, affirming that our coniunction with Christ, is carnally, and bodely.

HN.

CHrist himselfe is their light sayth HN. *which becommeth administred vnto them.* 1. Exhort. cap. 14. sent. 1.

Theophilus.

IT is true vnlesse ye will deny the scripture.

William Wilkinson.

YOu should first haue proued it by the Scriptures, & afterwardes haue affirmed it to be true: bare affirmations beare no weight. HN. his profe he quoteth John 1.9.a. (The light is the true light, which lighteth euery man that commeth into the world,) is a reuing profe.

1.Rom.20.c. The meaning of the which place is this, that all men are equally indued with the light of naturall reason to see God in his Creatures, and thereby to acknowledge him to be their creator. Which because they haue light other wheres, and Christ hath light of and frō himselfe, therefore Christ is God.

But this place proueth not that onely the Children of God are lightned with the light of Gods spirit, which assertion albeit it be true, yet is this place by HN. quoted without discretion: for it speaketh of a light generall to all that are borne, not proper to the regenerate: of this light Read. Esay. *9*. 1. 2. Mat. 4. 15. *16*. Joh. *9*. a. 5. Joh. 12. e. 35. HN. his other places John. 8. b. 12. I am the light of the world. And Ephes. 5. c. 14. Awake thou that sleepest and stand vp from death and Christ shall giue the light. The first proueth that without Christ is nothyng but darknes and condemnation, and out of the body of Christ, which is his Churche, is no health nor comfort of body or soule, which when ye can shew me by the Scriptures truly alledged that ye are, I will acknowledge my selfe to be in an errour: vntill ye can so do, say: not euery one that sayth the Lord. &c. Heretiques in crying the Churche haue alwayes sought to bryng in a schisme, to disturbe and disquiet the state of the Church.

HN.

1.Exhor.ca.15. sent.4. *ANd euen so out of this high Maiestie of God doth this true light shew forth his seruice through the illuminated*

ted or Godded man, with whom the most hyest through the selfe same light, and his seruice is also manned: witnessing and declaryng how that the true light consisteth, not in the knowledge of this or that, but in an vpright and true beyng of God, and his eternall life. Iohn. 17. c. Act.23.4.5.6. 2.Corin.4.a. 2.Pet.1.v. 1.Ioh.1.a.

Theophilus exposition.

THat is through the new creature which is incorporated into God by the power of his word.

W. Wilkinson.

IT is not in this place certaine to bee gathered by any apparaunt circumstaunce, wherfore, or to what end, all these authorities are wrong in by HN. for if he meane that no man ought to minister without a callyng (as it seemeth hee would fayne meane if hee could vtter it) the proposition I confesse is true: and I aske him what outward callyng he had, and by whom he was called, or who admitted him vnto that Propheticall function whiche so often he boasteth of? yet are these places by him very vnskilfully cited and vnaptly to the purpose, the whiche he doth alledge them, so that herein I blame his euill choyse for hee might better for profe haue quoted Iohn. 1. 25 Num. 17. 9. 2. Sam. 6. 7. Heb. 4. 5. Euang.cap.1. sent.1.

But if hee brought them for his *illuminated or Godded man*, as it is like that hee did, because vnto that place he made his directorie. g. I accuse him that he quoteth scripture with an euill conscience. For that in none of those places by him cited there is any word *of illumination Goddyng, or mannyng*. The places of the Actes he dealeth lyke a theefe that dare not make a playne stepe least he should be taken, for he treadeth but ouerly & dare not set downe either Verse or Letter to direct the Reader: but vsing onely his old ragged and running maner of quotatiōs very impertinently & to no purpose, doth he abuse the Reader. As also in the places of S. Peter and S. Paule he hath

 by

by his direction set vs to seeke that which we shall neuer finde. Lastly the place out of S. Iohn. 17.c.. is idle and emptie hauyng no one sillable tendyng to any such end as he alledged it for.

As for HN. it is very like that hee thought the worlde would allow his wordes without proofe: and as his Disciples vse to doe hand ouer head, he would take whatsoeuer commeth from him without examination, which his opinion is grounded of the old doctrine of the Papistes, that doctrine of teachers ought not to be further sifted or iudged by the hearer, of the which point we shall haue occasion to speake more Article.8. pag.89.

THE 7. ARTICLE

Conteinyng HN. his blasphemy what he boasteth of him selfe, and his miraculous and extraordinary callyng.

11.Epist.cap.2. sent.1.&.5.cap. sent.10. Euang.cap.1. sent.1.

HN. *Sayth that he is moued with the good nature of God: and that hee is raysed vppe from the dead to iudge the earth with righteousnesse.*

Theophilus.

HEre are his wordes wrested, and wrongly alledged, his meanyng subuerted, and misconstrued, Read Euang.cap.3.sent.11.cap.28.sent.3.and Dictata cap.5.sent.4.and ye shall see he pointeth on Christ.

William Wilkinson.

THis Article as it is one of the most blasphemous, and Hereticall of all the rest, so in the Exposition and saluyng therof *Theophilus* doth so freate and vary his old eloquence, as vnlesse I were acquainted with his melancholie, and what complexion, I should hardly beare such coales as he heapeth vpon me.

The

The houndes wherewith he persueth me are two, the first is wrestyng, the second is wrongfull alledgyng, subuertyng, and misconstruyng his meanyng: to the which vnlesse I withstand with playne dealyng, & naked truth, it seemeth that I shall finde small fauour at his handes.

And first whereas hee burtheneth me with *wrongfull alledging*, HN. him selfe shall explayne his owne meanyng, who will say agaynst him selfe much more then I in the former clause did accuse him of, or for these wordes of his, *He is indued with the good nature of God:* ẏ wordes be as playne as can be in the place by me alledged, which is also more clearely by him auouched in his wofull Euangely where he hath these woordes. HN. *out of grace accordyng to the prouidence of God and of his promises Iohn. 6. raised vp by the highest God from the dead, annointed with the holy Ghost in the Elderdome of the holy vnderstandyng of Christ. Iohn. 14. Godeified or Godded together with God in the Spirite of his Loue, made heyre with Christ in the heauenly treasures of the riches of God, Illuminated with the heauẽly truth, the very true light of the perfect beyng in the spirite, Apo. 21. Elected to be a minister of the gracious word stirred vp now at this last tyme accordyng to the promise Ieremy. 33.* Thus you see he hath word by word vttered that which you maliciously affirme that I haue wrongfully alledged: what blasphemy these wordes conteine no man can be ignoraũt but he that will not see, cõcerning his wordes I purposely abstaine to cõfute, for that they are learnedly by a godly man confuted already.

11. Epist. 2. cap. sent. 1.

HN. blasphemy Euang. 1. chap. 1. sent.

1. Raysed from the dead.
2. Annointed, &
3. Godded with God.
4. Heyre with Christ.
5. Lightned with the true beyng of God in the spirite.
6. Stirred vp in the last time, &c

M. Knewstub. Conf. pag. 1.

Concernyng his meanyng, I shall hereafter set down proofe that arrogantly and Luciferlike he taketh vppon him ẏ which is proper to Christ onely: where likewise I will touch the places by you cited, and proue that HN. pointeth not out Christ as ye affirme: *After the day of Loue seyng the same is last or newest day, wherin the vniuersall Actes. 17. d. compasse of the earth shalbe come iudged with righteousnes: There shall no (Apoc. 10. a.) day of grace appeare any more vpõ the earth but a seuere. (Heb. 10. c.) or*

HN. 1. Epist. 3. chap. 6. sent.

ſharpe iudgement ouer all vngodly. We acknowledge that there is none other light, nor liſe more that is true, nor hath bin neither in heauen, nor vpon earth, but this ſame light which is now in this laſt time, through the loue of God the father reueiled & come vnto vs, & that ſame whereon Moſes. Deut.18.6. and all the Prophets of God haue witneſſed. Eſay. 60.a. Iohn.5.c. and which the holy Apoſtles of Chriſt. Actes.2.3.4,7.10.13. &c. and the Euangeliſtes haue publiſhed. Theſe be HN. *his owne wordes, out of the which (becauſe they were to tedious to repeate) I made out of them his Collection.*

11.Epiſt.cap.5. ſent.4.

Scripture prophanely abuſed.

HN. *ſayth he is indued with the good nature of God, and that he is rayſed vp from the dead to iudge the earth with righteouſnes: alſo the day of Loue by him preached is the laſt day and there ſhall be no day of grace hereafter. Neither was there any trueth before him, or beſides him, or ſhalbe after him.* To the fourme of wordes he hath framed a wrangle, the matter he graunteth belike to be true.

11.Epiſt.cap.2. ſent.1.

1.Epiſt.cap.3. ſent.6.

11.Epiſt.cap.5. ſent.9.

Thirdly I affirme that HN. ſayth he was prophecied of by Moſes, and all the Prophets, and Apoſtles, and the Euangeliſtes: to proue this he alledgeth Deut.18.6. Eſay.60.a. Iohn.5.c. To the which Theophilus replieth thus.

Theophilus.

Reade the place againe, & you ſhall finde he ſayth that the light or lyfe is it which is prophecied of and not himſelfe, and leaue your lying for very ſhame.

William Wilkinſon.

To the which his reprochfull reply and childiſh cauill I thinke I ſhall aunſwere fully, and ſatiſfy ſufficiently: If firſt I be able to iuſtifie (which gods aſſiſtance I hope I ſhall) that HN. preſumptiouſly taketh on him, that which is prophecied on, and proper vnto Chriſt:

HN. Challengeth that is proper to Chriſt.

Second-

Secondly I will (cōparing him with Dauie George, and their hereſies mutually withother) prouc that it is very like to be true, which they deny, and Maiſt. Rogers doth charge him with HN. to be Dauie Georges ſcholler and that in impietye he goeth far beyond him. HN. Dauid George his ſcholler.

Thirdly by comparing him, and his opinions with Gods worde, I will ſhew that he is not the perfect Prophet, but the moſt peſtilent Archheretique that euer was: and that he was ſo prophecied of by the Prophets, Apoſtles, and Euangeliſtes. In the which place to diſplay all his wreſtinges of the ſcriptures, I neither am able they being infinit, nor willing becauſe I deſire to be briefe: onely I will by a few geue a taſt, what the reſt are which I haue not touched. HN. foretould by the prophets &c. to be an Heretique.

HN.

HN. *Alledgeth Eſay 60. a. to proue the light ſhewed by him, was forespoken of by Eſay.* 11.Epi.5.chap. 4.ſent.

W. Wilkinſon.

IT is manifeſtly ment of Chriſt his firſt comming.

HN.

HN. *Sayth that all the ſcriptures heauenly teſtimonyes, and ſpirituall voyces of the eternall trueth, which are gone forth from the holy ſpirite of Loue, (that is of God) are brought to light through him.* 1.Epiſt.1.chap. 1.ſent.

William Wilkinſon.

This is blaſphemous agaynſt the Prophecy of Chriſt, and agaynſt the Scriptures. Math. 17. 5. Marc. 9. 28. John. 1. 18. Col. 23.

HN.

HN. *Sayth yet once more he hath appointed a day in the which he will iudge the earth with righteouſnes.* 1.Epiſt.1.chap. 2.ſent.

Act. 17.g. and this in the next ſentence. 3. he doth apply to his appearaunce in theſe wordes, this day, and now is the day fulfilled in the Loue, and this once more ſayth he is meant of himſelfe: for profe he quoteth Act. 17.g.31. verſe.

Docum. ſent. cap.15. ſent.4. HN. publiſh. of peace. 1.cap.16.ſent.

W. Wilkinſon.

This is particularly ment of Chriſtes firſt comming in the fleſh, prophecied euen in ỹ ſelfe ſame wordes. Agge. 2. cap. 7. verſe. and in Chriſt fulfilled. Heb. 12. cap. 27. verſe.

HN.

11.Epiſt.2.cap. ſent.6. &. 2.

HN. *Quoteth Eſay.2.a.2. Miche.4.a,1. to be meant of the reſtoring of the decayed ſtate of Gods Church which is redyfied by him.*

William Wilkinſon.

This is manifeſtly meant of Chriſt.

HN.

Euang.cap.1. pag.

HN. *Citeth Math.24. verſe.14. Eſay.67.22.g. Pſal. 95.7.8. Heb.3.7. and the 4.7.8. Apoc.14.6. to be ſpoken of his Euangelye by him publiſhed.*

William Wilkinſon.

Which is vnderſtode of the preaching of the goſpell by Chriſt and his Apoſtles.

HN.

Euang. cap.1. ſent.1.

HN. *Sayth hee is an elected Miniſter of the gratious worde, ſtirred vp in the laſt time, according to the promiſes. Ierem. 33. read the whole chap.*

W. Wilkinſon.

It is meant of Chriſt.

HN.

HN.

HN. *Sayth the teſtimonye of his Euangelie is not alone the Euang. of the kingdome promiſed to be publiſhed in all the world, & to all people, but alſo all the teſtimonies which* HN. *hath ſet forth in the glaſſe of righteouſnes.* Præface ad Euang. ſent. 4.

William Wilkinſon.

Blaſphemous agaynſt the goſpell, and a thing accurſed. Galla. 1. chap. 8. ver.

He taketh that vnto him which belongeth vnto John Baptiſt. Mallachi. Math. 11, 10. Præface ad Euang. ſent. 3.

HN.

HN. *Sayth the miſterye of the kingdome of God, his righteous iudgements. Math. 25. d. Actes 16. 17. d. Iude. 1. and the comming of Chriſt now in the laſt tyme in the reſurrection. Ezech. 37, 6. Iohn. 5. c. Rom. 8. 6. Phil. 3. b. 11. ver. of the dead is declared vnto him, as an elected veſſel, from the mouth of God himſelfe.* Euang. cap. 2. ſent. 1.

God hath begone a new miraculous worke now in this day of Loue, whereof we witnes, with vs his elected ones wherin the ſcripture is fulfilled. Eſay. 43, 6. c. a. Eſay. 57, b. Euang. cap. 2. ſent. 4. Quoted in vayne.

HN. *Sayth he will declare the ſecret miſteries of God, and make relation of thinges hidden before the beginning of the world. Math. 13. 11. b. Iohn. 6.* Euang. cap. 2. ſent. 11.

The day of Loue. Pſal. 118. c. is the appearaunce and comming. Math. 24. c. 30. ver. Luk. 17. 20. ver. Actes. 2. a. of Chriſt Ieſu our Lord in the reſurrection. Eſay. 26. c. 1. Cor. 15. f. of the dead wherein the law, the Prophetes, and all that is written of Chriſt becommeth fulfilled. Luk. 24. e. Præfa. ad Euãg. ſent. 2. Scripture abuſed. Falſe Quoted.

The day of Loue preached by HN. *is the day of the laſt comming of Chriſt in iudgement with many thouſandes of Saintes. Eſay. 3. b. Math. 4. 24. d. 37. & 25. d. 31. Iude. 1. b.* Whiche places manifeſtly proue (beyng meant of the ſecond comming of Chriſt) that the reſurrection of Euang. cap. 1. ſent. 9. Impertinently alledged.

Euang.cap.25. sent.5.

his comming is perfected & past already. HN. *Sayth that this testimonie (that is his Euang) and publishing of the ioyfull message, is the same comming, and all seruices and prophecies which are gone out from God doe leade hereunto, and cease herein.*

Euang.cap.35. sent.1.

HN. *Sayth, Behold ye dearely beloued, presently euen from the selfesame day becommeth the scripture in all fulfilled of that which it mentioneth of Christ of his seede, and of his glory and Lordlynes.* Therefore all scriptures was vntill now vnperfect and not fulfilled, contrary to that which John sayth. 19.28.

Euang.cap.35. sent.3.4.5.6.7. After the end of the chapter.

HN. *Sayth that all the prophecies. Esdr.4.d.Esay.3.e.& 11.b.12.Ezechi.39.d.21.Zopha.3.b.9.ver.Zach.2.b.10.11 Numb.24.a.5.6.are in this day of Loue presently fulfilled all the which places are particularly meant of Christ, and applied blasphemously by* HN. *to him for to proue the day of his comming.*

The Familye compare and make equall HN. *his wrightinges with the holy scriptures, because say they, they are written with the same spirite.*

William Wilkinson.

Aunswere to the exceptions taken at the Euang.pag.

HN. seldome alleageth Scripture aright.

Thus with as great breuitye as I could, I haue set downe a few of his blasphemies, for that his vayne and blinde, idle, and impertinēt alleadging of Scriptures is infinite and without number: for almost he neuer citeth any scripture aright: for the children of God it shall not be vnprofitable to consider, that to leaue the Lordes hye way and the cleare sunne shine of his truth, is to entangle our selues with vaine, and endles Questions, which engender strife of wordes more thē godly edifying, of the which S.Paule geueth Timothy a straight charge to beware 1. Tim.1.4. and 4.chap. Titus.1.14. 2.Pe. 1.16. 1. Tim.6.4. The which watchword, if our Familye had diligently taken hede vnto, they had not so mightely ben deceiued with such strong illusions. For

this

this is the light vnto the which we muſt take hæde, as vnto a candle ſhining in a dark place, ſo ſhal we not faile of the reward after lyfe, nor in this lyfe make ſhipwrack of our owne ſaluation.

Now followeth the ſecond part of the compariſon of D. George his hereſies with HN. whereby we ſhall ſee the one not to be any whit in impietye inferiour vnto the other.

The Familye of Loue in their firſt Epiſtle to M. Rogers. pag. 72. lin. 7. &c. very vehemently ſtomack (as their maner is) becauſe M. Rogers enlinketh HN. *with Iohn a Leyde, and the Archheretique Dauid George* to haue ben confederates in ſpreading the hereſie of the Anabaptiſtes at *Munſter. Anno 1533.* And leaſt that M. Rogers ſhould ſcape vntarred with their opprobrious Eloquẽce they very louingly (as well becommeth their Familye) brande him with his marke, *An egregious vntruth vttered by this new ſhameles wrighter*. Furthermore they affirme that many learned wrighters teſtify the matter vz. of Dauid &c. to be Anabaptiſme, *and yet ſay they this man will haue it the Familye of Loue*: and here they triumph hauing taken M. R. tardye as though the Familye of Loue, and the Anabaptiſtes, were ſuch great ſtraungers, that at no time they had bin acquainted, nor euer yet talked, or met together. To remoue the which doubt if any ſhall happen to ſtand in doubt, which I thinke he will not that knoweth throughly what both the opinions meane, by laying of the ſchiſmaticall opinions of theſe two heretiques together, the Fam. ſhall not neede to be ſo ſtraunge with their kinne, nor be ſo nice becauſe their faction is more famous then the other of their Elder brethren, I meane the Anabaptiſtes.

> D.George and Fami.compared.
>
> Pag.3.
>
> Pag.72.
>
> Anabaptiſtes & the Fam.very neare of kinne.
>
> 1.Compariſon of D. George and the Fami.
>
> 2.booke.14. chap.fol.68.

The firſt opinion of *Dauid George* as M.Rogers alledgeth and M.Bullinger in his boke agaynſt the *Anabap-*

tistes auoucheth to be true was this : *The doctrine taught by Moses, Christ, the Prophetes, & Apostles, is vnperfect vnto saluation, but his heresie is perfect (as he sayth) to saluatiō.*

D.George and HN. their heresies all one.

The reasons which do induce me to thinke the heresie of *Dauid George, and* HN. is in effect all one, are because they iumpe both in this. They prefer their owne doctrine before the doctrine of Moses, Christ, the Apostles & Prophetes, and secondly affirme it is abler to saue those that heare theirs thē the other. Now to proue they prefer their doctrine before Moses. &c. This shalbe playne and an vndeniable reason.

The doctrine which in the Churche of England (the Lordes most holy name be praysed for it) is by Publike authoritie commaunded, by all that preache the same approued, and by the Fam. of Loue, confessed to be the doctrine of Moses. &c.

But they say that this is not sufficient vnto saluation.

Therefore are they *Anabaptistes*, and *Dauid Georges* Schollers.

For profe of the first proposition, that the doctrine by publique authoritie commaunded is the doctrine of Moses. &c. they will not deny it, for so much as they haue in

Confes. pag. 4.

their Cōfession of their fayth published An. 1575. openly protested that *they are not iustly to bee blamed, accused, detected, or burthened as transgressors of the law agaynst any of the Queene her Maiesties proceedyng in causes Ecclesiasticall, &c.* But all men know, that it is *an Ecclesiasticall cause*, concernyng the truth of doctrine Publiquely preached, therfore they are likewise obedient to her therein. If they shall here seeke to starte by affirmyng that they meane outward pollicie of the Church that is a thyng of lesse waight then the doctrine of the word of God openly professed: for that the truth of the word is alwayes one, and immutable, it is the same vnto all nations and people of the world: But the externall pollicie in gouerning the Church is mutable, neither alwayes one, but chaunged diuersly in diuers places, accordyng to the state of the

places

places,tymes,and people. Therfore they shall aunswere here nakedly: if they say that they agrée vnto the pollicie of gouernement,not vnto the doctrine of the Churche of England they shall shewe very plainly,and that they 1. deale doublely notwithstādyng they pretend in their foresayd *Confession,that they deale with all men vprightly, faythfully,and charitably.* Pag. 13.

Furthermore when as in their confession mēcionyng Religion they affirme that they *obey our soueraigne Lady the Queene, and the Magistrates our foregoers spirituall, and temporall.&c.* Conf.pag.12.

Whiche by the word of God they should not, neither ought to do vnlesse the doctrine by the Prince commaunded were from God: therefore secondly I conclude that they confesse the doctrine by vs professed publiquely to be the doctrine of Moses, Christ, and the Apostles, and Prophetes and this is the proofe of my first proposition. Actes.4.9.&.5.28.

But cōcernyng the second proposition, *vz.* that the doctrine of Moses is vnsufficiēt, is apparaūt. For no man in the choyse of two thyngs, wherof he must néedes chuse ye one, will chuse that, which is insufficient therefore is the particular Fam. (whiche they fayne vnto them selues) thought by thē more sufficiēt then the Publique doctrine & assembly of our Church & Christiā congregation. Now least they should shift, in saying that our Church & theirs is all one, as some times they do to dazell and deceiue the simple: I aunswere that in the third Epistle that is Extant of theirs to M. Rogers they affirme that *of such an houshold as we haue challenged to our selues they are straungers*. Therefore say I they thinke their Fam. to be more sufficient for to attaine saluation in, then the open visible Church of Christ in England, which doth impugne their Familie. And to this purpose very naturally they *Exhort such as be wise among vs to looke ouer the Scriptures agayne. For if their Fam. of Loue haue founde the true or old way correspondent with all the doctrine of the Apostles of Iesus Christ, and therfore so needfull that without it there shall* Fam. not of our Church, by their owne confessiō. Pag.94. 1. Epist. to M. Rog.fol.73. pag.2.

no man finde mercy with God, or els through Christ become saued. Item read the second Article of HN. pag. 23. and there this is handled at large. The places which further at large out of their bookes proue this matter are. *1. Exhort.cap. 12. sent. 42. & 20. sent. 7. Dictata cap. 9. sent. 3. Eu ã.cap. 3. sent, 3. & cap. 23. sent. 7. & cap. 24. sent. 25.* in all the which they affirme as *Dauid George* doth in his heresie that onely their Familie is sufficient vnto saluation, whereby is clearely auouched, that their Fam. of Loue are guiltie in the first degrée.

2. Comparison of D. George and his Fam.

Dauid George his second heresie was that he affirmed himselfe *Christ and Mesias the beloued sonne of God.*

HN. dare not expresly and definitiuely so affirme least all mẽ should hold him for a false Prophet, yet as it were a sloape and couertly affirmeth it in takyng vnto him the prophecie of Christ &c. as is declared before pag. 52. 53. so that yet in the second degrée. *D.G.* and HN. agrée very filthy in their heresies ech with other.

3. Comp. of D. Georg and his Fam.

Dauid George his third heresie was this: *that he would restore the house of Israell and the tribe of Leuy, he will rayse the tabernacle of God by the spirite of Christ.*

Letter of the Fam. to M. Rogers. pag. 82. lyn. 24.

That HN. is the minister by whom the Church is restored through the spirite of the Loue or of God, in many and sundry places cited already, is more thẽ manifest: & if (though they beyng incident to the matter) I should repeat them: they of the Fam. would charge me that I alleged thẽ often to make the volume arise ẏ greater. Let it therfore (besides the places quoted already in the pag) be sufficient for me, by one testimony out of his Euang. to proue this in him to be true wherewith I charge him.

Euang. cap. 3. sent. 21.

Scripture vildly quoted by HN.

2. King. 7. 1. Cron. 18. Esa. 2. Iere. 30. 31. Mich. 4. Luc. 17. Iohn. 4.

Now in the same day shall the Citie of the Lord be builded vpon her brief place or auncient roome of the tẽple of the Lord or tabernacle of his dwellyng shall stand euen as the same ought to stand. Namely inwardly in vs in the beyng of the holy Ghost, and therefore when HN. is disposed to boast of the restoring of the hill of the Lord and of the repaypayring of the Church, then straight he vseth to quote. *Esay.2.*chap.2.*vers.d.*and *Micheas.*4.chap.1.vers.d.and thẽ immediatly before or after straight hee putteth this *shall come to passe in this day of the Loue or now or in this same most newest day of the Loue. &c.* vpon the which places as those most often, wherein the redrsyng of the Church by Christ is prophecied and foretold of by the Prophetes, he that marketh this obseruation, well shall see him stumble very often. What may be gathered thereby is not hard to coniecture, *vz.* that he dreamed, and so would neede perswade his Disciples the instauration of the Churche should be perfected by him. *Euang.2.chapter 1.sect.2.leafe.* And in the third Chap. section the first and *9.* are notable places to verifie the truth of this verdict, which for breuitie I pretermit, onely notyng them not further meanyng to encomber the Reader with them: and thus much to proue that HN. agreeth with *D. George* in his iij. heresie. 1.Epist.cap.1. sent.1.4.cap.2. sent.2.*6.*

Dauid George his fourth heresie: That who soeuer speaketh agaynst his doctrine shall neuer be forgiuen in this world nor in the world to come. 4. Compa.of D. George and the Fami.

In this doth HN. fitly with *Dauid George* agree, & accord in one, as in my Additions may appeare at large to the 3. and 4. Articles: and *Theophilus* him selfe will not deny it. For hee expoundeth HN. his meanyng thus in the 13. Article in these wordes. *To the enemyes or enuious of the loue of Christ, and to the obstinate, which turne them away there from, there is no mercy promised.* If this be not all one both in wordes and sence with *Dauid George:* I cã not tell what it should bee to agree with him, at euery turne, both in wordes and sence.

And because by the way of comparison I haue in the former Articles declared that HN. and *Dauid George* do fully consent, and agree, in the principall matters wherewith we charge them: let it be lawfull for me (good Reader) to set one foote further in this comparison that I may shew more euidently how in as weighty a point as heretoo I haue layd agaynst them, that in the accord of their heresie they so conspire, either with other, that it clearely, and to HN. his perpetuall shame it may be affirmed which M. Rogers reporteth, that *Dauid George* layd the egge of this heresie, and HN. hatched the chickens. As for HN. though it seemeth his wit is pestilent enough to peruert ẏ truth: yet by *Dauid George* his Maisters whetting him forward, hauyng of him selfe a cankred mynde agaynst the truth, and a swellyng hart: he became x. fold more the sonne of perdition, in beyng wholy bent to seduce the simple that thereby he might not so much be holy as he pretended, as increase his priuate wealth, which by his fiskyng to and fro was not a litle empayred.

For to affirme that in word, which the deed it selfe auoucheth to be true, sufficiently apparaunt it is that *Dauid George* first put downe the principles of this secte: which when he had so done, and with writhyng and wrestyng had brought his heresie into tune, HN. was now by him further to be instructed how with a malitious mynde and perilous wit, he might runne descát at will, and quauer at pleasure vpon this straunge doctrine, and new tuned opinions.

The first straine wheron this further heretical accord was to be stretched, was this ẏ after D. George perceiued that openly in ẏ face of ẏ world to professe his opinions was not without spot, & godly Magistrates had diligently prouided that the Church of God should no lõger receiue any detrimẽt, straight way then did he forge this new found fond principle, as a soueraigne salue, to cure that mischeuous maladie and imminent perill which abode those that were defiled with that horrible infection. And seing the daunger was not smale to be outragious in so great a matter: he thought it sufficient that his sectary bare a good hart, & stode single in myndedly vnto his doctrine, to keepe their consciences to themselues, and for their further quietnes sake to cõforme themselues to any people whatsoeuer, amongest whome they liued & with whome they had to deale. This as it was a princi-

pall

pall point, so was it also a pestiferous poyson wherewith the diuel hath deceiued many a simple soule, and thrown many a stumbling block in the way of the wauering and weake harted Christian.

That this was David George his opinion, and that hereafter I be not sayd to slaunder him, let M. Bullenger be heard who testifieth thus of him: *Of this opinion was this beast D. George, whiche sect also is the most pestilent of all others.* Lib.2.pag.32.

To the which I further adde: Of this opinion is that wretched man HN. and by this bayte hath he choaked more Christians then by any other whatsoeuer.

For hereby in ye tyme of Papistry he had his faultors also whom by the Suthwarke Ioyner he licensed to be present at Idolaters seruice, and to kepe their consciences secret unto themselues, hauing taught them before, it was an indifferent thing to hould any thing, so they kept the doctrine of the Loue by him taught unto them. And this is manifest in his Euangelye, especially in that O yes which he maketh before his blasphemous proclamation, to the whole world, in these wordes following.

To the louers of the truth here and there, wheresoeuer or in what part of the world they dwell, or haue their abode of what sort or nation and religion as Christians in their Mahomet or Turkes in theirs, Heathen in theirs &c. To whom after HN. hath geuen particuler titles, immediatly he in the same section addeth. *And yet furthermore euery head properly for himselfe hauing then so diuers and many maners of groundes, beliefes, religions, ceremonyes, offices and administratiōs, as they will wherein they loue Gods truth and their righteousnes.*

Then the which wordes what may be sayd more Sathan like, or what euen belched out of the bottomles pit more blasphemous, if all the fiendes of hell would conspire together to afford a graceles and godles speach, whereby the hartes of them that stagger in the way of the truth: if not wholy they might be drawne away to superstition (for as for the worde Religion I feare me I haue attributed it to their scisme to often, albeit the Familye of Loue in their *Confession* would faine be counted religious) yet might they enioy the heresie of HN. with their opinions, and fauour whatsoeuer liketh them best.

Pag. 11.

So that certayne it is, whereas this his Euangelye, and the other of his bokes were nayled vpon euery post, in the common shops of stationers in dutch land commonly sould (vntill by the restraint of the maiestrate they were bridled and called in) they drew some Catholickes also to his faction, for whose cause, and with whome to créepe into fauour, to haue a shealter ready for any storme so notable he commendeth the popish Hierarchie, which order of popishe pollicye (to let passe that famous infamous booke, the Declaration of the Masse I meane,) after step by step he had extolled it aboue the cloudes, from the hyest to the lowest he falleth downe after this sort. *Section 4. he commendeth the Pope, and expoundeth Papa to signifie an olde Father in the holy vnderstanding: to whome he coupeleth his Colledge of Cardinals. sent. 8. thirdly, Primates sent. 9. Bishops. sent. 10. Priestes. sent. 14. who say their seruice in the formest part of the Church, that is in the chauncell. Parsons, Curates, Proctours, sent. 16, Deacons, sent. 17. Sextons, or keepers of holy thinges that the same muy be occupied in due season, and times conuenient. sent. 18. Monkes, which for the loue of righteousnes (as* HN. *sayth, are consecrated and sequestred from the world (from whome well it were if the world were seperated also) and from all that is worldly and fleshly. set. 19. and lastly the commen people. sent. 21.* To the which for a conclusion he addeth. *Behold all this hath bin euen so in tymes past in his very true being, when as yet the light of lyfe had the clearenes, and the beliefe her seruice, in the holynes of God, the renewed or Goddead men vpon the earth, all which shall now in the sam day, lykewise of the Loue through the comming of Christ, in the light of lyfe, and his holy spirite, be reduced or*

Euang. cap. 31. sent. 1. 2. &c.

Sent. 23.

HN. prophecieth of the restoring of Poperye.

or restored to his vpright fourme, in the very true being according to the Christian lyke ordinaunces, and florish in vigor or become forcible according to the promises.

Popish Hieracye shall flourishe sayth HN.

The which as I quake to wright so (to marke the ripenes of sinne that HN. is come vnto) must it nedes enforce the godly Christian, and tender childe of God to melt at the horrible outrage therein conteined. To the which if the *goodwilling in England which are named the Familye of Loue* shall reply and alledge, (for I hope they are not so far gone to defend this so great blasphmie, agaynst the kingdome of the sonne of God and his gloryous gospell) that they will not defend neither lyke in all thinges of his opinions to this I aunswere as M. Bullenger doth vnto the lyke obiection. Sometyme they are of this iudgement, sometymes of that, neither doe they all agree among themselues in the certaintye of their errour, for as truth onely is lyke it selfe error must nedes iar and disagre.

Bulleng in his preface.

But herein it had ben somewhat more tollerable for our Fam. if they had not set downe this in wrighting that herein they might shew themselues to be perfect schollers of a peruerse maister. But he that neuer kepeth touch with his seruauntes hath here betrayed them by their owne wordes to the world ere they were aware. For in their first Epistle which they make as an aunswere to M. Rogers boke. fol. 71. pag. v. lin. 30. they vtter these wordes.

You forget (say they to M. Rogers) many protestantes in Rome, Spayne, Italy, and many other places vnder the Byshop of Romes inquisition which hould it good pollicie to defend thēselues & their cōsciences from such tyranny: Will not you allow to others which you gladly chalenge to your selfe? &c.

Note how mānerly they speake of the Pope.

Whereby it is clearely proued and manifestly affirmed, that HN. and his scholers termed the Fam. of Loue in England, draw all in one line, and hould the same opinions with *Dauid George* that he doth: whom because they affirme by the testimonye of learned writers to be an Anabaptist nedes must it necessarye by the same consequence be urged, that they are Anabaptistes by their owne confession, and labour to bring Anabaptistrie into the church, from the which and other heresies, sectes, and scismes, the Lord deliuer both us and all his chosen dispersed wheresoeuer. Amen.

It remaineth that with the lyke breuitye or greater (if so large a matter may be conteined in a lesser rome,) as I before promised, so I compare HN. with those euident noates & manifest tokens of an heretique set downe by the spirite of God in holy Scriptures. For by that iudge both he and I must be tryed to be true meaning men in this lyfe before the Militaunt Church, and receiue our dome thereafter before the triumphāt Churche in the world to come.

Tokens of an heretique out of Scripture. 1. Tokē.

Cantic. 2. 5. The holy ghost in the Scriptures doth liken those heretiques, which disturbe the peace of the Church unto Foxes, which priuily, and by night, are wont to spoile and rauine. And in lyke manner our Sauiour Christ (Math. 13. 25.) doth describe not onely the father of heretiques, but his children also by the name of a enuious mā which soweth teares whilest men slepe. S. Paule (Gal. 2. 4.) termeth then false teachers, crafty creepers in: S. Peter (2. Pet. 2. 1.) sayth false teachers shall priuilye bring in damnable heresies. S. Iude (Iude vers. 4.) sayth certaine men haue crept in which turne the grace of God into wantones: upon all the which places it may very easely be gathered, that whosoeuer intendeth to broach any new and straunge doctrine, (as false coiners use to doe) he counterfaiteth in secret. That this hath bin the practise of heretiques from tyme to tyme nedeth no long profe: onely it is to be considered who it was, that renued Arius heresie in Constantine the Emperours dayes: (Ruffinus Hist. Ecclesia, cap. 11.) was it not a priest which priuilye bare Constantia the Emperours sister in hād, that the Counsell of Nice had

done

done Arius wrong, who thought not of Christes deuinitye as the Counsel supposed and the rumour was spread abroad of him &c.

And haue not the Familye of Loue this long tyme borne their schollers in hand and others whome they seeke to seduce: nay doe they not now at this instant perswade the simple, that *Henrye Nicolas and Christofer Vitels* are no such men as they are bruted amongest ye people.

The lyke is reported by *Iosias Simlerus* in his Epistle prefixed before M. Bullengers booke agaynst the Anabaptistes. Of the Anabaptistes themselues whom he sayth fly open conference, and creeping from house, and seduce the simple. Fol. 1.

M. Huldrich Zuinglius, in the same wordes doth utter the same sence of the Catabaptistes of his tyme, which sayth he, priuily spread abroad their bookes in the handes of their owne sectaries. Whereas when Christ taught any thing, he came first into the Sinagogue, priuilye sayth our Sauiour I haue sayd nothing. Fol. 11. & 93. Luke. 4. 16. Math. 26. 55. Iohn. 18. 20.

The Apostles in semblable maner whē they preached any thing, they came to the temple: and when the hye priestes called them and commaunded them to silence, committed them to prison: the Aungell of the Lord sayd unto them, goe your way, and stand in the temple, and speake unto the people. &c. Actes. 3. 11. 5. 20.

Furthermore S. Paule comming unto Antiochia on the Sabboth day, he went into the Sinagogue, and being at Athens when he saw the whole Citie geuen to Idolatrye, openly in the market place he disputed with the Epicures, and Stoick Philosophers, and such as he met, and Standing in the middest of the Mars streate he openly inueighed agaynst the superstitiō of that worthy Citye, and Uniuersitye, euen to the faces of the greatest Clerkes and wisest men (or naturall light I meane) in all the world besides. Neither was S. Paule affraid of all their learning, and countenaunce, but boldly hee preached unto them the unknowen God, and the resur- Act. 13. 14. Actes. 27. 17. 17 22 rection from the dead, vnto whome how vnlyke our Familyes are in zeale of profession, I leaue to the whole world that knoweth them to iudge, and their owne consciences to testifie.

For whether in the teaching of their doctrine, and in the defending of the same they are lykest to the auncient Anabaptistes, and to the ould heretiques, and vnto S. Paule the Apostle this one coullor wherby we see a schismatique discribed, can sufficiently testifie. For if the doctrine secretly taught by those, who are termed the Famlye of Loue, be such a truth and grounded vpon such inuincible profes as they in euery corner vse to bragge of: why follow they not that course which the sonne of God by his example shaped forth vnto them, that is euen in the presence of the ciuill and spirituall Magistrate, in the chiefest Citye of the Realme, and that in the concourse and greatest assẽblies of the people? why doe they not before them that openly blame them, and in sermõs publiquely confute them, protesting the truth of HN. his bookes openly at Paules crosse? Nay being at Paules Crosse for their fantasticall opinions, why doe they deny them and renounce them with detestation openly?

But herein did the Anabaptistes deale more orderly then our Fam. in England. For they procured an open conference, and disputation to be had in the presence of the Maiestrate, thereby to testifie their schisme to be truth, but our Fam. are so far from procuring an open that dare not abide a priuate conference, if they be thereunto vrged by any man priuately, without witnes, whereby they indeede betray their sect to be but a scisme, and shew how far vnlyke they are herein vnto the olde Prophets and Apostles of the Primatiue Church.

1. At. Tiguri. Bulling. lib. 1. cap. 5. 2. at. Bern. cap. 7. fol. 17.

2. Token of an heretique out of Scripture.

The second note of an heretique, saith S. Paule, is this, that those which sowe the corrupt seede of such

such erroneous doctrine,(as schismatiques most commōly doe,) they become vaine ianglers, desirous to teach, & yet vnderstād not what they speake, nor whereof they affirme. Whereby it is geuē to vnderstād,that they who in S. Paule his tyme began to sowe such sæde were but simple men, and in knowledge very base, in that they toke in hand to dispute they wot not what, and maintain that which they had no skill of. Such in times past were heretiques, and such as thought it a glorious and glittering thing in the sight of the world to set abroad straunge opinions,that they onely might cary away the prick and prise, not hauing so much as the emptye caske & smalest smacke of learning. And so alwayes hath it falne out that,those partyes which first taught heresies were least able to defend them, tel by little and little they gathered strength: Sometyme vaine heades being not altogether vnlearned toke part with them : and vnhapely labored to perfect that which was vngratiously begone.

An heretike out of Scripture.

The chief of the *Anabaptistes* in *Germanie* were men silly,for their wits,rather to be pittied for their follie, thē enuied for their knowledge. Which being weary of their seuerall craftes and occupations sought vp a more easie trade to get their liuyng. And beyng of meane and illiberall sciences, sought in the profession and interpretation of the word to shoulder and out face the Preachers thereof with reprochfull tauntes and scoffes vntollerable: such was *Cnipper Dollyng*,and *Iohn a Leid* beyng a Boatcher. HN. was a Mercer in *Amsterdam*,and those who are yet alyue both in *Emdene* and *London* & els where who haue kept him company and knew him very wel,affirme that his knowledge was but small, neither was he expert in any toung saue his owne Dutch toūg onely,neither was he euer trayned vp in any liberall Art,or had commendation for his learnyng.

Vitels was a Ioyner, and if his learnyng was so singular as his frendes affirme, it is lyke that he came by it rather by Reuelatiō thē by the ordinary meanes of study.

There is a *T*. in Cambridgeshyre, who was *Vitelles* companion, who was a flat *Arrian*, as by his owne hand I am able to auouch, and before men of worshyp *Anno. 1574.* March. 24. in Cābridge denyed *Christ to be God equal with his father. 2. He said that childrē are not by nature sinfull neither ought to be Baptised tell yeares of discretion. 3. The Regenerate sinne not. 4. S. Paule his Epistles be not to be more accompted of, then the letters of priuate men.*

This man beyng then a flat *Arrian*, since once recanted his errour, and secondly is falne into the same opinion. His name is *W. H.* of *B.* perhaps vnto the Family he is not vnknowen, for that *Vitels* had sometymes lodged in his house, and hee vseth to conferre with them concernyng their opinions: this man would sœme in the company of simple mē to be very learned, and they that haue talked with him affirme, that he hath many wordes but small wisedome, beyng of a wealthy occupation but smal in wit, and might be better occupyed to learne the first principles of Gods feare and him selfe bee instructed before he teach that, which he hath no skill of.

And so is it with the chief *Elders* of our *Louely Fraternitie*, some of them be Weauers, some Basketmakers, some Musitians, some Botlemakers, and such other lyke which by trauailyng from place to place, do get their lyuyng. They whiche amongest them beare the greatest countenaunce, are such as, hauyng by their smoth behauiour, and gloasing talke deceiued some Iustices of Peace, and other worshypfull of coūtrey, where they dwel, haue gotten Licences to trade for Corne vp & downe the countrey, and vsing such a romyng kynde of Traffique kœpe not commonly any one certaine abidyng place, but runnyng fiskyng frō place to place, stay not for the most part any where long together, saue where they hit vpon some simple husbandman, whose wealth is greater then his wit, and his wit greater then a care to kœpe him selfe vpright in God his truth and sincere Religion. His house if it be farre from company, and stand out of the common

Zuing. contra Catabap. fol. 39.

walke

walke of the people with whom he dwelleth is a fit neast wherin all the byrdes of that fether vse to méete together. Thus did the *Anabaptistes* in their tyme, and I wishe hartely in the loue I beare to some of the Fam. that our *Familiers* of Loue were far vnlike them. And thus much for the maner how, and the persons by whom their doctrine is set abroad in the handes of the simple.

¶3. Token to know an Heretique.

THirdly concernyng the doctrine, which is by all heretiques generally taught in corners, S. Iude sayth it maketh sectes. S. Peter saith it speaketh euill of the way of truth. S. Paul geueth them these titles: Men that cause diuision and offences, which serue not the Lordes Iesus but their owne bellyes, who with fayre speach and flatteryng wordes deceiue the simple. Vers.19. 2.Pet.2.2. Rom.16.17.

Now whether HN. haue made a sect, and be author of admission or not the subscription of those letters, whiche come from his Schollers with these wordes, *Your louyng Frendes the Fam. of Loue*, can sufficiently testifie.

That HN. speaketh euill of the way of truth is manifest, for these be his woordes. *Whose false beyng (vz. of the Preachers which through the false light haue taken on an imagination of knowledge) is the Deuill, the Antichrist, the kingdome of the Maiestie of the Deuill him selfe. &c. and in the same place the 10. sent. hee sayth they are but a neast of Deuils, and of all wicked spirites.* The hearers of the Preachers hee calleth *the Sinagogue of Sathan, or Schoole of the Deuill.* What God HN. and his confederates serue, I will not Iudge, but what speach they vse towardes the simple people in their day communication with them, whether they bee flatteryng and swéete wordes, they can at large testifie, who at any tyme haue vsed their company: may easely affirme with what sugred woordes they féede the itchyng eares of those, whō they labour to draw into their opinions. 2.Exhórt. cap. 15. sent. 17. fol. 38.d. 1.Exhort. cap. 16.sent.19.

2.Pet.2.7. Furthermore S. Peter he termeth the doctrine of heretiques. Welles without water, cloudes caried about with the tempest, speakyng swellyng wordes of vanitie.

Verse.12.13.&c. S. Iude sayth they are corrupt trees without fruite, twise dead and pulled vp by the rootes, ragyng waues fomyng out their owne shame, wandryng starres. &c.

The which excellent Metaphores here vsed by the holy Ghost, liuely and to the full describe vnto vs the properties of Schismaticall teachers, and their hereticall doctrine. For the nature of the cloud is, when the earth is parched with heate, & the fruite thereof for want of moysture begynneth to windell, and wither away with gladsome weate and siluer drops, to cherish and relieue the tender plantes, whiche by the hardnes of the earth doth hurt their sappy iuice, for want of water: euen so should the Preachers of Gods word, and Ministers of the Gospell, with wholesome doctrine and godly exhortations water the consciences and supple the hartes of their hearers, which are wounded with the feelyng of their sinnes, and inwardly in some measure touched with a conceaued grief, because they haue displeased God, whiche is their louyng Father and mercyfull redeemer. And this is that which S. Paule calleth the Preachers of the word waterers and planters. 1. Cor. 3. chap. 6. vers.

Now in so much as Schismaticall and phantasticall teachers make in worde great boast, and to the worlde wardes will needes cary a countenaunce of planters and waterers: Yet when the afflicted soule and tormented hart shall come to such welles to draw, thinkyng with their liquor to be relieued, when they looke for most succour, their comfort is the least, and all the hope they haue of moysture is turned into emptines: for the least storme that is will soone scatter such cloudes, and the smallest heate will so resolue them, that when our hope is the greatest, our helpe is very small. So that in false teachers it is assuredly true, whiche the holy Prophet long sithence complained of the halting Israelites their good-

nes

nes is like a mornyng cloude and as the dew that goeth early away.

Now whether HN.his writyngs haue in them ought but swellyng woordes of mans vanitie, and beyng fruitles trées, and starres that wander without a certaine motion, it is a litle further of vs to be considered. Hosea.6.4.

For, to examine the matter conteyned in HN. his bookes it is very small and silly: for let the diligent Reader pare and set aside his wrested and violent *Allegories*, his vnusuall and insignificant phrases, of beyng *United into the perfect beyng of the loue in the spirite, incorporatyng into God, consubstantiatyng with Christ.&c*, and such lyke wordes of course, he shall finde small substaunce and litle stuffe in matter that may be gathered by the order of readyng by pen or memory, and sometyme he shalbe so plunged in the wordes, and wander for matter, that hee shall very hardly or not at all make sence of that hee readeth. That this is true, they know whiche are occupyed in the perusing of them. HN. his scripture quoting.

As for his vayne and idle quotation they are innumerable whiche as Mutes vpon a stage called forth to fill vp a roome and make a shew, depart not vtteryng any word at all. His cityng of Scriptures sometymes for the phrase, wherein his greatest vayne is, and wherein oftentymes hee is vaynely occupyed, sometymes for one word onely hee clappeth out many places, without any further matter, sometymes neither for word, nor yet for matter. Yea sometymes he allegeth a place for a proofe, which cleane ouerturneth the Assertion why he induceth it for. As for example. *1.Exhortation.6.chap.sent.41.leafe 17.line.16.* to proue the resurrection he allegeth Ezechiell.36.chap.b. there is no such place, neither in that whole Chapter any word that maketh mention of the resurrection. In the.37.chapter v.vers.4.&c. the resurrection is clearely prophecied and by him rightly and to the purpose alleged. But Esay.26.c.vers.14.The dead shall not lyue, neither shall the dead arise.&c. Is alleged to the same purpose, where the woordes seeme to be cleane contrary, (where note also what HN.thinketh of the Resurrection) beyng meant, that the Lord will so scourge the wicked that euen in this lyfe, they shall feele in some measure the torment and worme of the conscience, that they shall haue in the world to come, when as the godly shall haue all ioye that can possible be thought, and more in deede then mortall man can imagine, the quietnesse of conscience that passeth all vnderstandyng: but this is meant of this lyfe, and not to be vnderstanded of the resurrection or the lyfe to come. For that, in all that Chapter the meanyng & scope of the Prophet is not to handle any such matter.

And thus much for the manner how, the personnes whereby, and the doctrine that is taught by them, whom the scripture termeth an heretique, which in my iudgement doth as fitly agree to HN. and is by S. Peter as fully foretold as if he had liued in HN. his tyme, and bin priuie vnto all his dealinges. Now in one word concerning HN. his stile, and the maner of the deliuerye of his opinions in his bookes.

2.Pet.2.

HN.his stile is hereticall.

His method is, take it among ye: The thred of his speach is sometymes knotty, and sometimes great, and sometyme small as vnskilfull spinners vse to afford, his grace and giftes in pẽning thereof is euen such as Marcion is reported to haue vsed in penning of his hereticall writings, Whose whole talke of the spirite was in such a straunge kinde of stile, that those which hard or read them at the first did wonder at them. And this being a part of that wherein our Familye doe as it were wonderfull loue, and make of themselues, so that in their speach which they dayly vse in talke with any man, if euer they may be gotten to confer of the knowledge of the Scriptures, of the law, of sinne, inner man and regeneration, of the humblyng of the soule, which are the largest Common Places of their studye, straight way by the vnusualnes of their speaches, and straũge termes ye

Caluin agaynst the Libertines, leaf.131.&.129.

may

may easely vnderstand what way they are enclined. So that when I my selfe haue spoken publiquely the great paynes which I haue taken in perusing their bookes, haue so acquainted my selfe with HN. his phrases, that I vsing them at vnwares haue by diuers, which knew me not, ben suspected to be priuie vnto their doctrine.

But concerning the generall noates of an heretique this shall suffice with the perticuler application thereof vnto HN. it remaineth that I confer his opinions with the perticuler fantasies of diuers heretiques with whom we shall finde him so to agrée, that it may easely appeare they haue had all but one and the same Scholemaister, who hath instructed them in the same principles, to ouerthrow and disquiet the Church of God.

HN. his opinions compared with Heretiques opinions.

THe *Origianists, Nepotians, and Priscilianists,* did altogether peruert the certaintye of the written word of God, by turning it into allegoryes: so doth HN. *Docum.sent.* or *Dicta-tis.* cap.3. sent.11.12, Euang. cap.8. sent. 3. 4.5.6.1. Epist.3. cap. 22. sent. and almost in euery side of euery leafe in all his wrightinges.

2. The *Montanistes, Praeputians, Donatists, Luthusiastes, Monkes, and Anabaptists*: boast of reuelations: so doth HN. Euang. cap.2. sent. 1, contrary to the Scriptures. 1. Gal.8. ver.

3. The *Cerdonians, Marcionites, and Appellites*, boast of their new Prophets, and prefer them before the olde: so did the *Anabaptistes prefer Thomas Muncer their Archheretique before Luther, and Zuinglius, Bulleng. fol. 9.b. Vitels in his reply to M. Rogers* display, termeth HN. a Prophet in these wordes. *Ye despise* HN. *because he sayth he is a Prophet sent of God, but the tyme may come that you shall finde his prophesie true. and in the same reply he sayth:*

whereas ye say that HN. *doth call himselfe Rectorer of all thinges. I aunswere that there is no such word writtē by him, and yet hath the Lord accomplished according to his promises through the spirite of Christ in him all what he hath spoken through the mouth of his seruauntes the Prophets.* And agayne *ye say we affirme* HN. *to be the true Prophet of God, sent to blow the last trumpe of doctrine, which shall be blowne vpon the earth: marke, what his workes testifie of him, and so is he: whether it be beleued or not.*

4. *Noetus* sayd he was Moses, HN. sayth he is *Malachias and Iohn Baptist. præface Euang. sent. 3.*

5. The *Heracleonites* made a double confession of God wherof either part was equall: one was with the hart only, and the other with the mouth to auoyd persecution. So doth HN. *Dictatis 16.* chapter 18. sent. and 11. Epist. cap. 6. sent. 3. So sayth Theoph. that the misteries ought not to be reueiled to the withstanders. &c. contrary to the scripture. 1. Pet. 3. 15. Heb. 10. 23. Phil. 2. 11.

6. The *Messalians* taught it was lawfull to deny God and the fayth of Christ. Theophilus sayth the beliefe ought to be declared to all men: But not the secrets no more thē we ought to cōfesse to a theefe what treasure we haue about vs: the Anabaptistes thought it was free vnto them either to confesse, or deny their fayth in persecution, the sam opinion held the *Priscianistes, and the Andiani* contrary to the Scriptures, Math. 10. 33. Luke 9. 26. and 12. 8. contrarye to HN. his owne doctrine. 1. exhor. cap. 5. sent. 9. cap. 6. sent. 1. cap. 4. sent. 5. 7. 8. cap. 12. sent. 22.

Bulleng. 2. boke 4. chap.

7. The *Hetianites, Cerinthians, Nazarenes,* affirmed that Ceremonies of Moses law are to be kept of necessitye: so sayd the false Apostles. Act. 15. 1. so sayth HN. Euang. 13. chap. 4. sent. contrarye to S. Iohn. cap. 19. 30. and the whole Epist. to the Galatians.

8 The *Nazarenes had more Gospels then 4.* the Papistes had S. Thomas and other gospels: HN. hath made a gospell of his owne, contrarye to S. Paule. Gal. 6. 8.

9 The

9 The *Basilidians* thought that the misteries of Fayth ought to be reuealed to few, so thought the Papistes, so thinketh the Fam.

10. *Hymineus and Menander* thought that sanctification and regeneration of the spirite was the resurrection of the flesh: cõfounding the first and second resurrection: so doth HN. 1. exhor. cap. 7, sent. 24. 11. Epist. cap. 5. sen, 10. and *Dictat.* cap. 6. sent. 3, he sayth the 15. chap. to the Corinthians. verses 50. 53. 54. are not meant of the earthly body in these wordes. *Verely the mortall, whereof S. Paule witnesseth, is not any creature of earthly flesh and bloud, but it is the liuing worde or being of God which in the beginning was mortall in the manhode, and is in vs for our sinnes cause, became mortall.*

11. The *Aerians, and Iouinians* refused to come to sermõs so doe the Familiers of Loue which be illuminated. For sayth HN. *As long as the yongons are childish and not yet growne vp into the Elderdome of the perfect being they are yet vnder the ordinaunce of the Lord or his word: not that they should alwayes remaine as subiect there vnder, but vntell the appoynted tyme, vntell the manly olde age in the godly vnderstanding of the holy worde, that is tell sinne in thẽ be subdued.* Docum. sentences. cap. 3. sent. 12.

12. The *Pelagians* and *Cœlestinians* denyed the doctrine of *Predestination* wholy, the Papistes deny it in part, the Familie in the first Epistle to M. Rogers blaspheme the doctrine callyng it *a licentious doctrine which filleth all the prisons almost in England.* Fol. 71. b.

Contrary to the whole body of the Scriptures particularly. Rom. 9. 1. Ephes. 1. 1. Tim. 3. 16.

13. *Nouatians & Donatistes* say that the Church ought to be spotles, the Papistes say that the Church can not do amisse or erre, so do the Fam. affirme that the Commaundemẽtes are able to be kept, and that there is a perfection in the godly and regenerate in this lyfe. *Docum. sent. cap. 1. sent. 7. 1. Epist. Præfac. sent. 2. 6. 1. Exhort. cap. 7. sent. 19. & cap. 12. sent. 18. cap. 15. sent. 26. cap. 17. sent. 18.*

Euang.cap.4.sent.1.cap. 21.sent.2.cap.25.sent.2.5.cap.27.sent.1.cap.28.sent. 13.cap.37.sent. 14. And *Vitels* in his reply to M.Rogers display. And the. 2. Epistle of the Family to M.Rogers *pag.1.fol.86.per E.R.*

14. The *Origianistes* and *Hierarchitæ*, denyed that Paradise was a certaine materiall place: HN. depraueth the Historie by wrestiyng it into an *Allegorie. 1. Epist. cap.3. sent.17.18.19.22.* And the Fam. by the picture of a hart of a man utterly deface the written word, affirmyng also Adam did not eate a materiall fruite.

15. The Family of Loue affirme that men that lyue wickedly cã not teach the truth. *1.Epist.* to M.Rogers. *fol. 73.a.* so affirme the *Anabaptistes.*

16. The *Nouatians &c. Arrians, Donatistes* affirmed that those which were Baptised by others then their fellow heretiques, were not truly Baptised, and therefore they ought to be rebaptized. HN. sayth that without the Familie of Loue by him founde there is no true Christian Baptisme. *3. Artic. pag.33.* of this booke.

17. The *Pellagiãs* affirmed that infants ought not to be Baptised, so did the *Anabaptistes* affirme, tell they come to yeares of discretiõ. So sayth HN. *Euãg.cap.19.sent.11.*

And thus much in few woordes (by the way of Comparison, first to declare that *Henry Nicholas*, is a *Blasphemer*. Secondly, A false *Prophet* foretold of by Christ the Prophetes and Apostles. Thirdly, that in 17. pointes he agræth with all the old *Heretiques* in their particular heresies, shalbe sufficient.

ARTICLE. 8. HN. *Videl. What is to bee required in his Disciples.*

T*He Disciples of the Family must giue ouer them selues to be obedient. Iam.1.b. Disciples of the gracious worde and the seruice of the Eldest of the Loue, and renounce all their selfe wisedome. 1.Cor.3 owne knowledge, and bee perswaded that before their new. Ioh.3.e. byrth that they know nothyng. &c.*

Videl.

Theophilus.

V*Idel. of the godly causes, or haue no experimented but a literall knowledge therof.*

William Wilkinson.

This whole 8. *Article* beyng framed of diuers seuerall propositions, with sundry interpretations of *Theophilus* vnto many partes of it, may for orders sake be reduced into these thrée especiall pointes.

The first is what HN. requireth at the handes of all them that desire to be incorporate into his Fam. & what it is, which he would haue them thinke cōcernyng them selues, *videl. They which desire to be Disciples, &c. must giue ouer them selues, and renounce their owne knowledge, and be perswaded they know nothyng, but they must stand single mindedly to heare right sentences of their Elder, &c.*

Secondly what opinion they must haue of their Elder in their Fam. that is, *They must not mistrust the Eldest in the Familie, nor suspect any maner of euill or vnwisedome by him, nor perswade them selues that the instructions taught by the Father of the Fam. of Loue, or Oldest Elder are to (1. Cor. 1 b.) slight or childish or to vnwise, for them to follow after, or to obey.*

Thirdly what deuotiō they must haue to the doctrine beyng heard of the Elder, and how they must be affectioned thereunto, that is, *Yet must not their Disciples cary the resolution and instruction* (of their Elders) *as in maner of acknowledge in their memory and vnderstandyng.* The other clause conteinyng reuelations & confession of sinnes to the Eldest in the Familie beyng thynges of great importaunce, I shall hādle them seuerall in particular Articles hereafter.

¶ The first part of the 8. Article, *videl.*
No learnyng, or knowledge.

T*He Disciples of the Familie must giue ouer. &c. and be*

 per-

perswaded that they know nothyng, &c. neither cā they iudge rightly, &c. First Theoph. expoundeth thus: It is very true for so shall they escape the deceipt of the enemy, and not remayne in errour nor yet be deceiued.

Euen as a certaine prophane Rhetoritian, which beyng desired to instruct on that was well mynded toward his Arte of pleadyng, when hee asked to great a stipende was aunswered by him that desired to bee his Scholler, that he was somewhat already entred into the principles of that facultie, whereby his Maisters paynes should be the lesse: The Oratour replyed that therfore he ought to haue a double sallarie: because first he must teach hym to forget and vnlearne that which he had already bene practised in, and then afterwardes he must enforme hym a freshe after an other Methode: right so dealeth HN. in this article with them, which by him desire to be instructed into his Louely Familie, *vz.* he affirmeth that none in his Schoole can profite sufficiently, vnlesse before he enter therein, he vtterly goe backewardes and vnlearne that whiche he hath learned before he come of him to be instructed.

Wherein the Deuill that old Serpent, and subtill Scholemaister very wily doth seeke to insinuate vnto vs, that vnto the knowledge of that errour, the which at his hand he would haue vs to receiue, there is no further vnderstandyng expedient, then wholy to submit our selues to embrace the doctrine, which he seeketh to set forth vnto vs: so that whatsoeuer knowledge any man hath in any point of learnyng (vnto HN. his further instruction in his sect) it is nothyng worth at all, but vtterly it must be reiected: and concerning any skill it doth not greatly matter whether the nouice, which commeth to be further instructe, be expert in any kynde of knowledge, vtterly or ignoraunt. It is very true that he which measureth the mercyes of God carnally, and accordyng to his sensuall vnderstandyng, doth erre with the *Capernaites*, and he whiche examineth the hygh and heauenly secretes of the

most

most wise God, accordyng to the crooked rule of mans reason, and in the ballaunce of flesh and bloud the incomprehensible wayte of so great misteries: can neuer aright vnderstand the thynges which are good. For euery man hath no fayth: without the whiche seyng God can not be pleased, how is it to be hoped, that without the brightnesse of that candle any man can see to do ought that God shall loue and like of. Heb.11.6.

Now if hereupon the *Familie* will gather as perhaps they will, and some *Anabaptistes* haue done heretofore, that seyng fayth commeth by hearing, and hearing by the word of God alone: and therfore all other helpes of learnyng are vnnecessary: I aunswere that vnto the begettyng and obtainyng of fayth the ordinary meanes and conduit whereby this gift of God is conueyed vnto vs, is the blessed written word of God sufficient and onely necessary, but to encrease and conserue fayth, the Lord hath left in his Churche many excellent helpe and meanes as prophecying (that is, interpretation and expoundyng of Scripture) which must not be neglected or contemned: furthermore the gift of tongues. &c. Whereby as by precious stones and costly pearles the pure gold of Gods word to the beholders and lookers on is bewtified, and adorned, so that albeit HN. him selfe were neuer instructed in the knowledge of any of the seuen liberall Sciẽces as *Grãmar, Rhetoricke, Logique, &c,* neither trained vp in the knowledge of the tongues: he must not contemne that in others, whiche he him selfe doth want, nor set downe his owne ignoraunce as an example and paterne for others to imitate. Neither is it reasonable that because some men be blynd, therfore other men, which haue their eyes should violently depriue them selues of that benefite, which God in his great mercye hath bestowed vpon them.

To beget fayth onely Gods word is necessarye.

1.Thes.5.20.

But it shall not neede I hope to make any long proofe that there are necessary in Gods Churche, diuers particular blessynges, and giftes, which serue to the buildyng vp of the same (for that no man herein will wrangle if he haue any skill at all and knowledge is most hunted and hated by those, who are least acquainted therewith) yet in a worde or two to preuent the cauilles of the barbarous and vnskilfull aduersary, it shall not be amisse, if with a fewe testimonies we stope vp that gape, at the which those beasts do enter in, to treade vnder foote, and vtterly lay wast all the seemely ornamentes of liberall Artes, and good literature, where by both the Church of God is excellently garded agaynst *Hereitques*, and their Schismaticall factions, but the common wealth also very much maintayned and defended agaynst the inuasion of those mischieuous *Machiauellistes*, which thinke that the obedience of subiectes doth especially consiste in the ignoraunce of all humaine Sciences, and commendable learnyng.

Gen. 11. 7. 8. The Confusiō of tongues, as first it was a punishmēt for sinne, so afterwarde the singuler mercy of the Lord made it an vnspeakable benefit, & blessing, the vse wherof serued to confirmation: first of the faith of the Apostles, Actes. 2. 11. Secondly to the encrease and enlarging of the flocke of Christ. wherein albeit diuers of the Apostles and sundry of the auncient fathers did notably excell: yet the sacred scriptures as a most plentifull storehouse is aboundantly fraughted with most cleare and euident examples, it shall be sufficient to fetch profes, from thence, thereby to defend such heauenly blessinges agaynst such rude *Barbarisme* as the Familie of Loue and other their complices doe labor to bryng in.

Actes. 9. 15. Rom. 1. 1. 5. The blessed Apostle S. Paule being chosen an especiall vessell to beare the Lordes name before Gentils, vsed none instrument more effectuall (to make them both one fould vnder one Shepheard) then the gift of tongues. And though he excelled in the working of Miracles, and in many other giftes which he doth singulerly commend, 1. Cor. 12. chap. 8. 9. 10. verses and 4. chap. 5. ver. yet in the same place verse. 18. he thanketh God very hart-

hartely, that very plentifully was endewed with the gift of tongues. Wherein how he excelled, read Actes the 12. verse of the 14. Chapter.

He disputed at Athens with the Epicures and Stoick Philosophers, defending agaynst them the doctrine of the resurrection. He disputed in the Sinagogue with the Jewes, and in the market place daylye with whome soeuer he met, he stode in the middest of the Mars strete and reproued the superstitious worship of the Atheniãs, which whole Action of his had not ben so profitable to those amongest whome he spake vnlesse he had vsed the tongue of that countrye, that is the Grœke tongue. How excellẽtly he vnderstode the Latin tõgue it is manifest in that he mentioneth there were some which did salute the Philippians: those who were of Cesars house shew that Paule conuerted some euen in the Emperours courtes, which he could not so conueniently haue done vnlesse he could haue priuatly haue instructed them in their natiue speach. But the Epistles of S. Paul to Seneca, & of Seneca to S. Paule do argue the mutuall conference they had at Rome vnder Nero in the Latin tongue. Furthermore it is apparaunt that the Appollogie, which he made for him selfe before the chief captaine was in the Hebrue tongue. Which gift of tongues he doth worthely commend 1. Cor. 12. 7. b. 28. d. where he sheweth lykewise the vse of them, which he neuer would haue done, if the knowledge of the tongues had bene a thing of so smale account.

Actes. 17. 18.

Vers. 22.

Phil. 4. 22.

Act. 21. 40.

But in the dispraysing of these and such like blessings, the olde prouerbe, which the Romanistes reproch those graces of God withall, in the mouth of HN. is lykewise (shewing what spirite he is of) verefied to be true, that is, the knowledge of the Hebrue, and Grœke maketh many an heretique. But what doe I bring in many examples, or sœke for any further profe? doth not HN. his translating of Hebrue names (out of that translation which the Papistes call S. Ieromes bible) brought forth so oft in the Euangely of *HN.* proue that the knowledge of the tongues is an excellent meanes to vnderstand the scripture: if it be so, how then doth *HN.* so vnskilfullye counsaile those which be his schollers to renounce their knowledge. &c.

But if the Familye shall obiect that I am not sufficiently acquainted with their meaning, neither *HN.* his sence: for that he will haue them that desire to be made pertakers of his doctrine to humble themselues, and to abiect and captiuate their owne vnderstanding, and that the vnderstanding of spirituall thinges is to be enquired of persons that be spirituall, so that onely the taking on knowledge which is learned out of the scientialnes of the letter, and the imagination which procœdeth out of the selfemindednes of the outward man, and vnrenewed creature is blamed by *HN.* and that he doth not contēne, nor dehort them, from the knowledge of Gods word, nor the study of tongues. &c.

I aunswere, albeit it were true that he sayth, yet seing vnder the mist and darknes of wordes, and termes he doth seke to rob and spoyle vs of the precious iuell of holy scripture, and the knowledge of the will whereby our Sauiour Christ dying and departing from vs hath left bequeathed vnto vs the Legacie of eternall lyfe: yet shall he not scape after that sort, neither shall he so start away: for the practise of his Familers shall clearely descry his meaning, and what that is in dœde which he in worde sœmeth to insinuat vnto vs. The behauiour I say of diuers of them that are sayd to be of that Fam, shall most assuredly affirme my assertion to be true. For diuers of thē haue priuely whispered abroad in the eares of the simple, as also with some men of wealth, who thē-selues haue tould it me, and are ready to testifie the thing it selfe to be true, that they of the Familye haue disuaded and dehorted some: not to put their sonnes to schole or vniuersitye, for that simple wrighting and reading (say they,) is sufficient for a Christian, without any further knowledge of the Latine or Greeke tongues, or any other

ther facultye of learning whatsoeuer. So that by this meanes they seeke to discredit learning, to deface the learned, and to strengthen ignoraunce to be the hye way vnto true deuotion, and to aduaunce the glory of God; which is flat Poperye: so that thereby they labour to put out the eyes of this land (the Uniuersityes I meane) the vtilitye whereof as it is vnspeakeable for that frō them come the most skilfull statesmen to gouerne, both the state ecclesiasticall, and ciuill in this land: so also is the antiquitie of such kinde of discipline and good nurture of youth most auntient, and in sondrye places of Scripture commended, and confirmed by the worde of God, and so hauing troden vnderfote this most precious orchards of the Lord, they might not onely runne vncontrouled, but also bring the commen wealth vnto that estate that the Anabaptistes brought the free Cityes of Germany vnto, in the tyme of their seditious tumult, and vnfaythfull rebellion.

1. Sam. 19. 18.
2. King. 2. 4. 5. & 6. 1. 2.
Actes. 6. 9.
Actes. 19. 9.

But for a playner and euidenter profe I desire thee gētle reader, (But thee especially which art haplesly gratious with that graceles company,) to marke diligently, & thou shalt see it to be true, ẏ very few of the Fami. (or none at all) be furtherers of learning, or fauorers of learned men, much lesse doe they traine vp their children in the knowledge of the liberall sciences, either in the commen scholes of this realme, or in the Uniuersities, to the robbing both of Gods Church & the common wealth of many a toward wit, being also vtterly vnthankfull to the florishing state and peaceable gouernement of this noble realme, wherein they might vse all meanes possible to further and promote the glorye of God, and also discharge some part of the debt wherein they are bound to the countrye wherein they were bred and brought vp.

Furthermore it is to be vnderstode, that if this first steine of the 8. Article, concerning the *renouncing of knowledge by the disciples of the Familye*, be thus to be expounded, that no man ought to seeke neither can attaine onto any knowledge but onely those which be spirituallye minded and regenerated, standing wholye subiect vnto their Familye of Loue, which is taught by the bookes of HN. then doth the Familye accuse all the churches in England (the perticuler congregations of the faythfull I meane, yea & the generall and visible Church in England to be vnrenued in spirite and vnregenerate, for that the visible and generall Church of England neither hath nor now doth allow the sect and schisme of the Fami) of vnregeneration. For that they affirme *they know nothing before they new birth* quoting for proofe John. 3.a. *Except ye be borne agayne of water and the holy ghost, ye cannot enter into the kingdome of God.* Thus couertly they affirme that there is no truth taught in the Church of England which is the second Article wherewith I charge HN. in this booke. pag. 23. he auoucheth here to be true, and that we haue nothing but a literall, not hauing yet attained vnto the experimentall knowledge wherof he dreameth. So that first they acknowledge no truth without their Fami. secondly he that is not regenerate can not speake the trueth. &c.

The Fam. what they thinke of the doctrine taught in England.

Herein then was HN. much ouerseene that whilest he would faine haue his sect to be some singuler thing, he put no difference at all betwixt the knowledge of the learned, and the blindnes of the ignoraunt, but either of them alike which came to be made free of his sect and incorporated into his Fami. and had a longing to be instructed by him, must equally cast of and renounce all their learning and knowledge whatsoeuer, albeit they had studied sore and swet not a little for it before they could obtaine it. So that betwixt the well practised and expert man in the holy word, and those which be simple and playne men, which neuer hard if there were any such thing as men vse to call learning, there is no great difference but all is one, wherein a man of meane witte may easely perceiue, that at the fist entring into HN. his schole, HN. maketh all his schollers to be a lyke and e-

quall

quall towardnes, placing thẽ all in one fourme to learne one lesson, wherein it had ben well if for his credit sake he had vsed a further forecast and more sober discretion.

The reason and Argument wherby HN. would fayne perswade vs that we should know and vnderstand more then we do, if we would suspect our knowledge and confesse it to be lesse, (and that beyng wholly naked of our owne skill, whiche we haue learned out of the word of God, we might be warmely clad with his exceedyng learnyng and so stand single myndedly obedient vnto his documentable Sentences) it is the same Sillogisme and seducyng fallations wherewith the Deuill beyng a subtill Sophister beguiled and blynded our graundmother Eue in Paradise. Gen.3.5.

That is, if he would forgoe that measure of knowledge, which God had bestowed vpõ her, and if she would be indued with a more excellent knowledge of good and euill she might easely attayne thereunto by eatyng the forbidden fruite, and breakyng the expresse commaundement, which she confessed she had receaued from the mouth of God.

This then is the iudgemẽt of HN. that we should abiure & recant all such knowledge of the word of God as we haue already learned out of the word, & take vnto vs such glosing Expositiõs, as he would teach vs. So that we should be alwayes learning, but neuer attainyng vnto the truth: contrary to the doctrine of S.Peter, which 2.Pet.1.19.
sayth That we haue a most sure word of the Prophetes, to the whiche if ye shall take heede ye shall doe well. And S.Paule sayth, we must not bee as children wauering and caryed about with euery winde of doctrine, Ephe.4.14.
nor as cloudes caryed about of wyndes, nor as vnstable Iude.12.
mynded men, whiche are vnconstant in all their wayes, Iam.1.
but we should be grounded and rooted in the truth, holdyng the mistery of fayth in a pure conscience, knowyng 1.Tim.1.19.
that if the Heathen writer onely indued with the light, which God gaue him naturally without the knowledge

of his word, could say,

Cognita iudicio constant, incognita casu.

That is, that which we know to be true it is vndoubtedly to be embraced, but thynges vnknowne proue true but vpon aduenture: therfore ought we not to forgoe the one to finde the other: for if we ware indifferent, whether we kept the word of God or no, the testimony of the Heathen shall conuince vs and our owne *Newtralisme*, and *Lukwarmenes* shall in the wyng of Gods sonne vtterly condemne vs.

But if the Familie shall hereunto further reply that their meanyng is not to depriue their Disciples of all knowledge, as I would seeme to burthen them. I aunswere their wordes shal discipher & explayne their meanyng, and the Scriptures quoted by HN. shall verefy my saying to be truth: where he sayth.

They must be obedient Disciples. Iam.1.b. (which place is vtterly falsified, for there is no such word) *of the gracious word and his seruice of Loue, and that they Heb. 12.1.a.* (cast away euery thyng that presseth downe) 1.Pet.2.1.a. *Turnyng them away according to the requiryng of the gracious word and his seruice from all their selfe wisedome and knowledge that riseth vp or becommeth imagined in them. 1. Cor. 3.18.d.* All these places doth HN. alledge to proue that they ought to renounce all their owne knowledge, the whiche how vnskilfully and vnshamefully he doth abuse may playnly appeare by the same wordes vsed by S.

Ephe.4.22. Paule, Cast ye of concernyng your cōuersation in tymes past the old man, which is corrupt through deceiueable

Colos.3.8. lustes. And agayne, Put ye away euen all these thynges wrath, anger, malitiousnes, &c. So that the meanyng of these places is that we ought to be at warre and hatred with sinne, &c. and as for renouncyng of knowledge in the word of God, there is no one word that tendeth vnto any such meanyng or renouncyng of knowledge, as HN. would seeme to importe. But more playnly doth he inueigh agaynst a particular knowledge of Christians in

Gods

Gods word. *1.Exhort.* where he sayth: *Verely to know the difference of all thynges. 1. Cor. 8. a. is no right knowledge of the godly wisedome, but the loue with her vertuous nature and beyng, is the vpright wisedome of the godly knowledge.* 1.Exhor.cap.13. sent.6.leafe.29.b And most playnly. *ibid. The true light consisteth not in the knowyng of this or that, but in an vpright and true beyng of God and his eternall life. Iohn.17.c.* 1.Exhor.cap.15. sent.4.sent.36.a.

By the which two places out of HN. it is apparauntly euident, that hee withdraweth his Nouices from the searchyng out of particularities in doctrine, onely he willeth them to stand subiectiuely obedient to the Loue, and her requiryng, beyng wholly resolued in the generall knowledge therof, and standyng simply counited thereunto. Whereas the spirit of God in the Scriptures doth not onely commend a generall, but also commaund a particular knowledge of the misteries of saluation. 1.Sam.2.3.a. Dan.1.17.c.

First that a particular knowledge of Gods fauour towardes vs is necessary. Secondly, that in matters of faith and Religion a knowledge in particulers is necessary the Scripture is plentyfull, neither doe I meane in many wordes to confute HN. his opinion therein: so that in one word to testifie a truth whosoeuer doubteth of Gods loue towardes him (as the Papistes would haue vs) shall in this lyfe neuer be certaine of his owne safetie in the day of iudgement, whiche euery man ought to be most carefull of. Secondly whosoeuer hath an intricate and doubtfull fayth of his Religion, whiche he hath reposed in any man (but in God and his word alone) he must nedes often haue as many faythes as there are Fathers in the Church concernyng many particular pointes of doctrine, as also hee shall stagger and reele in the worshyp of his God, seyng that man is mutable not hauing any certaine hold of him selfe in any thyng: yea the greater in countenaunce, the deeper in knowledge, the more zealous and earnest men shew them selues to be, when once they begyn to totter and swarue a to side, vnles the Lord vnderset them, their fall is more great and greuous. Iohn.11.22.c. 1.Cor.5.1.a. 1.Iohn.3.2.a. and.5.19.a. 1.Cor.14.20.d. Hebr.5.14.d. and 8.11.d. 1.Cor.2.8. and 10.1.a. Math.22.29. Math.16.26.

Furthermore that this knowledge in particularities is that which the Familie can not abide, I by myne owne experience whiche I haue had by conference with diuers of them, am able to testifie: for demaundyng of them how a man might fully and in déede become instructed in the loue, they haue aunswered me, that all the knowledge which I haue, must be of me vtterly forsaken: & askyng of them a reason of that speach, they haue alledged vnto me
1. Cor. 8. 1. 2. a. for profe hereof knowledge puffeth vp but loue edifieth. &c. And Pro. 26. 12. b. & Mar. 10. 15. c. wherby I am assuredly perswaded (myne experiense hauyng proued it true,) that the first part of this Article of *renouncyng of knowledge in the Disciples of the Familie* is assuredly true.

¶ The second part of the 8. Article, *videl.*
Mistrust not HN. vnwisedome.

HN. As in the first strayne he would not be content vnlesse his Disciples were witles, *In renoũcing of their former knowledge*, so in the second that he would haue them *not to suspect any vnwisedome by him, or thinke his instructions to be to childish, or vnwise for them to follow. &c.* He would depriue them of their common senses, and the wit which God hath bestowed vpon them by the benefite of nature. For what vnspeakeable childishnesse and extreme madnesse is this, that in buyng of spirituall thynges at the handes of the Lord his factours, he would haue vs more voyde of skill then the common chapmen of the world, which when they come to chuse or cheapen, bryng their eyes with them to iudge, if that whiche they are about to bargayne for shalbe for their turne or no. And euen as true meanyng and faythfull dealyng men are not displeased with those, which intendyng to buy bryng their wares to the light, and prie, and pore on them, and open them to sée if they be such as vnto them by a price pitcht they are deliuered out for: when as false men and dissẽblers desiring for true to vtter wares that

are

are braid and counterfaite, whisper in mens eares and leade them aside into the furthest part of their shop, and sometymes into their warehouses where partly with a true and false light, partely for want of light they beguile and deceiue them: so HN. in this place lyke a crafty marchaunt subtilly seeketh to leade his Schollers into the darke, where he offereth them doctrine and wholesome instructions which he telleth them is for them and shall fitly serue their vse, when in deede there is nothing lesse then he in worde pretendeth.

And whereas by his experimentall knowledge HN. can very well testifie, that he hath often tryed that those men which sell by whole sale haue a quicker dispatch, and sooner riddance then those which stand pelting out vntill the end of the market: the same pollicye vseth HN in vttering his spirituall traffique, not bearing any which may checkmate him in his doctrine lyke a franck marchant hee by wholesale deliuereth out his diuinitie, and taketh it greatly in the snuffe, that his stuffe which he deliuereth should be brought to light and be examined. Whereas he sheweth very clearely what his opinion is of those which he would haue to be his schollers, that they would straight way take for gould whatsoeuer glistereth.

But to stand vnto HN. his iudgemēt, shall we thinke that if *HN.* were in the open Marte of Emdē or Amsterdame that he would be such a want witte as to take all kynde of coine ÿ were brought him & neuer examine it? would he neuer bring his siluer to the touch, nor his gold to the ballaunce? so fareth it with Gods children in buying the precious pearles of Gods truth and heauenlye doctrine, they must touch all with the proportiō of fayth, Rom. 12. 6. and as in the meate wherewith our body is nourished the daunger of poyson is carefully to be auoyded and taken heede of, neither can we be to warye that the health of our bodyes be indamaged: so is the infection of doctrine by the contagiousnes whereof our soule is in hazard, it is most diligently to be considered of, for that as the one doth endaunger but the body, the other doth pitch down hedlong both body and soule into euerlasting torments.

Reuelat.22.15.

The principle which HN. doth publish in this place is mere Papisticall, as witnesseth M. Stapleton in his boke of *Controuersies*: the wares he offereth to sale he hath bought at Rome of the purpule strumpet, as ye by marke may sone discerne, which will bring it to light, and offer it to the triall: if they demaund vnto what light or triall: I aunswere vnto that candle which S. Peter sayth, shineth in a darke place, and we shall doe well if we will loke vnto. Let vs then in a word or two consider of HN. his doctrine by the Analogie of fayth, and light of holy scripture, and straight way espy the difference betwixt HN. his wordes, and the worde of God.

Stapleton.controuer.2.5.boke cap.2.3.4.5.pag. 161.162.

HN. sayth. He must not be suspected or mistrusted whatsoeuer he teach: Our Sauiour Christ geueth vs warning to take heede of false Prophets: HN. sayth if the Eldest say it, it must be beleued.

Math.7.15.

Herod demaunding of the Scribes, where Christe should be borne was aunswered, at Bethlem in the land of Iuda, for thus it is written Miche.5.2. so there vnto the truth of their aunswere, they ioyned a profe out of the scripture: yet will HN. haue vs beleue his resolution and that without profe, wherein he dealeth more vnequally with vs then Herod was delt withall by ye *Scribes and Pharisie.*

Math.2.4.5.2.

Furthermore HN. sayth that *right sentences must be heard of the Eldest in the Familye*. Christ sayth it must be learnd out of the Scripture.

Iohn.5.39.

HN. draweth his disciples from the examination of his doctrine, for sayth he *they must not suspect it to be to sleight, childish, or vnwise for the to follow.* The noble Berrheans when they heard S. Paule preach, searched the scriptures dayly, whether those thinges were so.

Act.17.11.

S. Paule biddeth vs iudge what he sayth, and proue all thinges, and S. John sayth: Try the spirites whether

1.Cor.11.13. 1.Thes.5.21.d.

they

they are of God adding also a reason for many false prophets are gone out into the world, and yet sayth *HN*. his doctrine must not be examined. 1. Ioh. 4. 1.

The spirite of the Prophets sayth *S. Paule* are subiect to the Prophets, and in another place speaking to the whole Church, and euery particuler member thereof, he sayth, that the Discerning of spirites is the gift of God. The kingly Prophet Dauid sayth that he was made wiser then his enemies, by the law of God, and that he had more vnderstanding then his teachers because he meditated in Gods lawe, he vnderstode more then the aged because he kept Gods preceptes. For by his worde he gat vnderstanding, which worde alone it is whereby the simple ons are lightned & instructed: yet would *HN*. haue vs leaue the broad and beaten highway, refusing all such meanes as holy Dauid was abettered by, and digge vnto vs cisterns out of his inuentions, where he first accused Gods reuealed worde and ordinarie meanes and fly to his strong methode, whereby he sayth his schollers may attaine perfect wisedome. 1. Cor. 14. 32. 1. Cor. 12. 10. Psal. 119. ver. 98 99. 100. 104. Psal. 19, 6.

But the same perswasion wherewith *HN*. seeketh to blinde his sectaries, yf they would profite vnder the instruction of the Eldest, not to suspect his doctrine which he termeth *right sentences*, but they should stand single mindedly to receiue the doctrine of the *Ouldest Father in the Familye*, is that wherewith Eue was beguiled in Paradice. But as many as are Christes sheepe, heare his voyce, and they follow him onely neither know they the voyce of straungers. Gen. 3. 5. Iohn. 10. 27.

Lastly whereas *HN*. would not haue the truth of his doctrine come in contruersie or be doubted of, he secretly would steale away with this Papisticall assertion that he can not erre: And so lykewise *Vitels* affirmeth of *HN*. saying, *I know not how he or any other should erre which are ruled by the spirite of God*. Which is all one with ye iudgement of the Papistes concerning the Pope, in determining of matters of religion. So that they will not onely driue vs to poysoned pastures, but in eating whatsoe- Vitels in his reply to M. Rogers his display.

uer they shall set before vs: we shall by them be compelled to be accessarye vnto our owne destruction. And thus desiring the Reader to marke how iust the Papistes and *HN.* doe iumpe in this point. I end the second part of this 8. Article.

HN. agreeth with the Papistes.

¶ The third part of the 8. Article.

The third and last clause of this Article as it is a palbable grosse and an absurde Paradox, so is the fondnesse therof more euident, in that it setteth it selfe not onely flatly contrary to the written word of God, but also it is manifestly repugnăt to HN. his own doctrine, deliuered in his bookes, and lastly to the very practise of humane Artes and the light of nature it selfe, in the iudgement of all the which witnesses it is most fonde and foolish.

1. HN. his doctrine contrary to Gods word. 2. To him selfe. 3. To naturall reason and common sense.

1. Exhort. cap. 13 fol. 30. b. line. 25

The wordes them selues are manifest and not able to be denyed *vz. And not for to cary the resolution and instruction as in maner of a knowledge, in their memory or understandyng*, in the helpyng and saluyng wherof the *Expositor Theophilus* is farre ouer the shoes, that beyng not able to shift the errour, or to get out of so manifest a slypp, he returneth the fault vpon me by a Rhetoricall Anticipation, and thinketh wholly to stoppe my mouth byddyng me *looke on the text and leaue my peruertyng*, whereas if I should looke vpon it neuer so often, I should not neither if I should vse his eyes finde any wordes then already I haue set downe. For that which he him selfe addeth for an Exposition, how I pray you doth it expounde, *vz. Yea verely but not to cary the resolution as in manner of a knowledge in their memory: looke the text and leaue your peruertyng*. But thus falleth it out with those whose heades labour with a Schismaticall phantasie, euen as a woman is payned in her trauaile tell she be deliuered.

Theop. Exposition.

But to come to HN. his wordes *The Disciples must not cary the instruction. &c.* Thinkes that these three seuerall and distinct phrases haue this meanyng: *To cary in maner*

of

of a knowledge in Latin, cognitione cõplecti, that is, to know, *to cary an instructiõ in memory: in memoria habere, to Remẽber or haue in remembraunce.* And to cary in *vnderstanding: intelligentia comprahendere, to vnderstand,* from the which proprieties of speach if either *HN.* or *Theophilus* shall seeke to slip, they shall straight declare how well they are ouersene in the tounges and common speach. So that if vpon all these we shall gather this sentence. *The Familie must not know, remember, nor vnderstand the doctrine or instruction whiche the Eldest in the Familie deliuereth forth vnto them, which Eldest sayth Theophilus is Christ him selfe and his holy worde.* How blasphemously and Papistically *HN.* and *Theophilus*, do play the heretiques is manifest. For what man is so blynd that he will not see or so graceless that he will not confesse that The word of God must be knowne remembred and vnderstode of the simple, if this be not Popery, what is Popery. And that First, the simple ought to know. Secondly vnderstand. Thirdly remember these places quoted for profe out of the Scripture shalbe sufficient.

Ierem. 31. 33. 34.
Deut. 4. 9. & 11. 19.
Prou. 8. 9.
Esay. 11. 9. & 52. 6.
Col. 1. 9.
Rom. 15. 4.
Math. 11. 23.
Luke. 10. 21.
Esay. 54. 13.
Prou. 2. 2.
Psal. 119. 104.
Dan. 2. 21. & 8. 17. & 10. 11. 12.
Math. 15. 10.
Mar. 7. 14.
2. Tim. 3. 16.

Furthermore HN. is contrary to his owne doctrine, which he him selfe teacheth, in his owne bookes whereas for his vsual *Embleme,* he taketh. *1. Exhort. cap. 12. sent. 10. b.* this sentence or posie for his cõmon badge whereby his bookes are knowne frõ others of his fellow Elders *Take it to hart.* Which is according to the best translations. Let thine hart hold fast my wordes. Where it is ment that his wordes ought wholly and throughly to be knowne, vnderstode and remembred, contrary to his former doctrine in the place first alledged.

Deut. 6. 6. 8. 9. & 11. 18.
Numb. 10. 10. & 15. 39.
Psal. 119. 52. 55.
Actes. 11. 16. & 20. 31.
Rom. 15. 15.
2. Pet. 1. 15. & 3. 2.
Iude. 17.
Prou. 4. 4. d.
1. Exhor cap. 13 fol. 30. line. 25.

But to let passe these two former partes of contrarietie: betwixt HN. and the written word of God: secondly betwixt him selfe and his owne writynges: if we diligently, way and consider we shall assuredly finde, that this thyrd clause concerning naturall reason and common experience it is as wholly agaynst *HN.* and impugneth his doctrine as truth is agaynst falsehode, and light darknes.

And herein to vse the same example, which the Scripture doth in like matter. The wiseman doth very excellently commend the diligence of diuers men in their sundry occupations and seuerall handlabours. As the Grauer in his Imagery, the Smith at his anuill, the Potter at his clay, all these (sayth the wiseman) vse wisedome in their worke, whiche they could not do, vnlesse their common practise had taught them experience, and vse makyng thẽ perfect, they should by remembraunce renew the same from tyme to tyme, which they before had learned.

Eccles. cap. 38. v. 27. 28. 29. 30.

And to vse yet more familiar example, thinkyou that it is lyke, that when *Vitels* Maister instructed him in his Arte of Joignerie, was it not conuenient for him, to instruct his Prentice *Vitels* often in those thynges, whereby he might get his liuyng in tyme to come? and was it not *Vitels* part to cary his maisters Arte, and his instructions in his memory and vnderstandyng? els if he had not remembred his maisters preceptes, how should he haue compacted that great knowledge, neither haue got the singular cõmendation, for to be so skilfull a Joyner as his Familie doth report of him that he is, albeit for greater matters sake he hath lefte that his trade & now professeth him selfe a teacher, in that his *Louely Familie*? What Scholemaster vnto his Scholers would so oftẽ take paynes to inculcate, and repeate the selfe same principles, with great labour vnto the one, and vnpleasauntnes vnto the other, if he thought it not expedient that it should be of him remembred? And blessed Esay saith Precept must be vpon precept, and line vpon line, here a litle and there a litle, to the end that by often iteratyng the same thyng, it might the better be remẽbred.

Esa. 30. v. 10.

But seekyng to conuince HN. by the ineuitable and most certaine rule of reason, why doe J alledge Scripture, seyng that the excellent Philosophers Themistocles, Simonides, Carneades, Sceptius, Metrodorus, are singularly praysed in prophane writers, for the worthy remembraunce which they had in Philosophy and other

Sci-

Sciences: and shal we thinke that seyng by the kéepyng Psal.19.11.
of Gods commaundements there is great reward ought
we not to remember those thynges for the remēbraunce
wherof, we shal receaue a reward: or how shal we kéepe
them if we do not remember them?

True it is that is wisely remembred by a Heathē O-
ratour. *Memoria non modo Philosophiam, sed omnē vitæ* Cicero.2.Acad.
vsum, omnesq; Artes vna maxime continet. Remembraūce
doth not onely conteine Philosophy, but also the whole
practise of mans lyfe, yea, she alone comprehendeth all
other Artes and Sciences whatsoeuer.

But what should I oppose the iudgement of the wise
agaynst him that is witles, and the Scriptures diuine
testimonies agaynst a prophane and godles *Atheiste*?
Whose scope iustly iūpeth with the *Romanistes* in this, HN.swarueth
to forbyd a particular knowledge in matters of salua- to poperye.
tion, and to teach that if men beleue as the Church bele-
ueth they can not do amisse. In the confutation wherof
seing that by these thréefold testimonies I haue throughly conuinced *HN*. his Assertion for this *8*. *Article*, and
all the partes therof let this be sufficient.

ARTICLE. 9. HN. *Of Reuelations.*

FOr vnto the Elders and Fathers God hath reue- HN.9.Errour.
led his word in this day of Loue. & Publishyng 1.Exhor.cap.6.
of the peace. cap.1. sent.12.6. sent.21.f.
The Lord hath reueled the true beyng vnto & cap.14. sent. 54.h.
me out of Sion and Ierusalem. Esay.2.a. Mich.4.a. 2. Pet.1.b. Euang.cap.2.
HN. sayth the mistery of the kingdome of God. Math.25. sent.1.
d. Actes.16.17.d. Iude.1.b. his righteous iudgementes, and
the commyng of Christ now in the last time in the resurrection
of the dead. Ezech.37.b. Iohn.5.e. Rom.8.b. Phil.3.b. is de-
clared vnto him as vnto an elect vessell: house or dwellyng of HN.speaketh
God from the mouth of God himselfe. with god mouth to mouth.
HN. sayth hee will declare the secret mysteries of God: &.sent.8.
and make relation of thynges that are hidden from the begin- Sent.11.

nyng of the world.

William Wilkinson.

Vnto many it may seme straunge, and scarse credible vnto some, that there should lyue a people vpon the earth, whiche not holdyng them selues content with the written word of God, would adde vnto it some tricke of their own deuising: which although they agreed as euill as a new peece of clothe vnto an old garment, yet fayne would they their toyes were pewefellowes with the sacred truth of God, not onely to match, but some tymes to geue a checkemate vnto the same.

Yet vnto him that equally considereth all things with an vnpartiall eye, it is easely to be sene, that it was not onely the practise of the Popishe Prelacie, so to outface the simplicity of the Scripture, partly with the bringyng their blynd and vnsauery traditions, partly with the burthenyng of the church, with the intollerable yoke of their vnwritten verities: but the dealyng of the *Anabaptistes* and *Libertines*, and all other like Heretiques hath agreed in this accord, that when the touchstone would not serue, and a naked truth would not so much hide as vnto all mē declare their misbehauiour, straight with the presence of the spirite & cloke of zeale they haue laboured to shroude this so great impietie.

For hereupō it ensued that the Romanistes so cloyed the church with their fond festiuals, leud Legendes, and so stuffed into the seruice of God such store of idle reuelations, and vnnecessary visions, that by the reading of them openly in the congregation, the holy and canonicall wrightinges of the holy ghost were wholy abandoned and cleane cast out of the dores. And this was that which the Anabaptistes, and other heretiques haue practised, which when they had no witnes or warrant from the written word and approued truth of God, they forged straunge euidence, and that which with blasphemie they inuen-

inuented, they vttered with vntruth. For being demaũded the ground of their misdemeanour, they aunswered: *The spirite thus commaundeth me, and thus the Father hath sayd:* so that when they wanted the worde they boasted of the spirite, and affirmed that they had their doctrine from heauen reuealed vnto them. This might by the inducing of many examples be proued to be true, and the historyes of them who haue noted their behauiour are many and manifest. Onely the testimonies of those learned men, which were acquainted with their dealinges shall vnto the indifferent reader be sufficient, for proofe of that which we haue in hand.

Bullinger. 2. booke. 1. cap. leafe. 35.36.

Bullinger. 1. booke. 1. chap. &. 2. booke. 1. chap.

Unto the which assertions of the Papistes and Anabaptistes, with the Libertines lykewise, if *Henrye Nicholas* should be added which in plainer wordes vttereth more pestilent impietye, their messe shall be the fuller, and the conuenticle of them more conuenient vpon the which the iudgements of God should fall in greater measure: seing they all haue bene partakers, fellow laborers in forging so great a heape of confusion, to set vp the same agaynst the truth of God.

Zuing. pag. 35. 77. 89. 100.

To proue that *HN*. is guiltye of the inditement wherewith I burthen him. vz. *That he is a coyner of reuelations*, my allegations are two: first his owne wordes vz. *That the Lord reueiled it vnto him out of Sion, and declared it out of the heauenly Ierusalem.* Secondly the places of Scripture by him misaleaged to quote and cõfirme this his dotage, wherein he will not onely be offensiue to men, but to the Lord also very wickedly iniurious.

As for his wordes the which are prefixed before this Article therin he claimeth vnto himselfe a more notable prerogatiue thẽ any mã liuing durst euer thinke or once imagine of. For whereas it hath ben an onely especiall thing which properly appertained vnto such as haue ben singularly beloued of the Lord, & vnto whom God hath shewed himselfe in more notable measure, as vnto Abraham, Moses, Iosua, Gedeon, Esay, Ezechiel, and the

Gen. 28. Exod. 3. 12. 3. Ios. 5. 13.

Iudg.6.37. rest of the heauenly prophets, and holy Apostles of Christ
Esay.1.1.2.10. whome the Lord had before adioyned to more excellent
Ezech.1.1.3. functions, and put them aside for some notable and extra-
Math.17.5.2. ordinarye ministration, vnto those the Lord hath more clearely discouered himselfe and reuealed his countenaunce, and in a greater measure opened and set abroad the brightnes of his glory, yet vnto none so far at any time, as HN. boasteth of hath hapned vnto him that he
Euang.cap.1. should *be codeified with God in the spirite of his loue, made*
sent.1. *heire with Christ in the heauenly treasures of the riches of God.* The which great and wonderfull claime as it farre surpasseth all that euer any of the Prophets durst challenge vnto themselues, so doth HN. herein very impudẽtly boast, and blasphemously arrogate more vnto himselfe then euer belonged vnto any mortall man, the son of God excepted. The which his vaine challenge as it is taken on by him with an harlots forehead, so hath he no specialtye to shew that can warantiz him therein, but onely the vngodly behauiour of the aũtient heretiques, which by their furious fantasies and vaine imaginations haue made a diuorce betwixt the spirite and the written
Esay.59.v.21 d. word of God, which alwayes are enlinked together: so
Ose.12.v.10. that the one of them is neuer seperate from the other. In
Iohn.16.13. the which poynt as he hath dealt very vnlearnedly,
Act.10.6. and vnskilfully before men, so hath he behaued himselfe
1.Thes.5.19.20. very vnthãkfull towardes the word of God: which before might haue ben vnto him a sufficient caueat, for that it
1.Sam.28.15. termeth such reuelations and Prophesies as his are, but
1.King.13.18. lying visions whereof none haue so much bragged as the
2.Cor.12.1. false Apostles.

But if here HN. his disciples shall reply, that their Eldest Father doth confirme that reuelatiõs are sent frõ God to him by the written word of the Canonicall scripture: then I aunswere that herein resteth the triall that HN. is a lying seer, and a seducing Prophet, which may more easely appeare, if the places which he alledgeth for the profe of his fained reuelations import no such thing

as

as he doth father vppon them.

As for the first place which is, *To the which Elders and Fathers God hath reueiled his word in the day of Loue:* There is not any one place quoted for confirmation of it, neither with Gods people will a mans bare worde be of sufficient warrant to countenaunce and confirme any thing. Scripture it is that is the true rule, and euen ballaunce, wherein Gods marchandise must be peised. This selfe same thing A godly and learned Father hath soundly proued when he sayth: Let it not be sayd, this say I and this thou sayst: but this the holy Ghost sayth. And agayne *Taceant voces humanæ loquantur diuinæ, ede mihi vel vnam scripturam pro parte Donati.* Let mens wordes be silent, let Gods voyce be heard, shew me but one text of scripture which defendeth *Donatus* assertion. Right so say I, set aside the persons of the speakers, let vs sift and examine that which is spoken, shew me but one text of scripture (truely cited) for the profe of HN. his doctrine. As for this profe, affirmations without ground, and miracles without the worde, as HN. doth commonly vse thē so is his vse not commendable.

Exhort.cap.16. sent.21.

August. de pastoribus.cap.8.

Euang.cap.1. sent.4.

The second place testifieth *that God hath reuealed his true being vnto* HN. *out of Sion and Ierusalem.* Esa. 2. a. Mich. 2. a. 2. Pet. 1. b. Wherein he depraueth the sence of the holy Prophets in wresting that into an allegorye of the Celestiall Ierusalem: which is ment of the Terestriall and earthly but this his fond exposition is more playne in an other place in these wordes.

Exhor.cap.14. sent.54. HN.

HN. *doth declare the same misterie of the riches of God agayne vpō the earth, and minister the selfe same liuing word which is the very true light haue out of the heauenly Ierusalem, to a testimonye of the truth receiued from Gods owne mouth. &c.* And in an other place he sayth that this opening of Gods misteries is come vnto him, out of the hyest heauen. So that here it is very plainely to be sene that he abuseth the scripture, and peruerteth the sence therof by turning the truth of a déede done in a place ma-

Euang.cap.2. sent.1.fol.6.

teriall, into a heauenly and spirituall vision, whereas the sence of the place is, that first the Gospell should first begin to be preached at Ierusalem, the which being long foretould, was by the Apostles of Christ most plentifullye fulfilled, as we all at this day are witnesses.

Icrem 31.vers. 31. Psal.110.1.a. Luke. 24.47. Math.15. 24.c. Ephes.2.17.c.

Secondly HN. & his heyre *Vitels*, beyng great postes in his new founde Family, herein do not agrée, for *Vitels* expoundeth *Sion* to be the *Familie of Loue*. HN. calleth *Sion* heauē, so that here it may be affirmed of the one of thē, whiche some tyme the Papistes affirme of their scholemen: *hic magister noster non tenetur*. Herein our maisters saying is not auouchable for to bee true. Furthermore whereas HN. quoteth this place Allegorically, it séemeth that his Reuelatiō came by the way of an Allegory also, & he would haue his Schollers fed with empty Reuelations, so that thereby the hunger they haue should be satisfied as the virgine Mary mentioneth. 1. Luke. vers. 53.

Scripture falsefied by HN.

Finally the thyrd place which cited out of S. Peter the 2. Epistle. 1. chap. is wholly *falsefied*, for that there is no one word in all that place, which maketh mētion of any *Reuelation*, or of the declaryng of the word of God to any person.

The thyrd place which I alledged to proue, that HN. boasteth of *Reuelations* is taken out of the *Euangelie cap. 2. sent. 1.* and it conteineth these two especial partes. The first is of *thynges reueiled* which are *foure in number:* the first is *God hath reueiled vnto HN. his kingdome*, the second *his righteous iudgementes*, the thyrd *the commyng of Christ in the last tyme*, fourth *the Resurrection of the dead.*

Thynges reueiled.

Math.25. vers. 31.d.

For prœfe of the first he alledgeth Math. 25.d. where is shewed in what maner Christ shall come and reward euery man accordyng to his workes, in the last day of the generall Judgement. Now if this hath bene reueiled vnto HN. then belyke that of Christes commyng was then reueiled whē Christ came, but Christs last commyng in his glorious kingdome (wherof S. Mathew maketh mention. 25. vers. 31.) is not yet come: for if he were come

our

our mortall should put on immortalitie, and our corruptible be without corruptiō. &c. Cor. 15. vers. 52. 53. But as yet we haue not made this chaunge, neither is death swallowed vp in victory, which shall *then* come to passe sayth S. Paule vers. 54. Therfore HN. hath vaynly affirmed that he hath sene Christ reuealed in his kyngdome, vnlesse it be possible that the resurrection be already past: which if HN. doth confesse then shall I tell him further. But if it be not passed (as by S. Paules wordes Then shall that come to passe which is writtē. &c. it is surely witnessed that it is not,) then *HN.* hath a quicke eye sight, which cā sée things so long before they are able to be sene.

The second place by him cited is takē out of the Actes the 16. chapter, where there is nothyng that tendeth that way. The 17. chap. d. vers. 31. there is, that all the world shalbe iudged by Christ, because he was raysed vp from the dead to that end. The meaning of this place is all one with the former: this place is by *HN.* abused in that he applyeth it to him selfe, that he is raysed from the dead to iudge the world. &c. This often tymes he wresteth in diuers of his bookes to this end. First in his Exposition vpō the *Beliefe sect. 28. publishing of the peace. 1. cap. sent. 16. D. 11. Epist. cap. 1. sent. 9. c. & ibid. cap. 5. sent. 10. c. and Euang. cap. 3. senten. 5. & cap. 28. sent. 3. & cap. 34. senten. 1, & cap. 35. senten. 14.* Act. 16. 17. d.

The whiche Assertion beyng grossly wicked in that it robbeth Christ of his honor, hauyng somewhat touched it before, I spare to speake further, referryng the Reader both for the sence of the place and the confutatiō of *HN.* his errour groūded thereon, vnto M. Knewstubs Confutation. Where the same is fully satisfied. Fol. 2. b. Fol. 61. b.

As for the place alledged out of S. Iude, it goeth most commōly in all *HN.* his bookes, which I haue sene, with the 17. of the Actes and Math. 25. so that place is altogether very vnskilfully cited and onely is brought in lyke a mute vpon a scaffold, which departeth dumbe. When I shall perceiue the application therof, I shall aunswere more at large.

Now for the secōd point of the first part. *vz the righteous iudgemēts of God are declared vnto HN*, he anoucheth no proofe to verifie it, and albeit God reueiles his iudgements that is both his word to instruct, as also his iudgementes agaynst the wicked, that is his sword to deuoure,
Psal.119.164. if *HN.* were one that were méeke the Lord would guide him in iudgement Psal.25.9. But because his speaches testifie that he feareth not God, therfore the Lordes secrets are not reueiled vnto him. vers.14.e.

The thyrd point, of *HN.* his Reuelation, *vid. the commyng of Christ in the last tyme*, is all one agréeyng with the first. His last and fourth note *videl.* that the Resurrectiō is reuealed vnto him is not so euident as he thought to haue made it. For the places by him alledged out of Ezechiell.37.9.10. vers. b. proue that the Israelites should certainly returne out of Captiuitie, and this was confirmed vnto them, by the visible signe of the raysing of dead bones, that God was as able to do the one, as the other. Howbeit yet I sée not how hereupō *HN.* would conclud his Reuelation cōcernyng the Resurrection, for that this place hath not any such meanyng. The place of Iohn.5. c.vers.28.29. truly proueth the Resurrection, yet it mentioneth not one word of Reuelation. Rom.8.b.11.vers. proueth that as God was able to rayse vp Christ beyng dead, accordyng to his manhode, so is God able to rayse vs vp that be his Children, both in soule and body to his eternall kyngdome. The Philipians.3.b.11.vers.S. Paule sheweth to attaine vnto the Resurrection of the dead was his great desire: where these wordes the Resurrection of the dead, are not taken (as *HN.* would séeme to alledge by his knittyng them with them which went before, conteinyng the same matter) for the Resurrection of the body before euerlastyng lyfe it selfe, and the participation therof after the Resurrection with the chosen Saintes of God.1.Thes.4.17.d. and 1.Cor.5.vers.4.a. So that *HN.* very vnskilfully hath alledged this place for the Resurrection,

ction which albeit it were by him rightly quoted, yet see I not how thereupon his proposition concernyng *the resurrection of the dead is reueiled vnto HN*. should be rightly concluded.

The second part cōteineth the person vnto whom this *Reuelation* was declared, where *HN*. because of euill neighbours is forced with shame enough to blase his owne commendations, *videl. that he was an elect vessell.* it is read of S. Paule] ẏ he termeth him selfe to be put a part to preach the Gospell of God. This was affirmed of him, first because his callyng was miraculous and extraordinary, as also because the sonne of God in the Actes geueth him the same title, he is sayth he, vnto me a chosen vessell. &c. now when *HN*. can iustifie his callyng to haue bene such as S. Paules was, then he shall proue some what, in the meane tyme our skill is not so meane as whensoeuer he vseth to alledge Scripture for the phrase that by and by it must materially be vnderstode as he will haue vs take it, or els all is marred. In the same sort he abuseth a place taken out of S. Paul to the Corinthes Cap. 3. vers. But these his vayne payntynges of his margent, shall hereafter make his cause more odious vnto them, whiche will diligently labour to take him haltyng in the alledgyng of the Scriptures: for to what purpose is it for an Archer to doe as HN. doth to set vp his markes and neuer commyng at them, to raunge vp and downe the fieldes at rouers. But of this somewhat before beyng spoken, shall herein stay my labour concernyng that matter.

Vnto whome reueiled. Vz. vnto HN.

Rom. 1. 1.

Actes. 9. v. 15.

1. Cor. 3. 15. Euan. cap. 1. sent. 1.

Unto the which also HN. addeth where he heard these his Reuelatiōs, *videli. From the mouth of God him selfe.* Wherein he doth open vnto the world his shameles and vayne boasting, beleue him he that will. And if it be truth that ẏ Israelites were so terrified with the voyce of God, and that Christes voyce drawe S. Paule to the grounde, with the wonderfull maiestie therof and the brightnes of his countenaunce; Which voyce also did smite the soul-

3. From whence it was reueiled.

Exod. 20. 19.

Act. 9. 4. 5. & 22. 1. 2. 26. 14.

John. 18.6. diours to groũd: The force and the working wherof, and
Psal.29. how mighty the operation therof is, holy David declareth at large by many effectes in the 29. Psalme through
out. Now then if this be true that God in his law hath
thus thundred, thereby to kepe vs in obediẽce to be wholy subiect vnto him, how can HN. auouch it to be true,
that he affirmeth hee hath heard these his Reuelations,
From the mouth of God him selfe. We know very well (as
many I meane as are the beloued of the Lord) that *Re-*
Heb.1.1. *uelatiõs* haue bene of old, but they are not nedefull. God
in tymes past in diuers maners spake in the old tyme by
1. the Prophetes, vnto our Fathers, but in these last dayes
he hath spoken vnto vs by his some. Miracles serued the
Church in her swadlyng clothes, but now fayth is sealed
by the death of Christ: and to cry for further miracles
were to crucifie the sonne of God a fresh, and to make a
mocke of the Sauiour of the world. Hath the earthly father an inward care to leaue his sonne his will sealed
with his owne seale, and subscribed with his owne hand,
to auoyde contention, and to cease strife: and shal not Jesus Christ the sonne, of the most wise God, which sonne
to testifie his loue towardes vs, often calleth him selfe the
sonne of man, shall not the loue of his manhode and the
vnspeakeable wisedome of his Godhead prouide for the
safe and quyet gouernement of his owne house, which so
dearely with his hart bloud hee hath purged and made
cleane? Thus then we se that HN. his bragges be but
bables, and trifles that he boasteth *he will declare the secret Misteries of God, and make relation of thynges hidden
from the beginnyng of the world.* Sathan albeit he hath ta-
Gal.1.8. ken vpon him the shape of an Aungell of light, yet if he
in the likenesse of the most glorious Aungell in heauen
will teach vs, or shall preach vnto vs any other Gospell,
then we haue receaued, be he ten thousand tymes accursed. But this doctrine, as it alwayes hath bene peculiar
vnto the *Papistes, Libertines,* and especially the *Anabaptistes*, for that they are mighty in such kynde of profes-

as

as for the true Church, it neither vseth, nor alloweth any such doctrine of *Reuelations*, as HN. in this place dreameth of: onely it is sufficiently instructed in the truth of Gods word, without any further search after fonde and curious visions, which are expresly forbidden by the written word of God, and holy Scripture, which onely is the power of God vnto saluatiō to saue the soules of Gods people: But of *Reuelations*, and extraordinary declarations of Gods word hetherto, for the 9. Article.

Deut.13.1.2.3. & 30.12. Esay.8.19. Actes.10.5. Luke.16.30. Gallat.1.8. Apoc.2.25. Rom.1.16. 2.Tim.3.17.d. Iam.1.21.

ARTICLE. 10. of HN. *Of Shrift.*

AND vnto their Elders (priuately) must they confesse all their sinnes, and make their lyfe naked, and bare before them.

1.Exhort.cap. 13.sent.12.

Theophilus.

FOr how should they otherwise receiue counsell, to auoyde the same? and thereto it is spoken, as reade forth the text, and leaue your priuate addition. (as priuately.)

William Wilkinson.

THe most conuenient method to deale with this, as with all the rest of HN. his erroneous, and absurd Paradoxes in my iudgement is, first, because the Famblers vse to cauil, that they are falsly and vniustly burthened, neither can that be proued by them wherewith they are charged, by their owne wrightinges to conuince them, to be guiltye of that which is layd agaynst them.

Brief rehearsall of the Familie, pag.2.lin.3.
1. Guiltie by their own wrytynges.

Secōdly to examine their groundes & profes, whereby they labour to auouch their heresie to be the truth.

2. Proofe of groundes quoted by the Fam.

Thirdly to shew whatparteners and fellowes they haue of other heretiques, which haue either held ŷ same heresie or hauyng held it, haue maintained it by the same profes, that they doe.

3. Fellowes to the Fam. in their heresie. who?

The Fa. wherein they swarue from the Scripture.

Lastly to shew wherein they in their opinions doe disagrée from the holy scriptures, & the iudgement of some wrighters cōcerning the same, which order he that well considereth the former Articles, shall sée hath by me ben obserued heretofore.

For the first pointe that *HN.* and the Familie hould an erroneous confession of sinnes, and a kinde of shrift more then Popish, shall not néede any long probation out of their wrightinges. For that the Elder Theophilus, confesseth the same boulstering vp his asseueration with this interrogatorye. *For how should they otherwise receiue counsell to auoyd the Fami. &c.*

Yet will I adde a place or twaine out of *HN.* to make ẏ matter more cleare, that hereafter it be not doubted of.

1. Exhort. cap. 11 sent. 7. b.

Let all your counsayles, enterprises, purposes, will, & deeds, (whether they be then secret, or manifest) appeare at all tymes naked, and bare before your Elders. Eccle. 4. &c.

Ibid. cap. 11. sent. 20. d.

But if ye chaunce to offend in committing any misdeeds yet binde not in any case your hart thereon: (Eccle. 5. a.) neither yet feare you to be ashamed (Eccl. 4. c.) to confesse the same before God, (Pro. 28. b. Esay. 29. b. Ierem. 23. c. & Esdras. 16. g.) and the priestes your Elders, but let it appeare apparauntly before them. &c. sent. 21. 22. 23. 30.

Esay. 29. falsefied Ierem. 23.

Ibid. cap. 13. sent. 12. c. fol. 31

Fourthly it is expedient that they should (Prou. 28. b. Eccle. 4. c. & 17. b. Iam. 5. b.) make manifest their whole harte, with all their counsels, mindes, willes, and thoughtes; together with all their doinges, dealinges, and exercises, naked and bare before the Eldest in the Familye of Loue: are not couer (Esay. 29. b. 4. Esdr. 16. g.) or hide any thing (be it what it is) before him. Also whereunto their inclination, kinde, and nature draweth them and all therewith they become tēpted or assaulted in their hartes.

The like place is in his Documentall sentēces. cap. 4. sent. 3. fol. 9. b. & cap. 13. sent. 18. fol. 28. g. & cap. 15. sent. 6. fol. 33. g. and cap. 16. sent. 4. fol. 36. b. the young Famlers must make manifest themselues, and their whole harts dealing and inclination to the Elders in the Familye of Loue.

That

That there is a confession in the Family of *HN*, more streight then euer was in the tyme of Popery is manifest, for that the one (namely the Fami.) requireth the very thoughtes, and naturall inclinations, which no man is able to expresse, for that he knoweth them not. Psal, 19. 12. but the other (Videl. Papistrye) demaundeth but a confession of the outward act committed, which in respect of the other is more easely to be performed, though in respect of the written worde both are false, and vtterly absurd, as by HN. his owne wordes hath ben sufficient playnely declared: now by what groundes & engines he would build vp this his heape of confusion, that remaineth briefly to be considered.

His profes which he vseth are all drawne either from the scripture Canonical, or Apocripha. For the last, in ye iudgement of all learned men it enforceth not any necessitye of doctrine, either by precept or example therein cōteined, as may by exceptiōs takē at diuers places thereof be substantially confirmed. Yet least our Familye should boast they cannot be aunswered to the first place. shame not to confesse thy sinnes, &c. that is, if any man that is a brother walke inordinately, and be thereof admonished according as Christ our Sauiour commaundeth, or if he be an open enemie & haue dew admonitiō, with such an one we ought not to be cōuersaūt, neither to haue fellowship with the vnfruiteful workes of darknes, but rather we must reproue him, and he that being so reproued is ashamed and amendeth not is a wicked man, as in the Gospell is to be sene by the example of the pharisies and Herod.

Profes Apocripha.

2. Mach. 12. 44. & 14. cap. ve. 41.

Eccle. 4. 26. d.

Ephe. 5.

Iohn. 9. 34. Math. 14. 4.

The second place Eccle. 17. 18. b. proueth nothing to the purpose. For it sheweth that God seeth all our sins, it speakes not a word of confession vnto any man, the which place he borowed of Peter Lombard, but erred in this that neither he himselfe nor the Papistes whence he had it, doth apply it to the purpose.

2. place aunswered.

Eccle. 17. 18. b.

Lib. 4. distinct. 17. a.

The third place which he citeth out of the Apocripha

4. Esdr. 16.57. 58.g. Scripture hath these wordes. When your sinnes are brought forth before men: ye shall be confounded and your own sinnes shal stand as your accusers in that day. HN. when he findeth these wordes sins shall be brought forth before mē, thinketh there is no remedie but needs it must be vnderstode of Auriculer confessiō in his Louely Fami. The which sence the very next wordes vers. 58. improue, shewing the former reueiling of sinnes before men to be ment of the opening of sin at the day of iudgement, How will you hide your sinnes before God and his Angels. which thing is also to be noted in the same sence. Apoc. 21. b. 12. Math. 25. v. 31. The which places albeit he draweth them by the puddles wherein the Papistes haue defiled them, yet he vsing them in his bookes very oft ouerseeth himselfe in that there is no such thing to proue by them for the which he doth alledge them.

Vers. 58.

HN. his Canonicall proofes. Prou. 28. 13. b. The profes out of the Canonicall Scripture are in number 4. the first out of the Prouerbes which sayth: He that hideth his sinnes shall not prosper, is to be expounded by the place of S. John. If we say we haue no sinne, we deceiue our selues. & by many other places of Scripture that no man is voyd of sinne, wherein *HN.* sheweth that he is wonderfull bewitched alleadging that for him which is directly agaynst his doctrine of perfection wherof the Fam. boast so often.

1. Iohn. 1. 8. 9. Prou. 20. 9. Eccl. 7. 20. 2. Chron. 6. 36. 1. Kyng. 8. 46.

2. Epist. to M. Rogers. pag. 86. The second place out of S. James. 5. chap. 16. v. b. Confesse your sinnes one to another. Where the illuminated Elder in the Loue, must likewise confesse his sinnes to the single minded ons, and to those which stand welwilling vnto his instructions as well as the simple disciple must confesse to the Elder in the Familie. But the Elder sinneth not, therefore the young mynded ones ought not to confesse vnto thē, for that such confession is mutuall and from either to other, but this place is likewise taken from the Romish Cleargie. For they long before *HN.* was borne, abused it vnto Auriculer shriftes and Lenton confession. Wherein also they argue not

HN. borroweth of Poperie.

M. Sentences. 4. booke Dist. 16. a

amongest

amongest themseles. For D. Scotus sayth: (vpon the same place from whence *HN.* hath filched this text.) *Nec mihi videtur hoc præceptũ dedisse Iacobus, nec a Christo acceptũ promulgasse.* In my iudgemẽt James gaue not this commaundement, neither had he from Christ any such authoritye: and the M. of the sentences, albeit he had alledged it before vnto ỹ same purpose, yet in the cõclusion he putteth a great doubt thereof. And Gratian sayth: speaking of the obseruing or not obseruing of this confession. *Whether of these two opinions it were better to follow, it is left to the discretion of the reader, for either side is fauoured by wise and godly men. Also M. Harding a great proctour of such popish palterye affirmeth that the expresse terme of secret confession is seldome mentioned in the auntient Fathers.* Thus we see wherein *HN.* and the Papistes agrée in the alledgyng of these two places as for the other two places. Esay. 29. b. and Jeremy. 23. c: they are vtterly falsefied, for they haue not any one word which *HN.* quoteth them for.

Ibid. Distinct. 17 Scotus quæst. 1.

De Pœnitendis. 1. quamuis plenitudo.

M. Hardyng. fol. 71. a.

HN. falsefieth the Scripture.

But straunge doctrine will haue straunge doctours, and children not legitimate when they come to claime inheritance as they bring forged euidẽce, so must néedes their seales be counterfeit.

Lastly to shew whence this doctrine of *Confession of sinnes enseweth*, as it is very easy, so néede we not in this part to vse any long or tedious circũstaunce. The Appollogie of the English Church refuseth it for Catholicke. *M. Harding* fighteth for it with tooth and naile, to the which if the diligent reader will haue recourse for his further instruction he shall finde this question handled at large, and learnedly debated.

Cap. 2. diuis. 2.

Bysh. of Salisbury defenc. of the Apollog. pag. 167. 168. 174. 175. 180. 181. 187. 188.

154477

ARTICLE. 11. HN. *Gospell a litterall seruice.*

Lam.com.s.7. 1.Exhor.cap.16 sent.17.& sent. 34.

They mislyke of the ministrye of the worde and terme it a ceremoniall seruice inuented by man, a false Gods seruice a seruice, of the letter.

Theophilus.

That is vntrue, read the lamentable complaynt, sent.6.7. and the rest also, and consider better thereof, least you vtterly shame your selfe.

William Wilkinson.

Whether there be any truth taught without the Familye of *HN.* and of the calling of him, that hath or shall teach any thing which the Fami. shall not lyke of, I haue somewhat before touched, the which that it yet may be more manifest both for the thing taught and the person that is the teacher, in this and the next Article is to be handled more at large. And though that those which know not Theophilus bringing vp, may by vnsemely and vnciuile speach, thinke it to haue ben very rude, in that at the first stoppe he breatheth out into this homely phrase, that is vntrue, and ye vtterly shame your selfe, yet being somewhat acquainted, and hauing as his phrase is an experimentall knowledge of his modestie, I toke him better then he meaneth, not measuring him by his owne ellwand. For I wot well it alwayes will be truth that the ould Oratour sayth to his frend *Qui semel vericundiæ fines transilinerit &c.* He that once hath raunged without the listes of honestye, he without all hoe must nedes be inpudent.

To proue that I haue vnderstode amisse, and falsified HN. his meaning in my places which I haue set downe: Theophilus referreth me to the Lamentable complaint. to the same sect which I quoted before, thinking (belike) that ŷ if I loked againe I should finde it otherwise in the section 6.7. The wordes ŷ I misliked in that place are these.

Euen as partely that same is well knowen and become manifest vnto vs of certaine, namely of those which are the auncientest in the scripturlearnednes or principallest in the Ceremonye seruice, which haue made vp themselues agaynst the truth of Gods testimonies, and his promises agaynst the holy spirite of Christ, and agaynst the Loue, &c. This place whome HN. in playne wordes auoucheth that ŷ Auncientest (that is the Bishops. and reuerend Fathers, and preachers of the word) in the Scripture learnednes the principallest in the Ceremonye seruice &c. is that wherewith I charged him. — Ceremonie seruice.

The same is more euidently also to be sene. 1. Exhor. cap. 15. sentence. 8. and 10. c. which is a slaunderous and a blasphemous section, which because it is tedious I refraine to set downe *verbatim* after *HN.* his copie. — False God seruice.

And Chapt. *16. sent. 3. For certaine take in hand & vse out of the imagination of the knowledge whereon they set their hartes at peace, false God seruices which they notwithstandyng institute or bryng in for true God seruices, Religions, Lawes, and Commaundementes of God: and plant the same knowledge into the people as though they ought of right to be obedient thereunto.* — HN. 1. exhort. cap. 16. sent. 3. — Col. 2. b.

And *sent. 14. Dare any man teach or set forth any thyng through the imagination of the knowledge (whether he then haue taken on the same out of the learnednesse of the Scriptures, or out of his good thinking wisedome as a word or Commaundement of the Lord? or yet to institute any seruices out of the letter of the Scripture accordyng to his good thinking, and so to plucke or make subiect the hartes of men, to dissention thereunder? &c. sent. 15. 16.* — HN. maketh the Gospell cause of discention.

By all the which places it is manifest, what opinion he hath of the preachyng of Gods word, that it is but an institute knowledge inuented by mans wit, to the breedyng of discord & dissētion, then the which I say not what *Papist*, what *Atheist*, or *Macheuile* in the world could write or inuent any thyng more vngodly.

Besides this I am able to auouch by myne own experiẽce that some, with whõ I haue conferred, which haue affirmed, that the Scripture is to hard for a simple mã, and therfore the bookes of HN. do make a more easie passage, and geue a readyer way to the vnderstandyng therof. In somuch as when that the Elders haue perswaded any man to become their sectarie, they haue for a tyme taken all the bookes of holy Scriptures from him, and all other bookes altogether and geue him the bookes of HN. to meditate, and be exercised in, and this is that which

1. Exhort. cap. 1. sent. 39.

HN. him selfe exhorteth them after this sort. *Glasse your beyng and minde in the glasse of righteousnes Iam. 1. c. and behold therein how many spottes and wrinkles there are yet in you.* Wherein he sheweth that he preferreth his booke,

HN. preferreth his own bookes before the Scriptures.

which he termeth, the *Glasse of righteousnesse*, before the word of God, in referryng them thereunto for to espy the spottes of sinne, cleane contrary to ẏ word of God, which

Rom. 7. 7.

teacheth vs that the knowledge of sinne commeth by the law. And this he doth not in this place alone but also almost at the end of euery Chapter in his *Euang.*

This horrible treason agaynst God and his word, as it would make any Christian hart to melt, so is it not for the manifest impietie therof by many argumentes or places so much to be confuted, as by the losse of the lyues of such gracelesse *Atheistes* to be chastised, which the sooner shall stay, if those to whom the Lord hath committed the care of his Church, and gouernaunce of this commõ wealth, shal by some waight of seuere, and sharpe lawes keepe vnder so horrible impietie and blasphemy agaynst the sonne of God. For herein is the infection more pestilent that the bookes of HN. beyng made of equall countenaunce with the word of God, the wrytynges of HN. are receiued as a playne and easie truth, the word of God either wholy abandoned, and set aside, or els read by the ouersight and allowaunce of their *Elders*, who often tyme dust the beames of the truth, by their vayne Allegories and idle Expositions.

But this is the iudgement of God, which is iustly in great measure come vpon vs, that whilest diuers of the ministers of the word haue not preached the word as the word of God, and the people haue heard it as the word of man, it is come to passe I say that our eyes are blynded least we should sée, and our eares waxed deafe least we should heare, our hartes are waxed dull least we should beleue, and so the secret though iust punishment of hardnes of hart is come vpon vs: so that thereby euery day we are nearer hell then other.

For what wickednes can be compared with this, or what blasphemie hath the world euer bene witnes of the like, that the fonde nature of our flesh as a swift streame hath caryed vs to the depth of such impietie, that we should loade and burthen the blessed word of the eternall God with such intemperate and graceles tauntes, as to doubt whether the truth be the truth or no. Well, I say no more, but he that is filthy let him be filthy still. And that Argument, which S. Paule thinketh to be of such weight to proue his preachyng to haue bene the vndoubted truth of God, the same would I vse to perswade all such as wauer in ẏ truth therof, Proue your selues whe- 2.Cor. 13.5.
ther ye are in the fayth, examine your selues, knowe ye not your owne selues how that Iesus Christ is in you except ye be cast awayes? &c. Wherein S. Paule appealeth vnto their owne consciẽce to approue the certaintie of his doctrine & truth of his Apostleshyp: Right so say I vnto the *Familie of Loue*, that whereas they affirme we teach nothyng, but our owne good thinkyng, I demaunde of them when they heare the word of God preached, and their consciences shaken with the terrour thereof, if all their glory in their perfection (wherof they rather boast in worde, then in déede are partakers of) if all the figge leaues, which they haue so fondly sewed together be able to garde them that they quake and quiuer not, when the Lord out of the mouth of his Ministers begynneth to me-

LEARNING RESOURCES CENTER
NAZARETH COLLEGE

nace them. If they tremble at the preachyng of the word of God, why then do they make accompt of it, but as a vocall word, & outward sounde? Why acknowledge they not that the workyng thereof is mighty, that it pearceth like a two edged sword and entreth into the deuidyng of the soule and the spirite. If they haue no fœlyng of ÿ word, when it is preached vnto thē, then is the Gospell therfore hid vnto them, because the God of this world hath blinded the eyes of their myndes, that the brightnes of the sonne of God should shine vnto them: but in this world in some measure the darknes of the world to come is begon in them, wherein is wœpyng and gnashyng of tœth: beyng farther gone in this lyfe in their impietie then *Fœlix* the prophane Deputie of Iudæa, which when he heard S. Paule preach of righteousnesse, and temperaunce, and the iudgementes of the world to come, hee trembled and was affrayde. Which tremblyng and quakyng of him which was an vnchristianed Heathen man, shall condemne the lose hearyng of Gods word in them, whiche count them selues Christians, and yet performe nothyng worthy of the seruauntes of Christ.

4.Heb.12.

1.Corin.4.3.4.

Act.24.26.

Wel let vs learne hereafter to heare Gods word with a more hungry and thirsty soule, to liue and dye thereafter: and as many as rue vpon the state of the poore seduced soules, made droncken with the dregges of this so fond a Familie, let them desire God that as many amōg them as are appointed to be of Gods flocke may leaue to wander in the wearynes of their owne soules, and layng the law of God to their hartes, may by the candle of his truth see from whence they are fallen, and so at the last returne backe agayne to the Archshepheard and Byshop of their soules. *Amen.*

HN.

1.Exhort.cap. 16.sent.14.

They say the freedome which commeth by the preachyng of the Gospell, there is not a more wickeder, falser, nor an

ab-

absurder, seducynger, arroganter, horribler, agaynst God and his vpright seruice, nor yet damagefuller nor destructionabler to the children of men then this. &c.

Which freedome also he termeth, a spirituall pride (Apoc. 17.a. 18.a. 21.b. there is no such places that hath any such word as he doth alledge them for) *a presumption, a great blasphemyng of God.* Ibid. sent. 13. HN. quoteth scripture in vaine.

Theophilus.

NOt so. *But that which is taken on presumptuously out of the learnednes of the letter, or out of the imagination of the knowledge, by the vnrenewed man for a word or cōmaundement of God, to a breedyng of dissention, and captiuatyng of mens hartes, vnto mens good thinking or imagination, is the worst or falsest fredome, as true it is. &c. and blaze your selfe therein.*

William Wilkinson.

HN. As in the former part of this Article, very vngraciously hath reproched the Gospell, by termyng it a ceremonie seruice inuented by man, and a seruice of the letter: So in the second part of the same Article he and his lewde Scholler *Theophilus* lay diuers accusations agaynst the same, prouyng that it is not the true light which we preach, neither the Gospell of the Lord: first, because it bringeth forth a most false, absurde, seducyng and arrogant fredome, horrible agaynst God, and his vpright seruice bringing daunger and destruction vnto the children of men. Unto the which *Theophilus* addeth a reason of his maister HN. his Assertion that therfore it is false. &c. because that we beyng vnrenewed or vnregenerate, out of the learnednes of the letter, and imagination of our owne knowledge take it vpon vs, because it breedeth dissention and captiuatyng of mens hartes vnto mens good thinking: therfore also is it the falsest fredome or libertie, and I must blase my selfe therein, *videl.* to be a false Libertine or Freeman. These be the chiefest notes of the second part of this 11. Article.

> The Gospell engendreth a false freedome sayth HN.
>
> HN. rayleth without proofe.

The first crime wherewith *HN*. chargeth the ministry of the Gospel is, that *it engendreth a false freedome or libertie*. The which his accusation albeit it is slaūderous and Godles, yet had it bene more glorious in the sight of men if in the approuing therof, as he otherwhiles doth, so in the confirmation also he had pretended some cloke of Scripture, that thereby also his meanyng might yͤ playnlier haue bene vnderstode. But seyng that neither in 14. or 15. sentences he citeth no proofe for any such matters, let vs examine his wordes, to see if his bare word be sufficiēt with proofe to be our warrant that his saying is true.

> Bulling. 2. book 2. & 3. chap.

The string that he harpeth on is the same, that all heretiques and schismatiques haue ben busie withall, therby to draw (by a plausible doctrine) many Disciples after them, *videl.* libertie, freedome. &c. And least HN. should seeme as grosse as his brethren the impure *Anabaptistes* in protestyng to the world an open and carnall libertie, by a cunnyng conueighaūce he couereth the same, shewyng vs in two dishes one meat, and onely telleth vs that they be twayne because he sauceth and setteth them forth after a diuers fashion.

> 1. Exhort. cap. 15. sent. 26.
>
> HN. his libertie what it is.
>
> Sent. 28. HN.

The liberty which he broacheth, he defineth after this sort, *when through the ministration of the gracious word vnder the obedience of the loue, man forgoeth or vnbindeth all taken on knowledge, with the purging of hart, spirite, & mynd is purged or purified from all wicked nature (Rom. 6. c. 8. a.) whiche hath reigned ouer hym, that there dwell nothyng in man but the true Godhead with his Louely beyng of the vpright loue:* this he termeth a definition the which he darkneth with many varying & diffuse termes, but how like a deffinition it is beyng a hotch potch without forme or matter, to him that knoweth what a deffinition is may easely be discerned.

> HN. definition of libertie discussed.

The partes whereof HN. his definition principally doth consist are in number 2. In the first he requireth *an*

vn-

vnbyndyng and forgoyng or as in an other place more fitly he termeth *it an vnlearnyng of all knowledge*. The which clause of this definition is flatly a Papisticall dotage which teacheth *Ignoraunce is the mother of deuotion* already cōfuted in this booke 8. Article. The second part of his definition *videl. a purging of the spirite from all wicked nature*, is also playne *Anabaptisticall* which dreameth that it is possible in this life to come to that perfection that mē should not sinne: whiche also our Familie mightly do maintaine by their open letters to M. Rogers in the quarell they moue against his displa. The last clause which doth after a sorte expounde, this *purging of the spirite. &c.* conteineth this palpable absurditie *that the true Godhead doth dwell in vs*. Which was the hereticall fantasie of the *Manichies*, wherof I haue spoken somewhat before: of ye which his definition sith already euery part is confuted, it shal in this place spare me a further labour. In the definition (as he termeth it) there are cōtained diuers outroades & extrauagant varying of phrases, altogether repugnyng vnto Arte, which willeth that euery deffinition be as brief and playne as possible may be, yet is HN. his definition so compacted together as if the one part of it stode at *Collen* and the other at *Amsterdam*: but herein rather pitie we his folly, then enuy his learning and dexteritie in formyng a fit definition.

Bulling. 1. book 21. cap. leafe. 26. b.

Epist. of E. R.

But seyng we haue founde fault with HN. his definition, of the *vpright fredome*, let vs see if there may a more playne and pithy definition be drawne then erst he hath set downe. Christian libertie is the forgiuenesse of sinnes. Psal. 32. 1. a. Rom. 4. 8. Purchased by the death of Christ, Rom. 4. 25. d. Ephes. 1. 7. b. Preached vnto vs by the Gospell. Joh. 8. 32. 2. Tim. 1. 10. c. sealed by the vse of the word. Actes. 13. 26. d. Rom. 1. 16. b. and Sacramentes. Rom. 4. 11. 1. Cor. 11. 26. The which definition I cease to amplifie, or to prosecute the partes therof, because the testimonies of the holy Scriptures shalbe my sufficient warrant in that behalf.

The difinitiō of Christian libertie by the Scriptures.

Second crime layd to the Gospell.

The second crime that HN. burtheneth our Ministry withall is that those that preach are vnregenerate, vnrenewed: which, that it hindreth not the truth of doctrine in that it is taught by a wicked person, is apparaunt by the testimonie of our Sauiour, who biddeth the Disciples and the people obey the doctrine of the Scribes and pharisies, which sit in Moses chaire, but do not after their lyfe: which he would not haue done if the Pharisies euill lyfe had made voyde the truth of their doctrine. But this is touched more in the 5. Article, where it is impugned by *HN*. that a man lewde in lyfe can not speake the truth in doctrine.

Math. 23.3.

The thyrd crime of preachyng out of the learnednes of the letter we shall haue a fitter place to touch it afterward in the next Article.

The fourth crime which *HN*, obiecteth is coalewortes more then tenne times sodden, and yet being refused by vs, eftsone is in the next seruice set downe. For how often doth he in his wofull exhortation still beate vpon this *a ceremonie seruice that maintayneth dissention: and agayne which stretcheth no further, but to the breding of schisme, partialitye, and sedition among the people, quoting Math. 24. a. 5. ve. and b. 24. v.* Where Christ sayth: *Many false Christes shall arise and deceiue many. HN.* expoundeth it of those which professe religion without his loathsom and schismaticall Familye, and in the same place he quoteth 1. Cor. 3. a. 3. Iam. 3. b. which conteineth a discription of the intemperancie of the tongue being abused, he vilanously doth aply it to those preachers which reuerētly handle the pure word of God without his hereticall secresie, and frentique conuenticle, and in the same 15. *Chap. of HN. The simple and vnlighted people, (Ierem. 23. c. d. Ezech. 13. b. ver. 8. 9. 10. &c.) become therewith seduced and beguiled. Math. 24. c. 2. Tim. 3. 4. 2. Pet. 2. a. Iude. 1. b.* still *HN*. applieth those places to the preachers of Gods worde which are ment of him aud such lyke bedlem heretiques, as he is as also captiued with many

1. Exhor. cap. 15. sent. 8. &. 10.

Sent. 12.

diuises,

diuises and sectes: the which knowledge of the worde that the same preachers haue, *HN.* termeth in the same blasphemous and schismaticall chap. *Variaunce renting or diuision bringing forth discordable disputations about vnprofitable argumentes.* Rom.1.d. Galla.5.c.1.Tim.6.a. Titus.3.a.Iam.3.b.then the which what can be vttered with more malice, or set abroach with more cancred hatred: and yet will *HN.* nædes be counted the Father of the Familye that in it hath nothing but loue and mæke mindednes. Sent.10.

The which accusation of his as it is most pestilent and full fraught with an hart wholy resolued to raile and backbite vnder the cloake of calmenes, so is it a thing that continually hath ben obiected agaynst the Church to infring the trueth thereof after this sort. *There are in such and such particuler Churches disagreementes in some pointes of doctrine & varietye of iudgemẽtes. ergo, there is no truth in those Churches.* This I say is an ould Argument framed first by heretiques, vsed by the Papistes as an Iron staple, and now againe furbushed and being new fethered is shotte againe cleane besides the white, and the butt also. For the auncient Fathers hauing it often obiected to them, & frier *Hosias*, and the graceles runnagate *Staphilus*, and *M. Harding himselfe hath often turned this stone which so is fastened by the Father of blessed remembraunce the Byshop of Salisburye*, that if all the Famblers of Loue and heretiques in the world shall set their shoulders vnto it therewith to ouerwhelme the truth, they neuer shall be able so much as once to stir it, and yet if they should, they must take hæde that in the rembling therof they crush not all their bones in sunder: to their vtter confusion. But that this gappe may finally be stopped that hereafter *HN.* neuer with his fellow hereticks breake in to disturbe the peace of Sion let it be remembred that is written. Gen.13.7.b.& 27.11.Luke.22.24.c. Actes.15,39.f.1.Cor.1.11.b. Gal.2.11.c.that alwayes in the Church of God there hath ben iarres aswell in

Staphilus 3. treatise from pag.78.& c.to 115.
Defence of the Apol.3.Chap. 1.diuisi.pag.378 379.380.& Replie.15.Artic.12 diuision.pag. 536.537.

maners as also in religion.

And thus much brieflye for this second part of *HN.* his doctrine of the dignitye of the word, and the opinion of the truth thereof. As for Theophilus who frendly geueth me counsell to blaze my selfe in the former definition of a Libertine, I doe him to know, that such libertye as is to be claymed by mercye and imputation of the death of Christ, that libertie from sinne I loke for and none other, and this is that which (in my poore iudgment) all the children of God doe loke for. Rom. 8. 20. 21. both in this lyfe, as also in the lyfe to come.

As for his Rhetoricall terme of blazing and Blazonrie, I wish him to spare it tell he come in place where he may haue occasion to vse it: for vnto me if he be that party whome some that wishe well to the Familye report to me that he is, he should not haue neded to haue shadowed him selfe by a terme of heraultrie, but if I were disposed to blase his coate, perhaps if I should say that he were like to be that E. R. which ouershot himselfe in his Epistle to I. R. I might so dissipher his personage that the bizard of Theophilus should not be sufficient to saue him that he be not knowne by blushing: but it is good for him to kepe him to that which he is called and rather to learne the principles of the Catechisme and the first groundes of Gods feare, then to busie bimselfe in that which he hath no skill of, to the hurt of the Church, the offence of the weake, and endamaging of his owne soule in the day of the Lord. And thus much of the 11. Article hetherto.

HN. his 12. Assertion.

The 12. Article what HN. thinketh of all preachers that be without his Familye of Loue. *1. Sent.*

11. Epist. of HN cap. 5. sent. 13. 34
1. Exhort. 15. sent. 7.
1. Epist. cap. 2. sent. 8. 5.
1. Exhort. cap. 15 sent. 8.

OF the preachers themselues HN. sayth they are false hartes of Scripture learned, vnilluminated and vnsent preachers, vaine praters through an imagination of knowledge, false hartes, and vnregene-

regenerate scripture learned, bould, presumptuous, selfewise, and good thinking wise, doctors of the letter. Lament complaint in the title. *which are yet fleshly minded and sowe nothing els but noysome and corrupt seede among the people.*

Euang. cap.4. sent.4.5.6. Pub. of the Peace cap. 1. sent.2.& sent.6. 20 24.27.

Theophilus.

HE onely speaketh of all such false hartes of the Scripture learned and vnsent preachers, which turne away from the true doctrine that serueth to the vnitye of the hart in Loue, which being fleshly minded geuing forth themselues (through the false light) to be teachers and ministers of the word, &c. loke better to the text before recited.

HN. 2. Sentence.

W*Hose minde (vz. of the preachers) or being is the deuill, the Antechrist, the wicked spirit, the kingdome of hell, and the maiestie of the deuill himselfe.*

1. Exhort. cap. 15. sent. 17. fol. 38. D.

Theophilus.

MEaning such preachers as are before expressed.

HN. 3. Sentence.

T*Herefore it is all (assuredly) false lyes and seducing and deceauing whatsoeuer the vngodded, or vnilluminated man. (Ier.23.c.10.& 29.a.8.) out of the imagination or riches of their owne knowledge, and out of their learnednes. 1. Cor.1.b.11. of the scriptures, bring fourth, institute, preach and teach. Ierem.8.a.27.9. verse.*

1. Exhort.cap.16 sent.17. Scripture prophanely quoted.

Theophilus.

BEcause they are not taught to the kingdome of heauen, in humblenes and lowlines of spirite, but in all arrogancie of hart, neither haue they receiued the word of lyfe from the liuing God. &c. reade 1. Exhort.cap. 6. sent. 16.

W. Wilkinson.

When as there is no such sent. in the Chapter as Theophilus eyes will beare me witnes.

HN. 4. Sentence.

1.Exhort.cap.16 sent.18.

They preach indeede the letter and the imagination of their knowledge (Ier.5.b.4. and chap. 6. 8. Ezech. 13. b. ver.6.7.8.9. and chapter 34.) but not the word of the liuing God.

Theophilus.

Can any man preach more then he hath by him?

William Wilkinson.

Iam.3.ver.11.

If it be true as no doubt it is very true, that in the gospel our Sauiour Christ sayth by the fruite the tree is knowne, and S. James also testifieth that the same fountaine can not send out swete and bitter water: yea and if HN. himselfe be to be beleued, when he sayth: *The perfect man can not geue forth any thing els from him but all humble and meeke vertues, and righteousnes which flow out of perfection*, surely if these be the fruites that *HN*. his Louely being doth afford, what rote is it from whence such a streame of frentique and furious eloquẽce doth abound? truely if these poysoned speaches, and tarrye Rhetorick wherewith he bradeth Gods ministers be as he sayth, his *humble and meeke vertues flowing from all perfection*: When *HN*. shall ebbe in his perfection, and his high tyde of his upright fredome become to a falling water, what ougly deformityes shall we see, when he is left naked? or being extremely euill how monstrous shal his impietye surmount it selfe, when being at his hiest pitch

Docum sent. cap.1.sent.7.

HN.his perfection, and the fruites.

pitch of perfection ye take him thus tardye?

But euen such perfect wightes were the Anabaptists which boasted that they kept the lawe, and liued sinles, and yet rayling on the preachers of their age they called them Lutherans. fol. 254. *False and carnal gospellours 255 erroneous and vnskilfull preachers. 256. a generation of vipers and hirelinges 257.b.*

And such vpright Christians are our Romish Catholickes, which boast so much of their good workes (which it were to be wished in many of thē were much better) and yet when they come by penne to proclayme, what hartes they beare in their bosomes, and how wholy they are mortified: their written treatises bewray the malice of their mindes, and wholy discouer their cancred stomackes, when as speaking of the state of the Church of God in the countrye whererein they were brought vp they terme it the *Synagogue of Antechrist and Lucifer, Harding confut. 212.b. The tower of Babilon. confut. 42.a.* and the preachers of the same they call *the limmes of Antechrist, confut. 202.a. Lecherous lourdaines. confut. 75.b. Chaines broode. confut. 114.b. Pulpet buzzers. R. pref.* Unto the which termes both of the Anabaptistes, and Papistes, whether *HN.* in the same vaine be behinde thē both or no, I leaue to be considered of them, that shall equally way all their speaches and the maner of their deliuerie in the same ballaunce.

Bulleng. fol. 260. Anabaptistes fulfilling of the law and the fruites thereof.

Papistes good wordes and workes, and a patterne of thē. Actes. 9. 5.

Unto all the which their immodest and vnsæmely snuffes and tauntes, truely be it aunswered that was said vnto S. Paule, whē he was prest to persecute ẏ hed in the members, and to persue the father in the childrē, it shall be hard for them to kick agaynst the prick. The children of darcknes may scatter cockle, heretiques whē men sleepe may sowe tares, yet can not any schisme be perpetuall, for great is the truth and preuaileth, heauen and earth shall passe, but the word of God endureth for euer.

Math. 13. 25. Esdr. 4. 38.

Math. 24. 35. Psal. 119. 89. 1. Pet 1. 25.

The meeke manner of *HN.* his reprehending ẏ preachers of Gods word, and whome he imitateth therein hath already ben declared: now resteth it yet further to be discussed what accusatiõ that should be, wherwith, he chargeth them, which is, they *are vngodded men, vnilluminated, vnregenerate &c.* The which his slaunderous accusation if it be by him vnderstode of all preachers, then is it manifestly vntrue, so néedeth it not any aunswere at all, but yf it be as Theophilus *HN.* his disciple sayth: (who explayning his maisters meaning) that it is onely to be vnderstode of those *Which will not receiue his louely doctrine.* Then haue I further to aunswere that albeit the persons were euill men as he misimagineth they are, yet to report that *their being is the maiesty of the deuill himselfe the Antechrist, the wicked spirite &c.* This is not so louely a phrase, neither doth it so well become the father of the Familye of Loue as he weneth that it doth.

But *HN.* his reason in this place as it is very waighty, (for so he taketh it) so he that shal consideratly weigh the 2. seuerall propositions gathered vpon the 2. first sentences by me in the forefronte of this Article set downe, and throughly loke vppon the *Therefore*, which he in stead of a conclusion laboureth to inferre, shall sée his argument briefly knitte together after this sorte.

Those which preache this or that doctrine are vngodded and vnregenerate. Therefore the doctrine it selfe is vntrue.

The reason framed Schoolewise is this.

1. Exhort. cap. 16 sent. 16. fol. 34. — *What soeuer the vngodded and vnregenerated man doth bryng forth, institute, preach and teach, is vntrue. But the Godded or vnregenerate mã teacheth there is * a Resurrection of the body, imperfection in the best workes of the godly, and that heretiques must be put to death. &c.*

* This perticuler standeth for any generall propositiõ though HN. expoundyng the. 1. Cor. 15. vers. 53. sayth that it is not ment of any creature of earthlyineshe and bloud. Docum. sent. cap. 6. sent. 3. fol. 13. b. linc. 15.

1. Exho. cap. 16. sent. 17. pag. 2. lin. 5 — *Therfore it is assuredly all false and lyes & seducyng and deceitfull what soeuer. &c.*

The reason, is framed out of *HN.* his owne wordes, the which is both mere *Anabaptisticall*, and also flat *Donati-* (Bullin. 3. booke)

nati-

natisticall by *Fulgentius* obiected vnto S. Augustine, *My Church is spotles, therfore the true Church*, sayth the *Donatist*, to the which S. Augustin aũswered. Who can bring, any cleane thyng out of filthynes? Because that as long as the Church is visible, in doctrine and lyfe euery part therof is attainted with ẏ dregges of imperfection. But the Donatist vrgeth Agge.2.cap.b.13. for proofe. S. August. aunswereth: Shew me where Agge departed from the middest of that people least he should be defiled amõgest them. And a litle after in ẏ same place followeth. We must depart from the company of the wicked with our myndes, not our fleshe: with our workes, not with our bodyes. Communicate not sayth S. Paule with the vnfruiteful workes of darknes, he forbiddeth them their workes, not their exercises in Religion, not their Sacramentes.

3.chap. D. August. contra Fulgentium Donatist. Iob.14.4.

Ephes.5.

And in an other place most playnly to the point we haue in hand, he sayth. No maruaile it is if good wordes which are vttered for the people by the Byshop in prayers are heard, for it is not because of waywardnes of the Prelate, but for the deuotion of the people.

August. agaynst the letters of Parmenianus.2. booke.8.chap.

And as learnedly so truly sayth Nazienzen, euen as the printed forme that is engrauen in any mettall, be it lead, or yron, brasse or gold, the thyng imprinted is still the same, and is not empayred by the basenes of the mettall: but alwayes it retaineth one fourme: and as a sealed letter is not preiudiced by him that doth deliuer it, if it be deliuered in such order as he receiueth it: so the message and proclamatiõ of Gods truth is alwayes the same to them, that heare it, what soeuer he be that vtter it, neither is the excellency of ẏ thyng adnihilated by ẏ wickednes of the person. For it were an incredible thyng that ẏ abuse of any thyng should make ẏ thyng it selfe to cease to be, and the holy & diuine Ministry of the Lordes word & Sacramentes, as first it was by him instituted, so therfore is it the more glorious, both for his sake that first founded it, as also for our sakes, and the safety of soules,

Exod.3.10. Ierem.1.10. Esay.6.9. Amos.7.15. Math.18.18.

whom the Lord in that behalfe hath most graciously prouided for. So that wee must beware that we defile not the Lordes Testament by our wantonnes, nor carelesly contemne the ordinaunce of the Lord by our misdemeanour: for he that thought in his secret counsaile these to be the fittest way for our welfare, if we shall make accompt of it, as worldlynges do, as of some common trifle or meane benefite, or with HN. rend them that deliuer the Lordes pearles vnto vs, albeit they come, but in earthen and trœ vessels, yet shall he inuent in his iustice such a plague to scourge vs with, that both as many as heare it their eares shall tingle at it, neither shall ÿ starre therof be forgotten of all posteritie.

Exod.20.12. Galath.4.19. 1.Sam.8.7. 2.King.1.11. & 2.23.

As for many that stumble at Christ, for because they know him not, or happlesly contemne him, because the day starre as yet is not risen in them, or thinke but basely of his bride, because she is but browne of coullor, yet they must know (if allready they haue not learned it) that the corne must not be contemned, because it lyeth hidden in the chaffe, that net must not be neglected for the fish that is vnprofitable, the great house must not be slaundered, because there are in it vessels of dishonour, the ayre not to be refused, nor the sunne thought lightly of, because the wicked, and the godly doe equally enioy them. Diuers Churches haue bene the Lordes swœte shœpfoldes, and yet haue had their wantes, and he that will leaue the company of the godly, because of the wicked & would goe out of the world for the wickednes thereof, must tary yet a while that hee may haue his way streightned, agaynst the tyme that the Lord shall come to call hym.

Cant.1.4. Math.3.12. Math.13.48. 2.Tim.2.20. 1.Corin.2.2. Galath.1.2. Ephe.11. Apoc.2. The Church there spotted in euery chapter. 1.Corin. Gal.3.1. Apoc.2.6. Apoc.14.15.

Euen as HN. in the former 3. Sections with great disdayne and despite hath slaundered the Preachers, in affirmyng that they could not preach the truth because they are not regenerate, wherein first he vttered an egregious vntruth agaynst their lyfe, secondly agaynst their doctrine: so in the 4. Sentence, or Section, he preuenteth an an obiectiõ that may be made by vs concernyng the thing that is preached, which he in playne wordes affirmeth to be but the outward letter, and therfore otherwhere he calleth vs *Doctours of the letter.* The witnes wherby he thinketh to conuince vs and to proue the allegation to be true, is taken out of Jeremy, and it is the slaunder, wherwith the Prophet was reproched by that people: for they termed his doctrine, which he did deliuer vnto them from the Lord, *a doctrine of wynde. &c.* the which their slaunder the Lord threatneth in that place shall be mightly recompenced by the Babylonians. As then Jeremy was slaundered by thẽ whom he calleth an adulterous people. vers. 7.8, so doth *HN.* slaunder the Gospell preached in these dayes without his Familie termyng it *a letter*, so that herein he notably sheweth him selfe to be a shameles railer, vsing euen the same accusation agaynst vs now, that was vsed agaynst the Prophet then. And if the people were scourged with the whippe of bondage then, for vttering this graceles speach, doth HN. and his Familie thinke for renuyng the same slaunder that he shall escape punishment? As for the other places which follow. Jeremy 6. and 8. there is no such thing in them to be found as *HN.* doth dreame of. Ezech. 13. chap. vers. 7.8.9. declareth nothyng, but the shamefull abuse of the word by the false Prophets of Iudæa he calleth their prophecies *vayne and lying visions.* The which if HN. do alledge generally to all Preachers, it is a shameles accusatiõ, and he alledgeth his Scripture without discretion. For whereas he often stumbleth vpon this terme *the vnregenerate Scripture learned*, he that marketh *HN.* well, shall finde that he quoteth most of his places for the phrase and maner of speach onely, and not for any matter or note to be founde in the place by him quoted: so that he whiche blameth other men vnworthely, may herein most worthely be termed *A Doctour of the letter.*

HN. lam. comp. in the title of the boke.

Ierem. 5. 13.

Vers. 15. 16. 17.

Neither is HN. the first that reuileth ỹ Gospell with this his most opprobrious reproch. For he doth but re-

HN. a doctour of the letter.

Hosius de verbo Dei expresso.
Illiricus in norma concilij.
3.booke of the Hierarch.3.cap. leafe. 103. and controuer. de Eccle. 3.
Kemnitius exã. of the Trident counsell.pag. 32
Staphilus Apol. fol.65.b.
Bulling.1. booke chap.3.and 2. booke cap. 4.5.

new the old slaunders, whiche haue by heretiques bene hatched long heretofore. *Hosius* an *Archpapist* vseth the like vnreuerent speach termyng the Scripture *a bare and dead letter*. *Lewes* a Canon of *Lateran* in Rome calleth it *dead ynck*: so doth *Piggius* wretchedly blaspheme, saying: it is, *a nose of wax, a dumbe iudge*. *Eckius* very graceleslly sayth it is but *a blacke Gospell and incken diuinitie*. *Staphilus* sayth it is *a new Idoll, set vp in the hart of man*. *Zwinckfeild* sayd it is but *a bare and dead letter*, not profitable say the *Anabaptistes*, for we are all taught from God. The *Messalians* sayd it was not *necessary neither yet the Sacramentes*: and so sayd the *Familie of Loue*: for in diuers places ye shall see them make small accompt of Sermons, so that some of them, will sit in the streetes in the tyme that the word of God is preached. Yet all these agreeyng amõg them selues, are at iarre with the holy Ghost, who in the whole course of the Scripture, doth singularly commende the hearyng of the word, but especially S.Paule to the Romaines, whiche maketh it the mother of Fayth, whiche fayth is the hand, whereby all the promises of God are apprehended and taken hold of: and without the whiche it is vnpossible to please God. Hebrues. 11. chapter. 6. verse.

Luke.5.1.
Luke.10.39.g. and 15.1.
Math.7.24.d.&. 13.20.c.
Mar.6.20.c.
Rom.10.14.17. c.
1.Tim.3.15.d.
Col.1.6.a.

Much more might be sayd agaynst this horrible heresie, but because euen the repeatyng of it doth strike a horrour and quakyng into the children of God, to thinke how wicked a thyng it is for a mortall man to mislyke that, which the Lord hath ordained as a meanes wherby he will haue the sparkles of his grace continually to to be kyndled in vs, the onely remembraunce shall rest herein, consideryng that the more myer is stirred, the sauour is the noysomer, and hurtefull to those that are standers by.

Article

ARTICLE. 13. of HN. *Of dissemblyng and concealyng Religion.*

HN. Sayth *it is lawfull for one of his Familie to dissemble and conceale his Religion, contrary to his owne doctrine. Euang. cap. 3. sent. 8. & cap. 25. sent. 6. & 1. Exhort. cap. 6. senten. 8.* where he biddeth them *confesse it before all men: amongest the adulterous, and sinfull generation. sent. 1.*

Theophilus.

THe adulterous and sinfull generation of the ignoraunt world, if they repent and turne, may finde mercy, but to the enemyes or enuious of the loue of Christ and to the obstinate which turne thē away therefrom. There is no mercy promised, looke the text.

W. Wilkinson.

T*Heophilus* beyng demaunded of Onions, aunsweareth of Garlike, for the question beyng, whether a man may hide his Religion, beyng demaūded of it, either openly by the Magistrat, or priuatly by his Christiā brother, he aunswereth that there is no mercy without the Familie, which is nothyng to the purpose. Therefore it were to be wished that his wisedome would be ruled by his owne counsell *videl.* looke better on the text. *2. sent.* Theophilus aūswereth not to the poynt.

Theophilus.

HE biddeth them confesse their beliefe among the sinfull generations and false hartes of the Scripture learned. &c. and not to reueile the secretes of God Math. 7. chap. 6. vers. to the bloud thirstie ones, and aduersaries to all truth, whiche lye in wayte to deuoure thē: more then a true man is bound to confesse his treasures to a theefe or a murtherer.

William Wilkinson.

First, I will aunswere vnto HN. his Article, and secondly to *Theophilus* Exposition.

Concernyng the certaintie of this Article, our Famblers will in no wise admit the same, albeit *Theophilus* in this place acknowledge it to be true. So that diuers that are sayd to be *welwillers* that way haue (being openly called to accompt before a Magistrate) set downe their hādes in a certaine schedule, the copy wherof I haue, wherein they affirme it altogether vnlawfull to speake one thyng with the mouth, and thinke the contrary with the hart. So that herein they and their Prophet *HN*. are at variaunce, for he as is before declared to auoyde trouble willeth them to conceale their fayth, as also *Theophilus* proueth by his thæuish similitude.

This I know to to be true by the report of a worshipfull freind in Cambridge that whereas one Allen a weauer being committed for the opinions of the Fami. and HN. he contrary to his promise made departed and fled away, and being afterwardes mette by a iustice of peace which knew him by sight, asked him his name, and he sayd his name wrs Allen, the iustice demaunded if he had about him no bookes of HN. he aunswered, no, the Iustice alighting from his horse searched him, and found diuers bokes about him. Now let the Famlers, and Allen himselfe confesse whether that herein he did dissemble or not, and whether by HN. his doctrine that art of his was lawful. I could by many liuing witneses proue this to be true, and shew wherein diuers of them haue dissembled, but I cease. And least the Familye should affirme that they are slaundered in this Article, *HN*. his owne wordes shall speake for himselfe after this sorte.

Famblers dissemble.

11.Epist.cap.6. sent.3.gag.24. lin.3.

Shew not your selues in any wise bare before the enemies: let them not see you: be now by them, whilest that the wicked world beareth rule, euen as though ye were dead and were not, and had no speach in your mouth. Psal,38.b.vers.13.and

walke

walke euē so as inuisiblie and vnknowen before all such as are without the Familie of Loue, and make manifest themselues as enemies there agaynst: as also before them that turne thē away therefrom. And in his documentall sentence HN. exhorteth his Fami. to the same thing, in the same wordes. *Thus haue not much prate or disputation with the straungers, or with them that fall away from the seruice of Loue, nor with the vnwilling ones and resisters.* Docum. sent. cap. 16. sent. 18. fol. 40. a.

The which places being throughly waied, no man can be ignorant that HN. geueth leaue to his Familie to dissemble, if to dissemble be as Salust doth define it *Aliud in linqua aliud in pectore clausum habere*: that is to haue one thing in the tongue, and another in the thought. But the profe of the truth of this Article, I leaue to the commen practise of the Fami, and to the knowledge of those men that haue had to deale with them concerning their Louely doctrine: albeit I must and will confesse, that I haue mette with a few which haue delt more playnely herein then they are commenly wonte to doe: wherein I doe geue them some better lyking in that they deale truely. To dissemble what it is.

Now if any man be desirous, to vnderstand further of this heresie, let him reade the excellent learned man, M. Lambert Daneus in his comentaries vpon S. Augustine, *de heresibus ad Quod vult Deum*, where the same is learnedly handled and art large, who reporteth among all the opinions of the Priscilianistes this was not the least that they held, a man must not open the secresie of their sect as appeareth by this verse. Eusebius historie. lib. 4. cap. 7. cap. 70.

Iura perinra secretum prodere noli:

Swere and forswere hid thinges doe not declare.

Of this heretique did that monster of mankinde and wild heretick Dauid George learne this opinion, of whome somewhat is sayd before, and of him it is very like to be true that HN. learned it, as he did diuers other pointes of this his louely doctrine, and from HN. his filthy pit drew Vitels that poysoned water, wherewith he infected diuers honest and godly men in the trouble-

Familie may be presēt at Masse.

some tyme of Q. Marye by perswading them that they might keepe their consciences to themselues, and be presēt at the masse, and other idolatours seruice, agaynst the which vngodly opinion, that excellent Christiā and blessed Martyr of God M. Bradford writ being in prison, as in the bookes that he published is to be seene at large. The which blind opinion of *HN.* is most clearely confuted by his owne bookes in the places by me before quoted, as also by the holy scripture in diuers places, which I refraine to set downe for that I will not be tedious, as also desiring the reader to vew these few places by me quoted in the margent for profe sufficient: as also let him reade further of his question. M. Bulleng. agaynst the Anabaptistes 2. boke 5. chapter. But to returne to Theophilus who laboreth to salue this sore and stoppe vp this breach with his headles distinction betwixt the beliefe and the misteries of God: I would that he knew that neither this wound will be cured with this salue, neither this breach stopped vp with this his vntempered head morter: For mightier is the shotte which the Lordes peeces affourd them with so smale a shelter they may be succoured.

M. Bradfordes treatise agaynst goyng to Masse.

Iob. 13. 7.
Dan. 3.
Math. 10. 33.
Mar. 8. 38.
Luke. 9. 26. & 12. 8.
1. Cor. 10. 21.
Ephes. 5. 11.

For whereas he would seeme not to haue spoken at aduentures, but to haue added his aunswere vpon a witty, and sober deliberation, albeit the other his expositions are very fond and fantasticall: yet this his distinction wherein he thought to haue wonne his spurres, is so frantique that therein he hath both ieoperded the horse, and lost the saddle. For whereas in a good and artificiall distinction, neither part can be affirmed of the other: yet in this diuision made by Theophilus both partes are but one, neither is there such difference betwixt them as he would beare vs in hand there is. For where as he insinuateth, that the belief, & misteries or secrets of god, cā not be one thing S. Paule handling that part (the chaunging of our bodyes in the resurrection) the belief, addeth these words *Behold I shew you a secret thing, we shall not all sleepe, but we shal all be chaūged.* Here he knitteth together

1. Cor. 15. 51.

the

the Article of our beliefe & a secret thing makyng thē but one which Theophilus maketh two. And speaking in an other place of the vnion betwixt Christ and his Church, whē 1 halfe especiall partes of the belief consist, straight he addeth This is a great secret: Still coupling thē to one which Theophilus will haue twayne. Ephes.5.32.

But whereas Theophilus his déepe iudgement alloweth that he will not haue the secrets of God reueiled to the enimies, he dealeth with vs euen as he doth with his owne fellow Famblers: for he doth not deliuer vnto them all the secrets of God, but the beliefe onely at the first wherein he discrieth himselfe at vnawares to be one of those of whome it is sayd by M. Caluine the chiefe and Rabbies doe alwayes keepe backe some point of theyr principall doctrine, that they may the better maintaine the opinion that their hangbies haue of thē. This also is the iudgement of Staphilus in his Appollogie, that he would haue the word God which is the bread of the soules of Gods people to be cut out and deliuered vnto them by péecemeale. Caluin agaynst the Libertines. Fol.76.&.77.

The scripture that Theophilus citeth to strengthen his assertion is the same that the Anabaptistes alleadged to the same purpose, being writtē in S. Math.cap.7.v.6. Geue not that which is holy vnto dogges, neither cast your pearles before swine. By dogges in scripture are ment those that are not conteined within the hedges of the church. Math.15.26.c. and open enemies which of set purpose persecute a knowne & manifest truth, which as yet Theophilus hath not proued ẏ doctrine of his Familie to be: And by swine are ment those that being once washed returne eftsones to their filth agayne, and making no accompt of the Lordes truth, become more beastly in lyfe, then they were before. 2.Pet.2.22. Pro.26. 11.b. the which place also of S. Math. before alleadged may thus be vnderstode that the word of God ought not to be preached vnto them which sinne agaynst the holy ghost. Heb.6.4.& 10.26. For that their sinne is so great Bulling.6. book cap.8.fol.227.a. &.cap.9.fol.229 Dogs in Scripture who. Swine who.

in the sight of God that is not to be prayed for. 1.John.5.16. of the which sinnes if Theophi: will say they are guiltye which withstand *HN.* his Fam. I desire him that he iude not neither to hastely pronounce the sentence til we haue hard the euidence red whereby he would that verdict should be gathered, which shall passe agaynst vs.

Furthermore whereas Theophili by the way of blinde similitude gathereth that those which seeke to suppres this their scismaticall secte are theeues by the high way, and therfore ought not the treasure of Gods word to be opened vnto them, I answere, that this reason is not so much to be confuted with wordes, as with whips, was it euer had, or being heard, was it euer suffered, ẏ Christian magistrates, into whose hands the sword of iustice is committed, that they should cut downe such weedes as trouble the growth of good trees in gods vineyard, and preachers which haue the sword of the spirite to cutt downe schisme, & heresie, was it euer hard that a graceles heretique as this *Theop.* is, durst terme thẽ Theues by the hyway as Theophilus doth in this place? God graunt all magistrates to loke to this betimes, least vnder this counterfeite cloake of Loue, that subiectes be drawne away from the obedience of their lawfull prince, when such rebellious wordes as these be blowne abroad in corners by such heretiques and their fellowes.

ARTICLE. 14. of HN. *Of Libertie to Sinne.*

Cap.13.sent.8. HN. *In a certaine booke of his entituled Dictata per HN. vpon the 22. chapter of Deutronom.vers.27. which sayth if a man rauish a womã, and she cry she shalbe free, the meanyng is sayth HN. when sinne commeth to a man and if he cry to God, and God helpe him not, he is free.*

Theophilus.

NOw forth whether your chosen out Errours may appeare to be in them selues very good and true sayings, sayinges, and your partiall additions to be mere lyes: we referre that to the iudgement of all those which shal read the text with an vnparciall eye. For he doth not say that she that is violently taken. &c. shall be free videl. to commit euill as you would seeme to haue it, but she shall be guiltlesse of the transgression (videl) for beyng condemned for the same.

William Wilkinson.

IN the aunsweryng to this Article *Theophilus* vseth this order. In his first clause he maketh a by speach to the collectour of the Article, in the secōd he setteth downe ẙ meanyng of the same Article. His first note in his speach is this, that they *are my chosen out Articles.* which, I vtterly deny for it followeth not *I chose out these Articles or errours* out of HN. to be resolued of the meanyng of them by the Fami. or some of that broode as time should serue, therfore these Articles are myne, this is a reason beyond all reason: that they are of my chosing out of HN. is truth, but that they are my Articles, that is vntrue for they are as I made the title in the inscriptiō of my Articles, which I deliuered to the Familie, *Errours out of the bookes of HN.* Agayne if they be true Articles and onely *my additions vnto them* be false, how cōmeth it to passe that *Theophilus* in his notes vpon my title afore the Articles where I say that they are *faythfully and truly gathered* there he aunswereth they are *vnfaythfully, lyingly, slaunderously, maliciously or vncharitably gathered?* But let it be that HN. sayth truth, as for *my additions*, whiche he mentioneth I deny that I haue added any one word, to the text of HN. whereby it might either be empared, or his meaning and sence peruerted, and herein I referre the whole determination therof, to him which shall peruse this my labour with an *vnparciall eye.* The place whereon I gathered the Articles is this.

But if they (videl. our old sinnes and paramoures which we loued: sent. 17.) take or lay hold on vs with force and violence Docum. sentences cap. 13. sent. 18. fol. 26. a.

that thē although we cry, there cōmeth not any power nor help vnto vs, for to withstand them in their force and violence: and euen so rauish vs agaynst our will, so are we giltles of the transgressing, for we haue cryed to be released from the Tyrāny of the euill, and there is no helpe come vnto vs. Of which guiltles transgressing, the law likewise witnesseth, where it sayth: a womā which is violently taken in the field, whereas there is not any helpe, and so rauished (and although she cry aloude yet gottē no helpe) she shalbe giltles of the trāsgressing.

HN. maketh an Allegóry of the Grammaticall senten. of the Scripture. Deut. 22. d.

Now the proposition, which *Theophilus* gathered vpō these wordes of *HN.* is this, *When we cry &c. and haue no helpe we shall be free from that transgression for beyng condēned for it.* The which interpretatiō of his is vtterly vntrue, for God is not bound by duety to geue ought to any man: his giftes are of his *mercy*, not of our *merite*. So y^t albeit being prayd vnto he yeld not vnto our requestes at the first, yet is not his withholdyng of his grace a sufficient warrant to geue vs libertie to offend. For who shall wryng from the Lord that whiche he will not geue, or if presently he doe not enable vs to resist and preuayle agaynst sinne, who (I say) shall accuse God to be accessary vnto our sinnes, as *HN.* and his *Scholler Theophilus* in this place flatly affirme. And be it true, as it is most true, that Christ sayd vnto his Apostles: Aske, and it shalbe giuen you: seeke, and ye shall finde: knocke, and it shalbe opened vnto you. &c. and S. Iames sayth, The prayer of a righteous man auayleth much if it be feruent, yet because our prayers are not so perfect, no not in the iust man as they ought to be, therfore cōmeth it to passe that we obtaine not at Gods hand because we aske amisse: neither did Christ obtaine at his fathers hād that the cup of his death might passe from him, for that it was not so agreable with Gods will, nor expedient for the accomplishyng of our saluation. So that when we accomplish not the cōdition in our prayers that God hath prescribed in his word, we are not to bynde or charge God with his promise, for that he knoweth better what to geue vs, thē

Math. 7. 7.
Iam. 5. 16.
Iam. 4. 3.
Math. 26. cap. vers. 39. 42.

we

we know what, or how to aske of him.

So that now we see that it is but a vayne kyndnes, which *Theophilus* in this place threapeth on God, when as either hee will haue God to bow vnto him at euery becke, or els by and by he will make him the authour of sinne. For what is this that *Theophilus* doth els burthen him withall: that if we pray & not helpe come, thẽ are we guiltles of the transgression. But to accuse God to be accessory to our misbehauiour, which thyng be far frõ him. Now if *Theophilus* cã not comprehẽd this, what, is it not truth, because he can not conceiue it? Gods iudgementes are alwayes true and iust, though often secret, and those thynges whiche we vnderstand not at the first, let vs rather reuerence and worshyp them then wonder at them. God when he leaueth vs to our selues and punisheth one sinne with an other, doth that most righteously in him selfe, that sinfull flesh doth see no reason in. Shall the pot reason with the potter, because he made him not a vessell vnto honor? shall the axe extoll it selfe agaynst him that Ierem. 18. heweth therewith? may God make his creatures as seemeth best to his singular wisedome, and shall he not dispose them as he will, when he hath created them? God geueth his children pardon in his mercy, yet he that flyeth to his mercy, not first fully hauing satisfied his iustice deceaueth his owne soule ere he be aware. So that when any man shall presume vpon repentaunce & fall in hope to rise, true it is he that hath promised pardon vpõ repẽtaunce, hath not promised that we shall liue till to morrow, that we may haue leysure to repẽt, he that is not fit to day, the Lord knoweth how fit he wilbe to morrow.

Now it is also most assuredly true that albeit God in respect of him selfe, for Christes sake, doth freely forgeue both the fault and the punishment, yet because he will not haue men dally with his iustice, vpon the opẽ sinnes of the godly committed before men, hee taketh open punishment least the enemy should haue a cause to rayle. This is manifest by kyng Dauids example, he sinned o-

penly in the sight of God and before Israell, God freely forgaue him both the punishment, and the fault: yet before men because the enemyes of God had openly a cause to blaspheme, therfore the Lord toke away the child that was borne in adultery. Furthermore when he numbred
2.Sam.24.10. the people, and had continued in the same sinne, without any notable repentaunce 9. monethes and 20. dayes, after albeit he prayed hartly, yet was his sinne punished by a great and seuere scourge, as is manifestly to be sene in the place of that History. By which places it is to be understode that we ought not to offend in hope of pardon, neither that God is faultie, who will not boullster vs in our faultes nor so easly be satisfied in his iustice as we imagine of.

But if *Theophilus* déeme that herein he is not fully satisfied, for that this question is of him that prayeth before sinne committed, and both these examples are not sufficiently playne, I further aunswere him, that before *Iudas*
Math.9.4.5. honge him selfe, he was sory and made a shewe of outward repentaunce as by his restitution may easly be perceiued: yet God stayed him not here, but because hee should be a notable spectacle of Gods vengeaũce to them that were then vnborne, that no man be so hardy to sinne agaynst his conscience: he ranne so farre that he caste himselfe willingly and wittyngly away, and yet albeit God did not bow to heare him nor vouchsafe him pardõ, will *Theophilus* say that he is giltles, for beyng condemned for that transgression?

So may it be sayd of *Caine*: before he committed that
Gen.4.v.6. horrible murther the Lord did not onely frowne vppon him, but gaue him likewise a watchword that if he stayd not his furie there was a punishment prepared for him, and the continuall torment of conscience should not departe from him. Dare *Theophilus* affirme that now seyng the Lord stayd not his hand from heauen in the slaying of his brother, is God therefore guiltie of that murther as well as *Caine*? because the tongues of them that teach

false

false doctrine, are not rent out of the mouthes of heretiques, and those that defile the Lordes Priesthode are not plagued, is God not iust? yes, *Theophilus* God will recompence the slownes of his punishment with the waight therof, our God shall come, and not stay for euer, looke you therfore before hand to your standyng, that ye be not cast out of the holy Citie, and haue your part with those that wepe eternally. And thus much to your Articles and aunsweres.

Nehem. 6. 14. & 13. ver. 29. 30.

Psal. 50. 3. Apoc. 21. 27. & 22. 15.

The summe of the opinions of cercertaine Libertines.

1 FIrst they affirme, that the preaching of the word is not the ordinarye meanes to come to the knowledge of the worde, but by reason.

2 Secōdly, that no man which is faulty himselfe can preach the truth to others.

3 Those preachers which doe take in hand to preach the word of God before man be regenerate, doe take the office of the holy Ghost out of his hand.

4 Those that be doctors and learned, can not preach the word truely, their reason is, because, Christ sayth, it is hidden from the wise and prudēt and is reueiled to sucklinges and babes.

5 There is no deuill, but suche as the painters make.

6 They which haue the spirite of God know all thinges.

7 That we ought not to geue our almes to beggers: for that they liue in the consumablenes, and that there was no begger in Israell.

8 Mariage is a ſacrament, and wonderfull ſpeculation.

9 That there were miſteries and great ſpeculations in the Maſſe if they could be attained vnto, and that it was a God ſeruice.

10 Alſo, the ſeruice that we haue taken for a gods ſeruice is not ſo, and in ſo taking it, both they, and we are deceiued.

11 That Adam did not ſinne at all, their reaſon is, Adam did not ſinne, but the woman.

12 There is no man Gods childe, but he that can ſhew his Pedigrue.

13 The martyrs in Q. Maryes dayes ought not ſo to haue died: for in ſo dying they diſtroyed the temples of God.

14 That whoſoeuer hath Gods Spirite can not ſinne, and that the Prophet Dauid did not ſinne after that tyme he had receiued the holy Ghoſt.

15 That a man ought not to wearie his bodye in trauaile, and labour. For ſay they the holy ghoſt will not tarye in a body that is wearie and yrkſame.

16 Where there is any contention, there is not the ſpirite of God: for ſay they the ſpirite is not deuided.

17 That the witch, which rayſed vp the deuill in the lykenes of Samuell, was no witch, but the wiſedome of God, and the ſpirit that ſhe rayſed vp was Samuell himſelfe.

18 That Adam was the ſonne of God, otherwiſe then by creation.

19 That there be many bookes beſides the Bible which Eſdras ſpeaketh of, ſhould be reuealed, and

come abroad before the end.

20 That the Bible is not the word of God, but a signification thereof, and that the Bible is but ynk and paper, but the word of God is spirite and lyfe.

21 That they may not speake the truth bouldly and openly because the truth will not be heard.

22 That there are Some which now are liuing which doe fulfill the Law in all pointes.

William Wilkinson.

ALbeit there be diuers of these *Articles* which I haue not read expressiuely in their bookes, yet haue they ben confessed by them in conference as it may be proued by the testimonye of thē which haue talked with them, vnto the which Articles exhibited at the same time with the former of *HN.* Theophilus aunswereth in maner as followeth.

Theophilus.

NOw forth for your conclusion that you make vpō the 22.forged articles, which you terme the opiniōs of the Libertines, and you would faine father thē on the Family of Loue, vpon the testimony of some priuate conference, had by some of that company (as you say) with such as are as ready as your selfe for to maintayne their lye, and yet shame not therein: Therfore it is briefly sayd: whatsoeuer accordeth not with the scriptures of God, therein that same may well be the opinion of the Libertines. (Whose God is their bellie, whose glory is their shame, and rest worldly minded. Which also with vncircumcised, and vnrenewed spightfull minded hartes, and all euill dedednes, as in contempt of his word, persecuting of his chosen, following of the fleshly lustes, forsaking of his crosse,

Theophilus aunswere to the former Articles.
1. Vntruth for they are not forged.
2. Vntruth for I would not faine father them.
3. Theoph. common eloquence.
Theophilus description of a Libertine fitly agreeth to him selfe.

seeking all ease in the flesh, by lying and slaundering of his worde and his chosen flock, doe seeke to honour the God of lyfe in maintayning of the contrary nature, the kingdome of Gods aduersary the deuill, to serue and worship, the Christ of the same God by maintayning of the lyfe of Antichrist. To reuerence his holy spirite by the vpholding of the Belialish spirite of Antechrist: but surely none of the right professours of the Loue, can in any wise maintayne any such errors as some of them be. **Therefore in some point Theophilus is a Libertine, and so is the Fam. also.**

Many wordes to no purpose.

That is of sinne for the Fam. say that sinnes onely is Antechrist.

4. Theoph. confesseth he houldeth some of the Libertines opiniōs yet dare he not say which

And by the way it is much to be maruailed at, that any such which take vpon them to professe the Christianitye can with such vehemencie contemne the loue of God and her louely ministration, whilest that all the Scripture enfouldeth all good, and the some of all what God and Christ requireth in his word therein. Vnles it were to be graunted that the enviers thereof are vtterly ignoraunt in that which they professe.

5. Vntruth for the loue of god is not in HN. his Fam.

6. Vntruth all that Gods word requireth is not fulfilled in HN. his Fam.

Therfore let this professed Loue vowed by the Familye of Loue, be proued a false and counterfaite Loue, by some euil fruites or deedes, that are in testimonye of truth, and meekenes, and not by lye and arrogancye: And eke by the rule of Scripture to breake forth and be gathered thereout, or els if better may be found to be proued by lyke effect, let it in peace be allowed to dwell by, and with you: Least ye procure by sucha continuall inueying agaynst God his righteousnes, God his seuere wrath and indignation to fall without remedie ouer you.

7. Theop. 1. reason whereby he proueth his Fam. the true Church.

8. Theop. 2. reason Scripture must iudge

9. Vntruth god nor his righteousnes are not in HN. his Familye.

For it is all in vaine to kick agaynst the pricke, or striue agaynst the Lord, for if it be out of the flesh and bloud it will surely goe vnder, or faile and spare you much labour, but being done by the finger of God small will be your preuailing, and much lesse your reward. &c.

10. Theop. 3. reason. Gamaliels coūsell abused by the Familye.

This

W. Wilkinson.

This whole speach of Theophilus may for orders sake be reduced into these two partes: the first conteineth his aunswere to the 22. Articles of the Libertines, where after his manner he is very eloquent in heaping up phrases to what end he wotteth best: if it be to describe a Libertine he did very unwisely in that for breuityes sake he referred us not to the 1. Epistle of the Fami. written to M. Rogers. pag. 73. b. lin. 15. where very artificially he defineth a Libertine in few wordes after this sort. *He that knoweth not the doctrine of* HN. *is a fre one, or Libertine*, thus if he had done in few wordes, thē should his wit and his wordes haue ben equal, whereas now running the furthest way about, it may be verified of him that was sayd in the lyke case of a person not far unlyke Theophilus, *satis loquentiæ, sapiētiæ parum*, many wordes but small wisedome. And thus much wt the notes in the margēt unto ye first part of his diuisiō. | A Libertine briefly defined by the Fam. | Salust of Cateline.

Theophi. first reason to approue that the doctrine of *HN.* is a true doctrine is taken from the effect thus, *The effect is good. Therefore the efficient*, in the which argumēt drawne from that profe it is failed when that is put for the effect which is not the effect, as thus, *The knowledge of the scripture is cause of heresie, Ergo, it is not good that scripture should be knowne. Agayne, The reading the histories of Lots incest, and drunkennes, of Lia, and Rachell, the wiues of Iacob, of Iudas and Thamar, &c. be euell examples and yet to be read in the olde Testament, Ergo, to read in the ould Testament is unlawfull for hurting of honestye.* | Theop. first reason aunswered. | HN. Fault not the cause put for the cause. | Gene. 19. Gene. 38.

This Argument is false from the effect for it putteth the reading of the Scripture to be ye cause of whoredome, whereas that is not such a cause, as *Staphilus* dreameth of, so that herein then ye see the fault of this Argument, wherein it ceasseth to be so strong as HN. would haue it. *Theophilus* reasoneth thus, the effect of the doctrine of the Familie is good, therfore the doctrine it selfe. To this I | HN. his doctrine not cause of godly lyfe. | Staphilus Apologic. fol. 76. a. lin. 22.

aunswere that *Theophilus* supposeth that whereas diuers liue honestly in the *Familie*, that is brought to passe by HN. his doctrine, that is to be denyed, for whereas they now liue an honest vpright and Christian life, this they learned of the preachyng of the Gospell, before euer they were infected with HN. his heresie, so that thereby they rather bewtifie it then are bewtified by it. And for proofe hereof it is manifestly apparaunt that the younger nouices mẽ be in HN. his hereticall doctrine, the honester they are in life and conuersation, but when they leaue once their *singlemyndednes and grow vp to the manly oldnes in the Loue, and come as they thinke nearer to the perfection of the vpright beyng*, then the wicked spirite beginneth to Lord ouer them, and sinne to haue a liuyng and dayly shape in them. So that ẏ deeper they wade in this mighty streame of ẏ louely ministration & the nearer they come to ẏ hiest pitch of being altogether Godded with the nature of their new foũd Idoll, which in stede of the true God they haue set vp vnto them, the greater rule and sway doth the wicked nature of sinne beare in them.

The preachyng of the worde, cause of godly lyfe.

The nouices in the Fam. more honest in lyfe, then the illuminate Elders.

And why so? truly because that in their childish yongnes of the loue the worde of the Lord, is of some credite with them. So that thereby they are bridled from sinnyng, but when they shall leaue that candle and light vpon false lightes as the perfect do, when they come toward this perfectnesse then their lyues are euery day more vngodly then other.

The leauyng of Gods word is the cause of all sinne.

Cap. 3. sent. 12.

That this is true in *HN.* his *Dictatis*, or *Documentall sentences* is manifest where he sayth. *As long as the beleuers of the word are yet young or childish in the procreation of the seede of the promise, that becõmeth borne in them out of the belief of the world. And are not yet growẽ vp to the Elderdome of the perfect beyng Ephes. 4. b. of the word (which is the appointed tyme of the father ouer all beleuers of the world) so stand they yet (although they beleue) vnder the ordinaũce of the Lord or his word, not therfore that they should alwayes remaine as subiect there vnder. But vnto the appointed*

Christ borne in the Fam. vpon the young ones.

ted tyme, to wit, till vnto the manly old age in the godly vnderstandyng of the holy word, as there is sayd, that is, till that the Sinnes be subdued. &c. The which wordes of HN. as they haue bene the rote of all *Anabaptistrie* and *Libertinisme*, (For that these sectaries haue boasted they could not sinne in their perfection, and therfore neded neither the word nor the Sacramentes) so doe they playnly confirme that, whereunto I haue alledged them *videl. So long men liue vpright as the doctrine of HN. is not knowen vnto them, and that HN. his Elders are more corrupt in lyfe then the simplest in the Familie.* The Disciples of the Fam. not alwayes subiect to Gods word sayth HN.

Secondly it is offended in this Argument, because it is drawne from the second table of the Cōmaundements vnto ẏ first, that *he liueth honestly before men therfore he is good in Religiō before God.* Whereas the reason should be cleane otherwise frō the first table vnto the second, & this is an vsuall maner in Scripture, wherby the holy Ghost laboureth to discry an hypocrite. In Esay the holy Ghost reasoneth thus, Ye secke me dayly and will know my wayes euē as a nation that did righteously and had not forsaken the statutes of their God: they aske of me ordinaunces of iustice, they will draw neare vnto their God, saying: wherefore haue we fasted, and thou seest it not? we haue punished our selues and thou regardest it not? Thus they reason as the *Familie* do, we fast &c. *Ergo*, we are Religious and godly men: but God turneth the Argument cleane otherwise thus. Ye are oppressours. vers. 34. ye are vnmercyfull to the poore, vers. 7. ye are oppressours. vers. 3.4. ye are vnmercyfull to the poore, vers. 7. ye are extortioners and ingraters. vers. 6. Therfore are not honest men in Religion neither feare God aright. The selfe same reason is vsed by S. Iames to reproue the dispersed Iewes which boasted of their vpright Religiō, they are proued to be hipocrites and dissemblers before God from the same table as before. Religiō not proued frō the secōd table to the first. Esay. 58. 2.

You refrayne your toungues but deceiue your owne hartes, therfore your Religion is in vayne. Iam. 1. 26.

And agayne. Ye visite not the fatherles and widowes in aduersitie. Therfore your Religiō is not pure and vndefiled before God.

And thus still we sée that the *Familie* reasoneth not aright for that they frame their Argument amisse: as also doth *Theophilus* in this place. But this is not *Theophilus* reasō in this place alone, but in ỷ *Brief rehearsall* ỷ same is likewise vsed as an inuincible Argument to proue the professed Religion by the *Familie* is the truth, where he likewise argueth thus.

Fam. proue by lyfe before men their religion before God.

The voyce of the countrey where we dwell approueth we are honest before mē: Ergo, *our Religion is good before God.* Where if the voyce of the countrey did iustifie them for honest men, as farre as they know them by trading with them, so farre I will confesse with them, that I know some few of them to be of an honest life, yet this proueth not the doctrine of HN. which they professe to be true, for that I know that some honest men of them in lyfe haue confessed vnto me diuers heresies in Religion. Agayne, it is extreme follie to be iudged by those simple men (amongest whom they liue) that are truly religious: for that some of those whom they desire to haue their Iudges haue no skill in those pointes that the Familie are charged, with all, so that in vayne it were to bring these men beyng blynd in this case to iudge of coullors not being expert in the knowledge of the Scriptures, whiche is the light, whereby these coullors must be sene.

Fam. put them for iudges of religion which haue no skill in religion.

By this then we vnderstand that the *Familie* is not so learned in vsing so vnlearned a reason, as they beare men in hand they are, for that hereby they deceiue the simple in makyng their liues before men to be Argumentes to proue their Religion to be true. For that in Scripture the Pharisies liued very vprightly before men, vsing many glorious ceremonies as washyng of cuppes and beds, &c. and yet Christ called them hypocrites, and sayd often woe be vnto them.

Mark.7.verse.4.
Math.23.v.23.

Math.7.15. Many false Prophetes shall come in sheepes clothing

sayth

sayth Christ and they are rauenyng Wolues within.

Staphilus a Papist handleth this Argument at large in his *Apollogie*, where he also confuteth this Argument of HN. and his *Familiers*: 1. the doctrine may be good sayth he and yet the lyfe euill. Math. 23. and many in the Romish Church liue not Catholiquely. *For they lead their liues clene contrary and repugnant to their owne Canons and Constitutions* (sayth he) 2. the doctrine may be euill and the lyfe good. Math. 7. beware of false Prophetes. Yea, heretiques are of great vertue in apparaunce as he proueth by sondry examples: So that sayth *Staphilus* the lyfe both must be iudged to be true by the doctrine, as also the doctrine by the lyfe both must agrée together, therfore it is not inough vnlesse both trée and frute be good. And our Sauiour sayth, that his workes therfore ought to be beleued, because the doctrine & the lyfe in him went ioyntly together. And to this purpose very fitly sayth he out of S. Augustin: The Argument that proueth mens doctrine by their lyfe is false.

Fol. 37. a.

Papistes liues most contrary to their owne lawes.

Fol. 38. a.

Math. 12.

Iohn. 10.

Staph. fol. 35. b. August. de vnitate Ecclesiæ.

Thus in the iudgement of the *Families* best frendes (the *Papistes* whom they magnifie so much) this their Argument is not true.

Furthermore as it is vnreasonable to finde fault with good séede, because it is sowed by an euill husbandman, so is not therfore euill séede the better to be liked of, because that a good husbandman, shall haue euill seruauntes that sowe it. Very aptly therfore sayth Origen concernyng this matter In myne opinion (sayth he) an Heretique of good lyfe, is much more hurtfull and hath more authoritie in his wordes, then he that doth discredit his doctrine with his lyfe: therfore must we take heede of heretiques which seeme to be of godly conuersation. God graunt all his children may be ruled by the ghostly counsell of this godly and learned father.

Origen. in 16. cap. of Ezech.

To all the which that hetherto hath ben sayd cōcerning this matter, if the Famblers will obiect: that euery man doth defend and maintayne that he lyketh best, and that here I shew my selfe a proctour of sinne as oftentimes they obiect, to this I aunswere that this obiection is *HN.* and Anabaptisticall, neuerthelesse I lyke not to smother sinnes or to boulster vp impietye in any person whatsoeuer: & albeit this accusatiō in some part be true, that many which professe thēselues to be Gospellers, & can talke gloriously of religion and regeneration, haue little list to lyue thereafter: abusing the pretence of the Gospell as a stalking horse to leuell at others by, therefore I counsaile that no man be accompted an honest man in religion what countenaunce soeuer he would beare, vnlesse he in lyfe expresse that in outward dealings which his tongue so often runneth of: so that to walke after, not to talke of the Gospell doth make a Protestant and a gospeller, otherwise when God shall in iudgement plucke of our Lyons skinnes, we shall be openly séene who we are to our owne shame and confusion.

A true Protestant who.

Neither are the Papistes to boast that the gospellers is but a schisme from the Romish Church, for otherwise it would yeald other fruites: I aunswere, that no land albeit sowen with neuer so good wheat bringeth out onely wheat but sometymes wéedes also. And as for the Church of Antechrist (the Romish harlot I meane) Staphilus in his Apologie shall tell her tale, and M. Harding which defendeth her open whoredome and commen stewes shall beare him witnes, that though some gospellers sinne, yet many Papistes sinck in impietye, and thus much for Theop. first reason.

Staphilus fol. 37. 38. Byshop of Salisb. in the Apolog. pag. 409. 410. 411.

Vnto Theop. secōd reason conteining a request concerning an vpright arbiter in this matter, as it is very equal (*vz. That his doctrine and the heresie of HN. be tried by the rule of Scripture,*) so do I in this behalfe thereto most willingly consent and agrée, wherein also I haue, as I am able, satisfied his request: wholy herein aunswering him as S. Augustine in the lyke case aunswered *Donatus a man in doctrine* not vnlike to Theophilus. Whether they hould the truth or no, let them shew me none o-

Theoph. second reason aunswered.

De vnitate Ecclesiæ.

therwise

therwise but by the canonical books of holy scripture.

And good reason it is that euery mã be heard by him to whome he doth make his appeale, seing therfore he hath appeald to the *Scripture, to the Scripture shall he go.* Wherin also I promes him very trulye that I am rather desirous of the defending the truth, then to contend with him in oppugning his errour. In the confirmation wherof, if he shall deale soundly, and set downe chapter and verse for his profe, I will as fully satisfie him as I am able, being euer ready to performe either priuately, or openly that which in priuate letters I long since did offer him: wherein also if at any tyme or in any matter I shall by him be thought not rightly to haue conceaued his meaning if by any meanes I shall haue intelligence thereof: and if he shall vouchsafe to deale by any reasonable profe, I offer my selfe to doe nothing out of euill will, being as ready to confesse mine ouersightes, as he shall be able to conuince me of them, onely mine earnest desire out of harty loue is if hee meane to deale heareafter with me any further, that he keepe him to the true gramaticall sence of scripture, expounding the same according to the proportion of fayth: this if he doe I shall be hartely glad: otherwise if he doe, in quoting scripture for the phrase, and in Allegorizing the text depraue the sence thereof: I promise him lykewise that hereafter I will not further medle with him or his: for I like not to spend good leasure (wherof I haue not such plenty) that in speaking in the ayre, I both may mispend my tyme, and abuse the reader with emptines.

The last and least reason whereby Theoph. would proue that no man ought to deale agaynst the Fam. is taken from the counsell of Gamaliell in the Actes of the Apostles. This reason is as it were by common consent receiued and alledged by all those that are any thing at all sene in the Fam. euer in their mouthes if it be of God it will stand &c. The which reason the Anabaptistes vsed very often, and is (by a learned expositor termed) *a rea-*

Theoph. thyrd reason aunswered.
Actes.5.38.39.

Fam. cõmon reason why they ought not to be spoken agaynst.
Caluin9 in Act.

son not fit for any man of wisedome.

First concerning Gamaliels wordes that they are not alwayes to be taken for a law, it is manifest: neither are they a right rule or conteine a generall doctrine, how at all tymes false teachers are to be delt withall (neither were the holy Apostles false teachers, as Theophilus comparison doth afford) but he onely upon that present occasion because of that imminent perill that hangeth ouer the heads of the Appostles at that instant, vttered that speach as a worldly wise and politique man, to stay the fury of the priestes, and set free the Apostles in so great a daunger. Wherefore he that shall stretch Gamaliels wordes further then he ment them, and of one priuate politique action, by and by publish a principle in Diuinitye, and thereupon ground a generall doctrine without an especiall precept to the warrant thereof shall of the lyke examples in the scriptures gather many and marueilous inconueniences.

Theop. falsly supposeth the Apostles to be false teachers.

Exãples without precepts proue not.

Concerning the doctrine of the first table if this example were generall, by this gapp many heretickes would stirre coles in the Church, and in the second tables many theues, harlots, and godles persons would swarue to the vtter ouerthrow of the common weale.

Inconueniences of Theoph. doctrine.

The first will not haue any man compelled to religigion, & therefore much lesse to be put death for the same.

The second is a plausible doctrine to fill the world full of theues, and harlots, to the confirmation whereof no honest man will once breath, to the confutation euery man both by the law of nature, and much more by the written word of God, is bound to agree with all possible resistaunce if he meane to keepe a good consciẽce towards God, or maintayne the dutye of Charitye towardes his neighbour,

But because the oportunitye and the instance of this place doth seeme to enforce a word or two concerning this question by sound and straunge reasons out of holy Scripturres I will approue that a Christian magistrate

both

both may and ought to punnish by death and otherwise, those that are heretiques agaynst the fayth, and blasphemers against religion. Heretickes both may and ought to be put to death by the ciuill magistrate.

1 The Manachies, Donatistes, and ould Heretiques were of the opinion, that all heretiques ought freely and without punnishment, professe what they listed, and not be compelled to fayth, but they might embrace what religion best they lyked without controulement, whome S. Augustine in many places confuted shewing, that a magistrate might lawfully compell heretiques to the fayth and sharpely punnish false teachers for broaching of their opinions. 1.

And therefore speaking to the heretiques he sayth very well, *Recte faciunt imperatores Catholici qui eos cogũt ad vnitatem*, the Catholique Emperours doe very well when they compel heretiques to come to vnitye. August de pastoribus. cap.16

The first reason is taken from S. Paule, who reasoneth from the end of the institution of the magistrate. *That he beareth not the sword for nought, for he is the minister of God to take vengeaunce on him that doth euill.* Seeing then heretiques and false teachers doe euill, in blaspheming the holy name of Christ, after the which we are named, in making a schisme amongest the people, in disturbing the cōmē quietnes of the land wherein they liue, and the state of priuate men also, therefore it is not to be doubted but they may, and ought to be punnished of him not onely in their wealth and goodes, but in their bodyes with the losse of lyfe also. Rom.13.4.a. 1. Reason.

Secondly, God by manifest precept and commaundement, hath prescribed how heretiques ought to be dealt withall: for when they stirre vp tumultes amōg the people, and drawe them from the doctrine deliuered out of the word of God, which teacheth that we should haue but one God, one fayth, one Baptisme. &c. And seeing I say there be perticuler preceptes of this matter, and God in his word hath commaunded that they should be slayne: It can not neither is it to be thought, that God hath com- 2. Reason. Leuit.24.14.16. Numb.15 30. 30.

 maun-

Deut. 13. & 17. 13. 14. 15. & 18. 20. 22. maunded that he hath not allowed of heretiques: Therfore lawfullye may by the commaundement of God be put to death by the ciuill Magistrate.

3. Reason. Thirdly the Lord hath not left this vnto vs, by precept onely, or as a thing indifferent in the pleasure of the magistrate, to chuse whether he will punnish them by death, or no: but he hath also hedged in this his law by example that whosoeuer shall transgresse in this behalfe shall be guiltye of a heinous transgression.

Numb. 15. 35. The man that gathered stickes on the Saboth day was slayne. Godly kinges by their example haue approued the same by their continuall practise. Asa put downe
3. Kinges. 14. 13. 2. Chron. 15. 13. his owne mother from her estate, because she made an Idole in a groue, and he destroyed her Idols and burnt them by the broke Kidron.

4. Kyng. 23. 5. Iosias put downe the Chemerims, he defiled Tophet, he brake downe the Images, and put downe the alters, sacrificing the priestes of the hye places vpon them.

2. Chro. 23. 17. Iehoiada destroyed *Baals temple*, brake his altar and his Images, and slew Mattan the priest of Baal before the altars.

1. Kyng. 18. 40. Elias put to death all Baals prophets and would not let one of them escape.

2. Kyng. 10. 25. Iehue put all Baals priestes to death.

Neither was this onely in the tyme of the law of Moses but after Christes assention when there was not a Christian Magistrate. S. Paule made Elimas blinde,
Act. 13. 11. Actes. 5. 5. 10. S. Peter slew Ananias, and Saphira because they lyed agaynst the holy ghost.

Lastly in the tyme of Christian Emperours, namely, Constantine, Gratiã, Valentinian, Theodosius, Archadius, Honorius, Valentinus, and Martianus. And many others which by waight of lawes did forbid all wicked sectes, and factions, contrarye to the word of God. And therefore did they commaunde, to all their Liuetenants, Proconsuls, and Presidents in all their Empires, that Idolatrye should be forbiddẽ, the temples of Idols should

be

be shut, that they should not be permitted to sacrifice in them, that all the herctiques as the Manichies, the Donatistes, the Arians, Apollinaristes, and Euchians, with their doctrine should not be suffered, their Churches should be spared, and their conuenticles forbidden. That their heretical bookes should be openly burned, that those which fostered them, or receiued them to house, should be greeuously punished, and the heretiques themselues, should be depriued of honours, goods, yea bodies and liues also, that by some meanes or other their wicked and schismaticall fantasies might be ouerthrowne. All the which they would not haue done vnlesse (by the worde of God,) it had ben assuredly lawfull, or if the counsaile of Gamaliell had bene as a generall lawe to all estates, tymes, and persons that followed. The which examples of Christian Emperours and godly kinges and gouernours both in the law, and the kinges of Judah, in and since the state of the Primatiue Church, I besech God to whome the care of his Church doth belong to put into the hartes of all Christian Magistrates to practise that they may in déede shew themselues nurses of the Church, to the maintenaunce of Religion and the assuraunce of their owne thrones, and estates, and to the quietnesse of their subiectes, that heresie may be suppressed, & sinne punished, and that God in all may be glorified, in and through his Christ our onely mediatour and redéemer. Amen.

Certaine profitable notes to know an Heretique, especially an Anabaptist. With the Opinions, and behauiour of them out of diuers Authors.

¶ *Out of M. Bullingers booke, agaynst the Anabaptistes.*

Simlerus epist. fol.1. ANabaptistes fly open conference and créepe from house to house craftely and priuily, seducyng the simple and ignoraunt.

2. 2. *Nicholas Storcke in Saxonie* the chiefe ringleader of the *Anabaptistes* boasted of *Reueilations*.

3. Bulleng. fol.1. 3. He boasted of a new world, wherin iustice dwelleth.

Anabaptisme commeth alwayes by contentious and troublesome persons, where the Gospell had bene preached before.

Thomas Muncer taught in word and writyng. First that the Preachers of his tyme were not sent of God, neither that they taught the word of God, but the dead letter of the Scripture: further that the scripture and outward word, was not the true word of God, but a testimonie of the true word: and that the word is inward and heauenly and cōmeth immediatly from the mouth of God, and that it ought to be taught inwardly by the spirite and not by Scriptures or Sermons.

Fol.2. He denyed Baptisme of Infantes.

He sayd that Christ did not fully satisfie for vs.

He sayd God reueiled his will by dreames, which he highly commended as inspirations from the holy Ghost.

His owne sect be termed the elect of God, all that were not of his sect he sayd they were wicked & woorthy to be slayne.

He sayd that goodes ought to be common.

Yea he sayd that Gedeons sword was geuen hym to abo-

abolish all Lordshyps, agaynst all tyraunts, to restore the former libertie, & erect the new kyngdome of Christ vpon the earth.

Muncer was put to death for his heresie, and repented before his death. Fol.3.

At Tygurie some contentious men though not vnlearned toke part with the *Anabaptistes.* Fol.9.

The *Anabaptistes* would not communicate with the wicked.

They sayd that the Baptisme of infantes was inuented by Pope *Nicholas* and therfore it was naught. Fol.10.

Anabaptistes were hartned by those which desired the ouerthrow of the Gospell and the restoryng of *Popery.* Fol.11.

Anabaptistes were sage men, they sighed often, they laughed not, they were vehement in reprehensions.

The simple were deceiued much by this Argument, Let mē say of the *Anabaptistes* what they will I sée their sobriety, I heare thē say nothing but this, that we must not sweare at all, but we must lyue holy and iust. &c.

The *Anabaptistes* complained that all thynges were done agaynst them by force, that the truth was oppressed, that simple and godly men which sought nothing but that which was conteined in the word of God, neither could they be hard or haue frée libertie to vtter out their myndes.

The *Anabaptistes* outwardly did lead a godly lyfe, they spake earnestly agaynst couetousnes, pride, othes, filthy talke, vncomely behauiour, chearyng and dronkennes, they spake much of killyng the old man. &c. Fol.17.b.

Briefly great and manifold was their hypocrisie. Fol.18.

They sayd they onely were the true Church, wherein Christians delighted, & that their Sectaries might kéepe company with no Christian Churches of the Gospellers for that their Churche were no more the Churches of Christ, then the *Papistes* Churches.

They sayd ỳ ỳ Ministers were not lawfully called to the Ministry, nor ordinarily, because they had not those qualities that S. Paule requireth 1. Tim. 3. e.

They allow of *Reuelations.*

They say that the Sermons of Preachers are of smal accompt, because in them is taught that Christ onely satisfied for our sinnes, and that men were iustified before God by fayth and not by workes.

They affirmed the law might be kept, and therefore they blamed the Preachers for saying the contrary.

They held Communitie of all thynges.

They affirmed that the old Testamēt ought not to be mingled with the new, because the old was abrogated.

They sayd that the soules slept untill the day of Judgement.

No Christian might be a Magistrat.

Magistrates must not medle with Religion.

Fol. 9. The last punishmēt of Christians is Excōmunicatiō.

No mā ought to be compelled to fayth, or put to death for his Religion.

Warre (say they) is unlawfull for Christians.

Their speaches must be yea, and no, without any oth.

None (say they) ought to be put frō the Lordes supper.

Cap. 9. Of diuers sectes and sortes of Anabaptistes.

Fol. 20. ¶Of Anabaptistes termed Apostoliques whose errours were,

1. They approued onely the bare letter of ŷ Scripture.
2. They used no weapō, staffe, wallet, shoes, money. &c.
3. They preached on house toppes.
4. They washed one an others feete.
5. They forsoke wiues and children.
6. They held communitie.

Cap. 10. ¶Of Anabaptistes Spirituall.

1. They had nothyng like the world, to proue it they abused. Rom. 11.

2. They

2. They had rules both for the matter and fourme of apparell. And affirmed, it was vnlawfull to weare silke. Fol. 23.
3. They had rules of eatyng, drinkyng, and sléepyng.
4. They might neuer laugh.
5. They sighed often & might not come in opē assēblies.
6. They condemne bargainyng and the vse of weapons.

Cap. 11. ¶Of Sinles Anabaptistes. Fol. 26.

These *Anabaptistes* sayd, they could sinne. For prœfe they cited.

He that is of God sinneth not. 1. Iohn. 3. 6. &.

He that sinneth is of the Deuill. cap. 3. 8.

Christes Church is without spot or wrinckle. Ephes. 5. 27.

And therfore did they intermit the 5. petition, Forgiue vs our trespasses.

They sayd there was no originall sinne, neither were infantes by nature sinfull.

The hatchers of this heresie were *Nouatus*, *Catharis*, *Auxentius*, *Pelagius*: it is learnedly and at large confuted by S. Augustin, Tom. 7. *Agaynst Cœlestius* of mans perfect righteousnes, in the last end of the boke.

Cap. 12. ¶Of Anabaptistes, that vsed to hold their peaces and pray.

1. They sayd there ought to be no more any preachyng, because the dore was shut. Apoc. 1.
2. The world was not worthy to heare the Gospell.
3. Beyng asked ought of their Religion, they held their peace.

2. Booke, 1. Chap. Of Anabaptistes Enthusiastæ.

They were often in a trayne and boasted much of the spirite and Reuelations.

Their common by word was, *The father sayd it*.

They saw by Reuelation that the day of Iudgement was at hand.

Cap.2. Of free brethren or grosse and impure Anabaptistes.

Fol.37.
1. They had (as they thẽ selues affirmed) fleshly knowledge either of other.
2. They sayd Christ made them free from all lawes.
3. They might haue no landes, nor pay tithes or obedience or subiection to any man.
4. They had communitie of all thinges.

Cap.4. Of Libertine Anabaptistes.

Fol.42.
1. They grãted that othes Magistracie, and Baptisme might indifferently be vsed or not be vsed.
2. They passed not for Scripture, for say they we are all taught of God.
3. They sayd Sacramentes were needeles, for the faythfull hauyng the thyng signified *vz.* the holy Ghost needed not the outward signe of water.
4. They sayd it was free for them in persecution, either to confesse or dissemble their Religion.
5. They sayd it is sufficiẽt for them, to keepe their harts cleane although they do cleane cõtrary in their deedes.
6. No man say they ought to put him selfe in dãger for his fayth, for God is not pleasured by any mãs death, neither wil he haue any man leaue his wife & childrẽ.
7. For their quietnes sake (they say) they may cõforme them selues to the Religion of any people, among whom they lyue.

And of this iudgemẽt (said M.Bulling.) was ẏ beast *Dauid George*, and this is the most pestilent sect of all others.

Fol.43.a.

Cap.6. Of the sect of the Hutties.

They thought they were the Israelites bodely.
They had terrible dreames and visions.

They saw in their dreames, that domes day was at hand, & therfore spent their goodes rioteously.

In continuaunce of tyme when all was wasted, they professed wilfull pouertie.

Cap.7. Of the sect of the Augustines, of Augustine a Bohemian.

They sayd that heauen is, was, and shalbe shut vntill the day of Judgement.

They thought that neither the good were in heauen, nor the wicked in hell, vntill the day of Judgement, but they were put in seuerall places, which places are vnto vs vnknowne.

Cap.8. Of the Anabaptistes of Munster.

1. They inueyed agaynst all excellencie, wealth, and honour.
2. They despised and spake agaynst the Magistrate.
3. They despised the world and worldly thynges.
4. Their talke was wholy of ye mortifying of ye old mã.

Cap.13. Melchior Hoffmã an Archheretique and an Anabaptist and his sectaries affirmed,

1. That the Baptisme of infantes was of the deuill.
2. That Christ toke not flesh of the virgin Mary.
3. That our saluation is of our selues.
4. That there is no hope of pardon for those, which fall away after they haue receiued the grace of God.

Cap.14. Of the heresie of Dauid George.

1. David *George* affirmed that all the doctrine giuẽ vs from godly Moses, Christ and the Prophets and Apostles is vnperfect & vnprofitable to saluation, but sayd that his heresie is perfectly profitable vnto lyfe euerlastyng.

2. *Dauid George* sayth he is Christ, and the Messias, the beloued sonne of God, borne not of the flesh but of the spirite.

3. *Dauid George* sayd he will restore the house of Israell and the tribe of Leuie.

4. *Dauid George* sayth, it is he that must forgeue sinnes.

4. Libertines.

1. They sayd God made the sinne of *Cain* and *Iudas*.
2. They denyed the Resurrection and sayd it was spirituall.
3. They sayd the deuils & all ÿ wicked should be saued.
4. They sayd the old Testament is abrogate.

3. Booke. 1. Chap.

THe Anabaptistes withdraw themselues from their Churches and Ministers. cap. 2. your Ministers liue not well say the Anabaptistes: therefore your Church is not the true Church.

The Anabaptistes in ioyning to the Churches where the Gospell hath with much labour bene preached there they stirre vp tumultes. They say the Ministers are not rightly called.

Chap. 6. Anabaptistes reasons why they refuse to come to Church.

1 THe Ministers refuse and depart from Christes doctrine.

2 No man ought to be compelled to fayth.

3 Ye resist euill, and Moyses sword should not defend doctrine but Christes.

4 Your Ministers liue not as they teach, *Ergo*, their doctrine is vntrue.

4. Booke 3. Chapter.

THe Anabaptistes say we may fulfill the law.

They affirme they are not heard as they ought to be.

vz. openly, and as the law requireth, and Nichodemus counsaileth, and yet not one of thē dare once professe their doctrine openly. 1. Reason.

They quoted much scripture.

Wee ought not say they be compelled to Religion. 2. Reason.

It is not lawfull to defēd Religion by the ciuill sword 3. Reason.
For Christ sayd resist not euill.

The preachers rayled on them, and delt vncharitably 4.
with them, yet were they the most scoffers of all others.

No man say they ought to be put to death for Religiō, 5.
but be excommunicated onely: for excommunication is the last punishment of the holy Ghost.

They rayled on the Lordes supper, and sayd it was 6.
no sacrament, they sayd they might not companye with any but of their owne sect, & other they sayd are wicked.

They affirmed none ought to be baptized, but they 7.
which are of age which can professe their fayth, and yet for profe hereof they quote no scripture.

Yf any of the Gospellers lyue godly they call him an Anabaptist.

The reprochfull tauntes of the Anabaptistes, Lutherans. Fol. 254. False and carnall Gospellers. 255. errors and vnskilfulnes of preachers. 256. Succeders of the Pharesies. 256. Hipocrites, blind guides, Fooles, blind serpents, Generations of vipers. 257. fellowes of theues whome Dauid maketh mention of. Psal. 50.

They say we hate thē because they would lyue without sinne. Fol. 260.

They say we may keepe the law, to the profe whereof they abuse much scripture.

The preachers (say the Anabaptistes) would haue vs professe openly because they would haue the Magistrate persecute vs.

FINIS ex Bullingero.

Out of Caluin agaynst the Anabaptistes.

They say that they ought not to receiue ẏ Lordes Supper, where there is no true excommunication. Fol. 38.

Fol.35. They say they may not participate in the sacraments with any man whome they know to be wicked.

Fol.53. Cathariſtes, Donatiſtes, and Anabaptiſtes, ſéeke a Church without spot.

Fol.58. The Anabaptiſtes say no man that is miniſter may haue a certayne charge, alledging for profe the Apoſtles example.

Out of Caluin agaynſt the Libertines.

THe sect of the Libertines is that sect which S. Peter and S. Iude foretould.

Fol.129. The whole speach of the Libertines is in such ſtraũge kinde of ſtile, that those which heare them at the firſt doe wonder at them, and so dealt Marcion in the hatching of his heresie.

Fol.131. The Libertines denied the resurrection.

Fol.133. The Libertines, were deuided into orders of men.

The firſt sort were called bleſſed ones, which whẽ they vsed their office in purging their religion, they were termed Puritanes.

Secondly there were ij. kindes of their disciples, the firſt they vnto whome they did reueale their miſteries of their sect, and them they termed Elected ones.

Others whome they a farof by little and litle made acquainted with their heresie, they termed Hearers.

Fol.164. In the beginning the Libertines bouldly reiected the scriptures, they tauntingly ſcoffing at either of the Apoſtles sought to weaken their credite that thereby they might the more magnifie their owne authoritye, they termed S. Paule a broken veſſell, S. Peter a forſwearer of his Maiſter, S. Iohn a ſely young man, S. Mathew an vsurer, neither were they aſhamed to blaſpheme them openly.

But afterwardes, when the Libertines perceiued, that all men abhorred them for those their vncomely speaches, they deuised more ſlyly and iuſtly to behaue them-

themselues, and saying then that they reiected no scripture, they did writh it into allegories, and wrested it into wonderfull straunge interpretations.

In the ordering of their disciples, they folow altogether the Manichies neither come they commonly abroad that they may the better be knowen, nor tell any man what they thinke: but kéepe them lōg in doubt, & by farre fetched circūstaunces, they winde in them whome they desire to make their disciples, neither doe they tell the watchworde of their mighty assemblies to any man, before they perceiue they haue so bewitched him, that they may easely perswade them whatsoeuer they list. 135.

Their secrets they open onely vnto those which first are sworne vnto them, & the chiefe Rabbies doe alwayes kéepe backe some especial pointes of their doctrine, wherby they may the better maintaine the opinion that their hangbyes haue of them.

Quintinus the Archlibertine and other of his felowes of botchers were made doctors, and so chaunged their calling: the reason was they faine would liue daintely, and idlely, neither thought they that they were fit to labour. 139.

The Libertines bookes were written in such a lofty stile, that hardly they could be vnderstode. 155.

One of the chefest pointes of their doctrine was, that they ought to vse a certaine crafty kinde of dissembling, & cōterfeiting that they may easely deceiue the simple. 156.

They think they may lawfully runne to Idol seruice. 157.

They are not content with the simple sence of the Scripture, but they writh it vnto Allegories, neither will they kéepe them to the letter: for they say the letter killeth. 165.

They affirmed that euery one of the children of God are Christes, and Quintinus the chiefe heretique being asked how he did, aunswered how can Christ doe amisse. Fol.215.

They say that regeneration is the restoring of the estate wherein Adam was placed before his fall. Fol.217.

Fol. 218. They make an Allego. of the historie of Adam Gen. 3.
Adams innocencie say they is nothing els but this, not to be able to iudge betwene black, and white.

219 If they see any mã strock with a feare of Gods iudgement: oh hast thou yet say they a tast of the Apple?

237 They surely hold these 3. principles, the first there is no Arte in the world which they do not allow of although God haue condemned it in his word, as for example. They thinke that the Popish priesthode is good, & Quintinus being at the Masse of a certaine Cardinall, affirmed that he saw the glory of God there.

238 Secondly they affirme that the abuses and corruptiõs wherewith the world is infected, is no harme.

240 Thirdly they affirmed that all mans inclinatiõ whẽcsoeuer it come, be it from corrupt nature, or euil custome is it is euery mans calling.

The bookes which M. Caluin sawe *of the Libertines.*

297 1. An instruction, and wholesome admonition how we should liue in this world, and be patient in aduersitye.

2. The Glasse of Christians.

¶Out of M. Zuinglius agaynst the *Catabaptistes.*

Fol. 5. The *Catabaptistes* cry God, the truth, ỹ word, the light, the spirit, holynes. &c. not onely mighty but if hypocrisie were not, worthy, and excellent were their speaches.

7 In what vice soeuer they are takẽ, be it adulterie, mãslaughter, theft. &c. they aunswere. I haue not sinned for I am not any more in the flesh, but in the spirite, I am dead vnto the flesh and the flesh vnto me.

9 Those that take part with the Gospell, they rayle worse on them then on the *Papistes.*

11 They spread abroad their bookes in ỹ hãds of their disciples

ciples, boasting euery where ẏ they could so cōfute Zuinglius ẏ they would make him haue neuer a word to say.

Their Captaines beyng franticke and brainesick men 12
complained to the Ministers, that they could not lyue among the wicked, and therfore would they separate thē selues frō the Church, because that in their cōmon assēbly and Church, there were many that were openly wicked.

They rayled vpō the Baptisme of infants & sayd that 14
it is a great abhominatiō come frō the deuill & the Pope.

They say they will proue their doctrine, by sheddyng 16
their bloud whē as they cā not proue it by the scriptures.

They rayled on the Ministers and sayd, that the Ministers hated them, because they founde fault with their euill lyfe.

They sayd no man was Gods child, but they which 33
fulfilled the law and wrought righteousnes.

They boasted much of the spirite, when they had no 35
Scripture, and vnder the pretence of the spirite they 62
wrought much filthynes.

They prophecied domes day should be on the Ascen- 63
tion day two yeares after.

They held freewill. 75

They reiect the authoritie of the old Testament. 76

They bragge of ẏ certainety of knowledge in doctrine 77
without the word and say *We are thus certified from God.*

They say there is no Sacrament of the Lordes Sup- 81
per, without their congregation.

Those which are not of their sect are abhominable be- 89
fore God, neither can they doe any thyng that is not abhomination.

They must in this lyfe depart from all euill, and those that be vngodly, for proofe they quote Apo.

¶They make three sectes.

videl. { *Romanistes Papistes.*
Protestauntes halfe *Papistes.*
Anabaptistes perfect Christians.

92. When they haue drawne any mā vnto their sect they straitly charge him, not to come at the table with him that is not of their faction, neither at the Sermons of any man that is an enemy to their sect.

100. They boast perfection.

They haue aunsweres reueiled vnto them.

107. All that are not of their owne sect, they say that they are infidels.

182. They say that the dead sleepe, both in soule and body till the day of Judgement.

187. They affirme that both the deuil and the wicked shal be saued.

190. They deny that Christ is Gods sonne by nature.

¶Out of Zuinglius.

The reason wherefore (gentle Reader) I haue out of these thrée excellent learned men, gathered the particular opinions of these heretiques, was not that I thinke the *Familie of Loue*, to be culpable in all those pointes, which I haue set down although I dare auouch the most of these errours out of HN. his writynges and other the letters & writynges of the *Familie*: but this especially moued me, that when any either of ÿ ministry, which know not neither haue read, and also the simple, which are acquainted by conference with the opinions of the *Familie* may hereby hereafter haue some light and skil both of the short propositiōs by me gathered, and also of diuers Reasons of the *Familie*, beyng mere hereticall beyng set down in this end of the booke might hereafter (when they shall here any of the *Familie*, slide into any of these affirmations) know whence such speaches haue bene learned and auoyde them: gentle reader the Lord geue thée vnderstāding in all thinges; and lighten all thy wayes by the candle of his word, that the day star arising in thy hart thou maiest grow to a further knowledge of the Lord, with a feruent desire to doe his will, and to liue to learne, and

learne to lyue, to tread the steppes of Gods sonne, and to dye his seruaunt: He this graunt vnto thée, who hath geuen himselfe for thée, to whome be eternall prayse, power, and glorye. Amen.

Tim. 4. chap. 6. vers. 8 7.

YF thou put thy bretheren in remembraunce of these thinges, thou shalt be a good Minister of Christ, which hast bene nourished vp in the wordes of fayth, and of good doctrine, which thou hast continuallye followed. But cast away profane and ould wiues Fables and exercise thy selfe vnto godlines. So be it.

FINIS.

AT LONDON

Printed by Iohn Daye, dwelling ouer Aldersgate *Anno. 1579.*

Cum priuilegio Regiæ Maiestatis.